PRACTICE
PRACTICE
PRACTICE

BOOK II +
Percents
Integers   Timothy A. TRINKLE
Rationals   Steven G. SELBY
Geometry   Thomas R. FITTS
Equations
Problem
Solving
ST² Publishing

ABOUT THE AUTHORS.

TIMOTHY A. TRINKLE—Received his BA from UCLA and Masters in Education from Portland State University. He has taught mathematics in the Longview, Washington School District since 1968. He taught previously in the Los Angeles School District.

STEVEN G. SELBY—Received his BS and Masters of Education from Oregon State University. He has taught mathematics in the Longview, Washington School District since 1973.

THOMAS R. FITTS—Received his BA from Washington State University. Received his Masters Degree from Lewis & Clark College in Portland, Oregon. He has taught since 1973 in the Longview, Washington School District.

Second Printing 1992
ISBN 0-943542-04-9

ST² Publishing, 203 Si Town Road, Castle Rock, Washington, 98611
360-274-7242

PREFACE

Book II of *Practice, Practice, Practice* was written, as was Book I, to: (1) provide the classroom teacher with an abundant source of practice problems in addition to their regular textbook; (2) provide the classroom teacher with a source of enrichment problems for those students who need the little extra practice or those who want to get ahead of the regular program; and (3) provide parents with a source of problems to work individually with their children at home.

An added feature of these books is that on most pages the problems get progressively harder as one works down the page. The pages on each topic are also arranged in order of difficulty. With this feature the user of the book can adjust the level of difficulty for each topic covered.

Proper use of *Practice, Practice, Practice* books can save the teacher time and their school district money. By using the detailed Table of Contents, the classroom teacher can produce an instant lesson plan, a review, or extra problems to augment a normal lesson plan. A classroom set of *Practice, Practice, Practice* will eliminate the expense of running off dittos, using a print center, and the time of making up new problems and answers.

This is the second book in the *Practice, Practice, Practice* series. Book I covers whole numbers, fractions, and decimals. Future books in the series are being planned and organized.

All questions or comments about this book, Book I, or any future books in the series can be addressed to:

ST² Publishing
203 Si Town Road
Castle Rock, WA 98611

Thank you,
The Authors

Practice Practice Practice was written by math teachers to save time for math teachers. Practice problems are essential for students to learn new concepts and review old ones. Both Practice Practice Practice Book I and Book II provide quality, organized, practice problems in large enough quantities for students to learn the mathematical concepts covered. (look below for book I.)

There is no need to reinvent the wheel every day. With a copy of Practice Practice Practice on your desk, you have over 10,000 problems and answers at your fingertips.

The classroom set concept:

A classroom set of books shared in your math department will save:
1. Hours of teacher time.
2. Money off your math duplication costs.

A classroom set of books will really cut down on your math duplication costs. Some schools have saved enough on their math ditto costs in a year or two to pay for a classroom set of books.

Practice Practice Practice Book I contains the following concepts:

Whole numbers	Fractions
Decimals	Prime numbers
Rounding	Greatest common factor
Comparing	Least common multiple
Money	Basic facts

Plus over twenty-five review and combination pages!

Compare the amount of money a classroom set will cost with the amount of time it will save teachers.

The easy review lessons you can use for substitutes will save you and your principal time and stress.

For more information contact: ST^2 PUBLISHING
203 Si Town Road
Castle Rock, WA 98611
(206) 274-7242

TABLE OF CONTENTS

PRACTICE PRACTICE PRACTICE BOOK I

Whole Numbers
Basic Facts
Decimals
Rounding
Comparing

Money
Fractions
Prime Numbers
Greatest Common Factors
Least Common Multiples

Plus over 25 review and combination pages!

Just think of the topics listed above. Book I can provide you with an abundance of quality, organized, practice problems on these topics.

Classroom set:

Think of the time you will save if you have or share a classroom set of books.

Save ditto costs.

"The publication costs in our math department decreased enough in one year to pay for the books" Henderson, Kentucky

For more information contact: ST^2 Publishing
203 Si Town Road
Castle Rock, WA 98611
(360) 274-7242

WHOLE NUMBERS—ADD THE FOLLOWING

1)	45	2)	496	3)	2916	4)	2916	5)	2716
	67		52		9		4728		4996
+	58	+	718	+	458	+	3856	+	3048

6)	483	7)	264	8)	9056	9)	5876	10)	14580
	4062		728		983		1987		6486
	7183		59		4865		8164		29486
+	215	+	644	+	7485	+	2858	+	58984

SUBTRACT THE FOLLOWING

11)	415	12)	248	13)	256	14)	140	15)	266
−	6	−	88	−	87	−	126	−	189

16)	4000	17)	3046	18	24158	19)	67159	20)	52815
−	2946	−	1539	−	2415	−	29843	−	26598

MULTIPLY THE FOLLOWING

21)	56	22)	74	23)	642	24)	1706	25)	2184
×	8	×	7	×	9	×	5	×	4

26)	25	27)	13	28)	497	29)	3680	30)	4158
×	42	×	63	×	59	×	78	×	81

31)	249	32)	657	33)	803	34)	2187	35)	3895
×	358	×	296	×	405	×	394	×	787

DIVIDE THE FOLLOWING

36) 5 ⟌ 436   37) 3 ⟌ 2146   38) 7 ⟌ 71582

39) 8 ⟌ 30605   40) 9 ⟌ 291586   41) 12 ⟌ 156

42) 34 ⟌ 2153   43) 56 ⟌ 41823   44) 78 ⟌ 92634

45) 90 ⟌ 210186   46) 215 ⟌ 1065   47) 514 ⟌ 24510

48) 318 ⟌ 21538   49 745 ⟌ 184915   50) 689 ⟌ 421863

ADD THE FOLLOWING

1)	63	2)	713	3)	2156	4)	317	5)	21643
	48		28		385		1764		2915
+	9	+	643	+	2978	+	189	+	18378

6)	29	7)	2143	8)	2150	9)	71583	10)	21583
	378		215		6938		2915		15996
	65		6173		7215		65348		20638
+	718	+	2975	+	2834	+	486	+	15818

SUBTRACT THE FOLLOWING

11)	743	12)	295	13)	208	14)	2134	15)	2050
−	86	−	176	−	156	−	866	−	394

16)	6158	17)	7900	18)	2061	19)	61583	20)	71830
−	2862	−	1938	−	1565	−	9846	−	27642

MULTIPLY THE FOLLOWING

21)	46	22)	82	23)	68	24)	90	25)	39
×	85	×	70	×	32	×	49	×	61

26)	265	27)	279	28)	415	29)	2068	30)	7983
×	58	×	86	×	79	×	47	×	83

31)	215	32)	793	33)	718	34)	293	35)	483
×	106	×	249	×	718	×	675	×	379

DIVIDE THE FOLLOWING

36) 6 | 496   37) 9 | 4186   38) 7 | 31456

39) 3 | 418362   40) 8 | 914168   41) 48 | 718

42) 36 | 4168   43) 73 | 91543   44) 99 | 718146

45) 40 | 914163   46) 869 | 2914   47) 703 | 91643

48) 563 | 106343   49) 914 | 700050   50) 692 | 791882

WHOLE NUMBERS—ADD THE FOLLOWING

1) $68 + 39 + 53$

2) $10 + 39 + 48$

3) $29 + 64 + 47 + 85$

4) $295 + 71 + 683$

5) $645 + 738 + 697$

6) $293 + 413 + 516 + 243$

7) $24 + 6918 + 363$

8) $4183 + 7186 + 283$

9) $41632 + 718 + 2915$

10) $6234 + 18953 + 18976$

SUBTRACT THE FOLLOWING

11) $683 - 29$

12) $275 - 196$

13) $7183 - 2184$

14) $6005 - 2589$

15) $72000 - 5163$

16) $49106 - 28793$

17) $41618 - 15983$

18) $215463 - 99548$

19) $695 - 215 - 58$

20) $2065 - 598 - 784$

MULTIPLY THE FOLLOWING

21) 29×8

22) 368×7

23) 706×9

24) 3125×6

25) 52683×5

26) 59×67

27) 48×39

28) 615×20

29) 7186×54

30) 31872×78

31) 215×613

32) 738×956

33) 209×605

34) 2185×642

35) 4687×789

DIVIDE THE FOLLOWING

36) $418 \div 8$

37) $1015 \div 7$

38) $51516 \div 4$

39) $61561 \div 9$

40) $607971 \div 6$

41) $849 \div 15$

42) $4146 \div 32$

43) $95591 \div 70$

44) $86805 \div 92$

45) $916187 \div 63$

46) $7150 \div 810$

47) $51567 \div 486$

48) $90700 \div 293$

49) $108873 \div 709$

50) $249168 \div 283$

WHOLE NUMBERS—ADD THE FOLLOWING

1) $68 + 93 + 48$
2) $78 + 63 + 43 + 90$
3) $214 + 63 + 794$
4) $318 + 643 + 943$
5) $2146 + 79 + 493$
6) $4163 + 987 + 8143$
7) $2987 + 2987 + 2987$
8) $716 + 71 + 7983 + 23$
9) $7186 + 914 + 7183 + 7168$
10) $7218 + 8694 + 798 + 888$

SUBTRACT THE FOLLOWING

11) $586 - 243$
12) $1482 - 868$
13) $2416 - 1952$
14) $16842 - 9843$
15) $72834 - 15986$
16) $70605 - 29859$
17) $28403 - 17847$
18) $108649 - 56494$
19) $7154 - 689 - 2593$
20) $64895 - 34853 - 2154$

MULTIPLY THE FOLLOWING

21) 68×7
22) 295×6
23) 658×8
24) 8783×4
25) 25648×9
26) 63×57
27) 83×92
28) 784×75
29) 4015×43
30) 23869×68
31) 256×529
32) 789×935
33) 700×708
34) 2914×167
35) 7815×478

DIVIDE THE FOLLOWING

36) $786 \div 7$
37) $2754 \div 8$
38) $78643 \div 6$
39) $25900 \div 9$
40) $716583 \div 5$
41) $709 \div 25$
42) $2954 \div 43$
43) $78648 \div 67$
44) $28586 \div 48$
45) $715409 \div 37$
46) $6180 \div 543$
47) $90534 \div 256$
48) $28344 \div 743$
49) $618953 \div 946$
50) $295088 \div 158$

WHOLE NUMBERS—ADD, SUBTRACT, MULTIPLY OR DIVIDE THE FOLLOWING

1) $46 + 85 + 97$

2) $29 + 48 + 63 + 89$

3) $218 + 49 + 346$

4) $368 + 418 + 248$

5) $2061 + 29 + 385$

6) $5648 + 786 + 2948$

7) $7154 + 8908 + 6437$

8) $785 + 295 + 86 + 481$

9) $2956 + 2583 + 482 + 9864$

10) $5958 + 7184 + 2065 + 3953$

11) $652 - 189$

12) $4186 - 294$

13) $7864 - 5095$

14) $50643 - 2958$

15) $79436 - 25843$

16) $41803 - 25649$

17) $106438 - 94386$

18) $343852 - 4186$

19) $7946 - 3856 - 295$

20) $41860 - 15643 - 4863$

21) 45×6

22) 346×8

23) 485×9

24) 4054×7

25) 95786×5

26) 38×43

27) 473×20

28) 594×19

29) 6535×86

30) 61438×74

31) 396×52

32) 485×31

33) 2948×952

34) 7906×864

35) 84753×739

36) $384 \div 6$

37) $4054 \div 8$

38) $51516 \div 4$

39) $61654 \div 5$

40) $971463 \div 9$

41) $418 \div 72$

42) $4085 \div 34$

43) $41555 \div 65$

44) $61003 \div 70$

45) $394158 \div 59$

46) $4158 \div 248$

47) $515618 \div 619$

48) $61083 \div 743$

49) $29408 \div 208$

50) $718643 \div 651$

WHOLE NUMBERS—WRITE THE WORD NAME FOR EACH

1) 17	2) 46
3) 78	4) 264
5) 385	6) 752
7) 994	8) 625
9) 239	10) 4,812
11) 1,873	12) 2,956
13) 8,888	14) 9,005
15) 21,864	16) 34,863
17) 248,635	18) 543,856
19) 2,000,437	20 7,714,682
21) 15,658,743	22) 25,718,947
23) 105,284,678	24) 616,616,616
25) 7,005,008	26) 719,068
27) 5,856,443	28) 23,467,238
29) 202,487	30) 319,425,237
31) 11,294	32) 14,243,333
33) 328,219,396	34) 4,380,456
35) 45,298,273	36) 689,478
37) 3,040,000,296	38) 2,000,468,000
39) 75,465,394	40) 485,319,243
41) 3,265,450	42) 86,265,398,005
43) 4,248,356,279	44) 4,284,343,090
45) 23,235,446,657	46) 384,296,446
47) 43,295,387,358	48) 315,294,574,080
49) 13,483,295,440	50) 2,000,416,053

WHOLE NUMBERS—ROUND TO THE NEAREST TEN THOUSAND'S PLACE, THOUSAND'S PLACE, HUNDRED'S PLACE, TEN'S PLACE, AND ONE'S PLACE

1) 61,584

2) 3,183,496

3) 2,015,638

4) 212,648,153

5) 31,589,164

6) 2,555,564

7) 30,607,090

8) 995

9) 61,459,153

10) 79

11) 615,715,834

12) 918,648

13) 61,458

14) 184,998,171

15) 78,189,186

16) 29,158,648

17) 218,638

18) 3,954,164

19) 718,171,906

20) 10,563,834

21) 4,991,496

22) 25,564,198

23) 71,814,345

24) 718,648,914

25) 2,961,483

26) 7,777,777

27) 8,194,687

28) 719,189,946

29) 221,221,221

30) 9,964,183

31) 12,345,678

32) 89,643

33) 2,618,943

34) 21,867,723

35) 2,212,638

36) 4,545,454

37) 71,943

38) 4,444,445

39) 48,699,618

40) 718,100,609

41) 6,154,561

42) 3,945,186

43) 2,915,864,183

44) 6,000,916

45) 29,743

46) 156,015,834

47) 17,801,819

48) 718,697

49) 21,634,818

50) 999,999,999

DECIMALS—ADD OR SUBTRACT THE FOLLOWING

1) 41.4 − .7

2) 3.6 + 8.54 + 9

3) 41.4 + 7

4) 1.014 + 28.5 + 3

5) 41.4 − 7

6) 17 + 6.147 + 39.04

7) 41.4 + .7

8) .8 + .9 + .6 + .5 + 3

9) 7 − 4.14

10) 2.06 + .99 + .8 + 6

11) 9 − 6.48

12) 241.176 − 39

13) 241.176 − .39

14) 54.351 − 53.3496

15) 4.68 + .071 + 8.8

16) $20 + $3.19 + $43.07

17) $20 − $13.85

18) $20 − $.63

19) $20.81 − $7

20) $50 + $5.17 + $1.01

MULTIPLY THE FOLLOWING—
ROUND MONEY TO THE NEAREST CENT

21) .41 × .06	22) 3.52 × .89	23) .015 × .017	24) 456 × .30	25) .456 × .009
26) .042 × .72	27) 7.6 × 1.3	28) 18 × .89	29) .249 × .61	30) .55 × .39
31) .026 × .007	32) $48.41 × .06	33) $153.12 × .91	34) $650 × .035	35) $453.41 × .89

DIVIDE THE FOLLOWING—
ROUND MONEY TO THE NEAREST CENT

36) 8 ⟌ .14

37) .08 ⟌ .14

38) .08 ⟌ 14

39) 9 ⟌ .126

40) .7 ⟌ 4.263

41) .25 ⟌ 1.1

42) 75 ⟌ .015

43) .14 ⟌ 428.4

44) .007 ⟌ 14

45) 8 ⟌ 2.317

46) 43 ⟌ 8.6215

47) .09 ⟌ 432

48) .06 ⟌ .303

49) 15 ⟌ $7504.59

50) .07 ⟌ $43.41

DECIMALS—ADD OR SUBTRACT THE FOLLOWING

1) 34.6 − .28

2) 34.6 + 2.8

3) 34.6 − 28

4) 18 − .93

5) 57.1 + 48.92

6) 7.5 + 15 + 8.87

7) 56 − .9

8) 56 − 9.8

9) 4.73 + 10.6 + 14

10) 1.9 + 19 + .19

11) 57.3 − .48

12) 57.3 − 48

13) 65.9 + .36

14) 65.9 + 36

15) 72 − .69

16) 72 − 6.9

17) 5.4 + .89 + 3.076

18) 6.3 + 28.99 + 15

19) $20 − $1.73

20) $2.58 + $67.94 + $30

MULTIPLY THE FOLLOWING—
ROUND MONEY TO THE NEAREST CENT

21)	45.3 × .7	22)	9.86 × .2	23)	51.7 × .08	24)	65.9 × .007	25)	$41.71 × .09

26)	346 × .28	27)	44.5 × 7.9	28)	2.08 × .009	29)	.404 × .068	30)	$350.75 × .25

31)	.007 × .002	32)	584 × .53	33)	10.7 × .010	34)	987.6 × .054	35)	$743.02 × .38

DIVIDE THE FOLLOWING—
ROUND MONEY TO THE NEAREST CENT

36) 8 ⟌ 56.64

37) .9 ⟌ $29.36

38) .07 ⟌ 42.63

39) 6 ⟌ .5442

40) .05 ⟌ .4515

41) .05 ⟌ 4515

42) .04 ⟌ 3

43) 18 ⟌ .009

44) .014 ⟌ 4256

45) 25 ⟌ .03

46) 3.6 ⟌ 5.4

47) 50 ⟌ .0013

48) 9 ⟌ $456.37

49) .7 ⟌ $214.25

50) .05 ⟌ $320

DECIMALS—ADD OR SUBTRACT THE FOLLOWING

1) 41.4 − .8

2) 41.4 + .8

3) 41.4 − 8

4) 41.4 + 8

5) 41.4 + .08

6) 8 − 4.14

7) 8 − .414

8) 3.3 + 7 + .114

9) 6 − 1.8

10) 4 + 3.33 + 13.1

11) 24.1 − 5.18

12) .3 + 18 + 6.47

13) 28.71 − 5

14) 28.71 − .5

15) 5 − 2.871

16) 1.8 + 18 + .18 + .018

17) 9.07 + 15.3 + .7 + 6

18) $50 − $2.71

19) $50 − $41.07

20) $6 + $4.11 + $15.94

MULTIPLY THE FOLLOWING—
ROUND MONEY TO THE NEAREST CENT

21) 24.19
 ×   .8

22) 42.76
 × .005

23) 1.35
 × .17

24) 6.111
 × .13

25) 4.013
 × .0009

26) .015
 × .006

27) 419
 × .24

28) 7.07
 × 3.09

29) .076
 × .25

30) .004
 × .07

31) .206
 × 2.06

32) $47.75
 ×   .6

33) $58.91
 × .07

34) $65.12
 × .008

35) $75.75
 × .51

DIVIDE THE FOLLOWING—
ROUND MONEY TO THE NEAREST CENT

36) 9 ⟌ 7.218

37) .08 ⟌ 5.3

38) .004 ⟌ 3

39) 2 ⟌ .503

40) 7 ⟌ .01428

41) .006 ⟌ 24.3

42) 24 ⟌ .07212

43) 4.5 ⟌ 27

44) 1.8 ⟌ .0144

45) .008 ⟌ 113

46) .75 ⟌ 300.3

47) 25 ⟌ $3056.75

48) 9 ⟌ $726.37

49) .005 ⟌ $3.91

50) .015 ⟌ $911.71

DECIMALS—ADD OR SUBTRACT THE FOLLOWING

1) $41.4 - .91$

2) $5.63 - 5.6$

3) $3 - .54$

4) $15.3 + .97 + 1.8$

5) $19.747 - 9.7$

6) $14.6 - 8$

7) $14.6 - .8$

8) $3.3 + 2 + 17.55$

9) $.76 + .4 + 3 + 9.11$

10) $14.6 + 8$

11) $14.6 + .8$

12) $24 + 917 + 3.1 + 2.44$

13) $61.7 - 9.4$

14) $61.7 - .94$

15) $86.07 - 9$

16) $86.07 + .9$

17) $14.6 + .536 + 4$

18) $5 - .914$

19) $5.5 - 5.473$

20) $\$20 + \$3.13 + \$917.07$

MULTIPLY THE FOLLOWING—
ROUND MONEY TO THE NEAREST CENT

21) $\begin{array}{r} .95 \\ \times\ .08 \\ \hline \end{array}$ 22) $\begin{array}{r} .68 \\ \times\ .7 \\ \hline \end{array}$ 23) $\begin{array}{r} .243 \\ \times\ .01 \\ \hline \end{array}$ 24) $\begin{array}{r} 147 \\ \times\ .19 \\ \hline \end{array}$ 25) $\begin{array}{r} 6.52 \\ \times\ .032 \\ \hline \end{array}$

26) $\begin{array}{r} .81 \\ \times\ .304 \\ \hline \end{array}$ 27) $\begin{array}{r} 12.4 \\ \times\ .6 \\ \hline \end{array}$ 28) $\begin{array}{r} 1.009 \\ \times\ .005 \\ \hline \end{array}$ 29) $\begin{array}{r} .050 \\ \times\ .002 \\ \hline \end{array}$ 30) $\begin{array}{r} 16.78 \\ \times\ .77 \\ \hline \end{array}$

31) $\begin{array}{r} 5.08 \\ \times\ .75 \\ \hline \end{array}$ 32) $\begin{array}{r} .0004 \\ \times\ .156 \\ \hline \end{array}$ 33) $\begin{array}{r} \$95.67 \\ \times\ .07 \\ \hline \end{array}$ 34) $\begin{array}{r} \$83.52 \\ \times\ .008 \\ \hline \end{array}$ 35) $\begin{array}{r} \$172.91 \\ \times\ .0015 \\ \hline \end{array}$

DIVIDE THE FOLLOWING—
ROUND MONEY TO THE NEAREST CENT

36) $.07\overline{)17.115}$

37) $.005\overline{)9}$

38) $.005\overline{).9}$

39) $.16\overline{).5}$

40) $45\overline{).27}$

41) $.8\overline{)14.31}$

42) $.32\overline{)18}$

43) $24\overline{).6}$

44) $144\overline{).18}$

45) $.007\overline{)3514}$

46) $.09\overline{).4563}$

47) $.09\overline{)7254}$

48) $.012\overline{)\$72.48}$

49) $15\overline{)\$754.59}$

50) $.016\overline{)\$32.01}$

DECIMALS—ADD OR SUBTRACT THE FOLLOWING

1) $71.3 - 9$

2) $71.3 + .9$

3) $71.3 + 9$

4) $71.3 - .9$

5) $241.376 - 5.34$

6) $2.184 + 5 + 6.88$

7) $44.1 - 3.98$

8) $6.04 + .7 + 8 + 9.9$

9) $11.4 - 6$

10) $11.4 + .6$

11) $11.4 - .6$

12) $11.4 + 6$

13) $17.016 - 3.4$

14) $4.19 + 6.8 + 82.28$

15) $50 - 3.19$

16) $\$20 - .70$

17) $\$20 - \$7$

18) $\$20 - \$.07$

19) $\$50 + \$4.25 + \$6.17$

20) $\$50 - \$24.75$

MULTIPLY THE FOLLOWING—
ROUND MONEY TO THE NEAREST CENT

21)	.035 $\times$ .06	22)	.19 $\times$ .84	23)	452 $\times$ .78	24)	3.007 $\times$ .009	25)	6.06 $\times$ .015
26)	.404 $\times$ .023	27)	.0688 $\times$ 1.9	28)	30.50 $\times$ .06	29)	.75 $\times$ .87	30)	69.5 $\times$ .0009
31)	.789 $\times$ .066	32)	.455 $\times$ .086	33)	\$47.69 $\times$ .05	34)	\$53.28 $\times$ .036	35)	\$394.67 $\times$ .809

DIVIDE THE FOLLOWING—
ROUND MONEY TO THE NEAREST CENT

36) $4\overline{).2434}$

37) $.07\overline{).4263}$

38) $.09\overline{)5436}$

39) $8\overline{).7}$

40) $.012\overline{)24}$

41) $25\overline{).0003}$

42) $.14\overline{)429.8}$

43) $.16\overline{)5}$

44) $75\overline{).003}$

45) $.009\overline{).3132}$

46) $9.8\overline{).245}$

47) $.036\overline{)27}$

48) $.12\overline{)\$45.33}$

49) $8\overline{)\$311.31}$

50) $.0024\overline{)\$356.97}$

DECIMALS—WRITE THE WORD NAME FOR EACH

1) .8	2) .07
3) .005	4) .0009
5) .00002	6) .000003
7) .17	8) .107
9) .1007	10) .239
11) .05063	12) .1111
13) .340142	14) .496
15) .0808	16) 3.2
17) 888.36	18) 6140.641
19) 25.4188	20) 6.10648
21) 500.005	22) .505
23) 7.316491	24) 80.39
25) 56.9156	26) 48.3
27) 4.00538	28) 800.140008
29) .0773	30) 700.0073
31) 1640.6	32) 46.2164
33) 7.47856	34) 818.18
35) 11581.364	36) 378.0599
37) 518.64155	38) 580.63
39) 153894.7	40) 764.459378
41) 348.7995	42) 17.37298
43) 61583.9	44) 491.448
45) 599.996	46) 43.3649
47) 28000.028	48) 46895.09
49) 17.341891	50) 74.61980

DECIMALS—ROUND EACH TO THE NEAREST TEN'S PLACE, ONE'S PLACE, TENTH'S PLACE, HUNDREDTH'S PLACE, AND THOUSANDTH'S PLACE

1) 47.1837	2) 630.7941	3) 82.7114
4) 6.89942	5) 674.9384	6) 176.3849
7) 99.0895	8) 9.47283	9) 108.7739
10) 248.6363	11) 4.82175	12) 53.6831
13) 272.1795	14) 8.11472	15) 4,239.6147
16) 989.8989	17) 2.79942	18) 699.8437
19) 86.4729	20) 90.0909	21) 714.0814
22) 503.7956	23) 6.0724	24) 85.7203
25) 5.0007	26) 453.8025	27) 17.9954
28) 700.0534	29) 896.3794	30) 9.5788
31) 38.4772	32) 56.6636	33) 342.7939
34) 21.5555	35) 87.8778	36) 0.47892
37) 70.4963	38) 4,784.8837	39) 4.93992
40) 76.5845	41) 22.2282	42) 600.0060
43) 72.4926	44) 58.7666	45) 94.7233
46) 8.42671	47) 346.8147	48) 609.7354
49) 4.67891	50) 99.9999	

FRACTIONS—ADD, SUBTRACT, MULTIPLY, OR DIVIDE THE FOLLOWING, AND EXPRESS IN SIMPLEST FORM

1) $4/5 + 3/5$

2) $7/9 + 2/9$

3) $6/15 + 7/10$

4) $9/20 + 5/6$

5) $3/8 + 15/16$

6) $7/12 + 4/9$

7) $1/2 + 5/13$

8) $3/4 + 9/10$

9) $15/36 + 2/45$

10) $5/24 + 11/30$

11) $17/18 - 13/18$

12) $12/21 - 5/21$

13) $8/15 - 1/6$

14) $5/9 - 1/12$

15) $11/16 - 3/20$

16) $5/8 - 3/14$

17) $27/42 - 9/28$

18) $36/45 - 7/30$

19) $12/25 - 1/4$

20) $21/27 - 7/36$

21) $7/14 \times 18/20$

22) $24/28 \times 15/16$

23) $36/45 \times 12/30$

24) $9/40 \times 25/35$

25) $8/11 \times 33/48$

26) $27/60 \times 30/50$

27) $15/70 \times 0$

28) $16/51 \times 17/32$

29) $18/39 \times 26/54$

30) $45/75 \times 85/120$

31) $5/6 \div 5/6$

32) $30/42 \div 5/8$

33) $12/25 \div 14/15$

34) $22/32 \div 11/16$

35) $9/21 \div 6/7$

36) $14/35 \div 7/10$

37) $13/40 \div 26/60$

38) $19/72 \div 3/8$

39) $34/81 \div 17/27$

40) $15/36 \div 21/24$

41) $6/15 + 4/9 + 3/5$

42) $19/20 - 2/5 - 3/10$

43) $17/18 + 5/6 - 2/3$

44) $3/4 - 1/8 + 7/12$

45) $30/35 + 4/7 - 3/10$

46) $8/9 \times 10/21 \times 7/15$

47) $18/28 \times 4/9 \div 3/7$

48) $27/40 \div 14/15 \times 45/75$

49) $42/60 \div 9/12 \times 5/8$

50) $22/26 \times 15/44 \div 6/13$

FRACTIONS—ADD, SUBTRACT, MULTIPLY, OR DIVIDE THE FOLLOWING AND EXPRESS IN SIMPLEST FORM

1) $\frac{1}{2} + \frac{3}{4}$

2) $\frac{5}{6} + \frac{5}{9}$

3) $\frac{7}{8} + \frac{4}{5}$

4) $\frac{11}{12} + \frac{4}{15}$

5) $\frac{9}{25} + \frac{1}{10}$

6) $5\frac{3}{20} + 7\frac{6}{7}$

7) $14\frac{6}{15} + 6\frac{3}{5}$

8) $52\frac{5}{21} + 18\frac{7}{9}$

9) $36\frac{13}{36} + 7\frac{5}{27}$

10) $68\frac{11}{18} + 14\frac{17}{24}$

11) $\frac{13}{16} - \frac{7}{20}$

12) $\frac{6}{7} - \frac{3}{8}$

13) $\frac{3}{4} - \frac{9}{12}$

14) $\frac{7}{11} - \frac{2}{5}$

15) $\frac{19}{30} - \frac{11}{25}$

16) $17\frac{9}{14} - 8\frac{17}{21}$

17) $36\frac{12}{13} - 15\frac{2}{3}$

18) $9\frac{7}{12} - 4\frac{8}{9}$

19) $47\frac{7}{45} - 16\frac{5}{6}$

20) $113\frac{65}{72} - 8\frac{35}{48}$

21) $\frac{24}{27} \times \frac{18}{21}$

22) $\frac{12}{15} \times \frac{35}{42}$

23) $\frac{32}{40} \times \frac{9}{16}$

24) $\frac{25}{65} \times \frac{45}{70}$

25) $\frac{28}{49} \times \frac{21}{48}$

26) $3\frac{3}{4} \times 2\frac{2}{3}$

27) $9\frac{3}{5} \times 1\frac{5}{12}$

28) $5\frac{4}{9} \times 3\frac{6}{7}$

29) $12\frac{1}{2} \times 7\frac{1}{5}$

30) $4\frac{8}{11} \times 3\frac{5}{13}$

31) $\frac{14}{27} \div \frac{2}{9}$

32) $\frac{15}{24} \div \frac{9}{16}$

33) $\frac{25}{28} \div \frac{7}{30}$

34) $\frac{12}{13} \div \frac{20}{21}$

35) $\frac{72}{100} \div \frac{27}{40}$

36) $6\frac{1}{8} \div \frac{7}{12}$

37) $5\frac{3}{5} \div 2\frac{1}{10}$

38) $3\frac{5}{9} \div 4$

39) $7\frac{7}{10} \div 4\frac{2}{5}$

40) $16\frac{2}{3} \div 2\frac{1}{7}$

41) $\frac{7}{9} + \frac{1}{6} + \frac{3}{4}$

42) $\frac{9}{10} - \frac{3}{5} - \frac{1}{6}$

43) $6\frac{2}{7} + 5\frac{2}{5} - 4\frac{5}{14}$

44) $8\frac{7}{12} - 4\frac{1}{8} + 3\frac{5}{6}$

45) $12\frac{7}{9} + 4\frac{3}{8} - 7\frac{5}{24}$

46) $\frac{7}{12} \times \frac{6}{28} \times \frac{9}{15}$

47) $\frac{18}{30} \div \frac{14}{25} \div \frac{27}{48}$

48) $\frac{21}{32} \times \frac{15}{16} \div \frac{11}{12}$

49) $3\frac{2}{11} \div 2\frac{1}{7} \times 4\frac{2}{5}$

50) $8\frac{1}{3} \times 6\frac{3}{4} \div 2\frac{4}{5}$

FRACTIONS—ADD, SUBTRACT, MULTIPLY, OR DIVIDE THE FOLLOWING, AND EXPRESS IN SIMPLEST FORM

1) $3/8 + 5/12$

2) $7/9 + 1/6$

3) $14/25 + 7/10$

4) $6 3/4 + 5 2/3$

5) $14 5/27 + 4 7/18$

6) $5 3/5 + 8 4/7$

7) $15 5/8 + 13/14$

8) $9 6/21 + 8 5/7$

9) $38 7/36 + 9 8/9$

10) $49 1/3 + 16 4/5$

11) $7/12 - 3/10$

12) $9/25 - 18/50$

13) $4/9 - 2/15$

14) $4 5/8 - 2 1/12$

15) $12 1/6 - 8 5/24$

16) $11 5/13 - 6$

17) $24 - 17 3/7$

18) $42 3/11 - 16 5/8$

19) $823 4/15 - 16 1/10$

20) $89 17/72 - 19 7/8$

21) $16/25 \times 15/18$

22) $45/48 \times 12/60$

23) $56/63 \times 21/40$

24) $3 4/7 \times 3 1/5$

25) $12 \times 5 1/4$

26) $18 1/3 \times 2 5/11$

27) $4 1/6 \times 6 3/5$

28) $4 7/8 \times 9 1/3$

29) $6 2/3 \times 0$

30) $8 4/7 \times 4 2/9$

31) $15/24 \div 12/42$

32) $49/100 \div 28/35$

33) $18/40 \div 14/15$

34) $12 1/4 \div 14$

35) $28 \div 2 5/8$

36) $7 6/7 \div 1 5/28$

37) $6 8/9 \div 5 1/6$

38) $8 4/5 \div 3 1/15$

39) $9 1/3 \div 6 5/12$

40) $1/8 + 5/6 + 3/4$

41) $6/7 - 1/4 - 1/2$

42) $6 2/3 + 1 1/5 - 4 5/6$

43) $8 1/9 - 3 4/5 + 2 7/15$

44) $12 3/10 + 4 1/3 - 2 13/30$

45) $12/14 \times 6/9 \times 15/48$

46) $21/35 \div 7/15 \div 18/25$

47) $3 3/4 \times 3 1/3 \div 4 1/6$

48) $9 1/3 \times 2 1/7 \times 5 1/5$

49) $7 1/8 \times 4 1/3 \div 2 3/8$

50) $15 3/4 \times 0 \div 6 1/3$

FRACTIONS—ADD, SUBTRACT, MULTIPLY, OR DIVIDE THE FOLLOWING, AND EXPRESS IN SIMPLEST FORM

1) $\frac{3}{5} + \frac{7}{10}$

2) $\frac{9}{16} + \frac{5}{8}$

3) $\frac{1}{12} + \frac{4}{9}$

4) $8\frac{6}{7} + 5\frac{1}{5}$

5) $12\frac{6}{21} + 4\frac{5}{7}$

6) $35\frac{9}{20} + 15\frac{7}{15}$

7) $435\frac{13}{24} + 6\frac{5}{16}$

8) $9\frac{9}{14} + 6\frac{7}{18}$

9) $81\frac{9}{28} + 8\frac{9}{10}$

10) $15\frac{11}{25} + 8\frac{7}{30}$

11) $\frac{8}{9} - \frac{2}{3}$

12) $\frac{7}{12} - \frac{3}{8}$

13) $\frac{10}{18} - \frac{5}{27}$

14) $48\frac{2}{15} - 9\frac{1}{6}$

15) $70\frac{5}{9} - 14\frac{9}{21}$

16) $481 - 7\frac{6}{13}$

17) $97\frac{11}{14} - 6\frac{14}{56}$

18) $59\frac{25}{36} - 3\frac{13}{27}$

19) $19\frac{5}{12} - 7\frac{7}{8}$

20) $63\frac{9}{40} - 5\frac{7}{30}$

21) $\frac{8}{15} \times \frac{21}{40}$

22) $\frac{7}{16} \times \frac{20}{35}$

23) $\frac{24}{33} \times \frac{27}{32}$

24) $6\frac{3}{5} \times 3\frac{1}{3}$

25) $7\frac{1}{2} \times 5\frac{5}{9}$

26) $15\frac{3}{4} \times 3\frac{1}{7}$

27) $0 \times 6\frac{11}{12}$

28) $8\frac{2}{5} \times 2\frac{8}{21}$

29) $9\frac{4}{9} \times 7\frac{2}{7}$

30) $29\frac{1}{2} \times 2\frac{3}{14}$

31) $\frac{35}{72} \div \frac{42}{56}$

32) $\frac{28}{32} \div \frac{19}{20}$

33) $\frac{27}{50} \div \frac{18}{45}$

34) $3\frac{1}{8} \div 5\frac{5}{6}$

35) $12 \div 4\frac{2}{3}$

36) $8\frac{4}{9} \div 2\frac{4}{15}$

37) $9\frac{3}{8} \div 2\frac{11}{14}$

38) $7\frac{4}{5} \div 2\frac{1}{10}$

39) $4\frac{7}{8} \div 6$

40) $30\frac{1}{4} \div 1\frac{5}{6}$

41) $\frac{5}{12} + \frac{9}{14} + \frac{7}{8}$

42) $\frac{21}{25} - \frac{4}{15} - \frac{3}{50}$

43) $6\frac{4}{9} + 2\frac{7}{12} - 4\frac{7}{36}$

44) $47\frac{7}{10} - 18\frac{5}{6} + 4\frac{1}{3}$

45) $90\frac{11}{21} + 4\frac{9}{14} - 3\frac{3}{7}$

46) $2\frac{4}{5} \times 3\frac{1}{3} \times \frac{19}{20}$

47) $4\frac{3}{8} \div 2\frac{1}{6} \div 15$

48) $6\frac{3}{7} \times 4\frac{1}{5} \div 8\frac{1}{4}$

49) $7\frac{2}{9} \div 2\frac{1}{27} \times 3\frac{1}{8}$

50) $14\frac{2}{3} \times 2\frac{1}{16} \div 1\frac{1}{5}$

FRACTIONS—ADD, SUBTRACT, MULTIPLY, OR DIVIDE THE FOLLOWING, AND EXPRESS IN SIMPLEST FORM

1) $7/12 + 11/15$

2) $4/21 + 7/24$

3) $5/8 + 3/10$

4) $6^{15}/16 + 4^{7}/18$

5) $17^{9}/25 + 8^{4}/15$

6) $53^{17}/20 + 46^{13}/30$

7) $100^{7}/9 + 47^{5}/6$

8) $9^{9}/22 + 4^{5}/12$

9) $39^{9}/14 + 8^{12}/35$

10) $91^{4}/7 + 23^{3}/8$

11) $15/28 - 5/21$

12) $41/42 - 3/8$

13) $17/36 - 3/14$

14) $15^{13}/48 - 9^{15}/16$

15) $24 - 16^{5}/9$

16) $138^{5}/13 - 17^{2}/7$

17) $41^{4}/27 - 18^{7}/12$

18) $9^{15}/26 - 4^{5}/39$

19) $71^{7}/10 - 46^{11}/12$

20) $503^{4}/15 - 74^{3}/20$

21) $21/30 \times 45/51$

22) $33/63 \times 54/57$

23) $42/56 \times 72/100$

24) $4^{3}/8 \times 2^{2}/7$

25) $16^{2}/3 \times 7^{1}/7$

26) $7^{1}/12 \times 6^{2}/5$

27) $4^{6}/21 \times 9^{3}/4$

28) $15^{7}/13 \times 26$

29) $8^{1}/15 \times 4^{1}/11$

30) $5^{7}/10 \times 6^{4}/9$

31) $18/25 \div 24/40$

32) $34/81 \div 28/90$

33) $75/120 \div 45/65$

34) $8^{4}/7 \div 3^{3}/14$

35) $12^{3}/5 \div 4^{6}/15$

36) $7^{4}/5 \div 4^{7}/10$

37) $35^{5}/6 \div 8^{2}/9$

38) $0 \div 38^{7}/12$

39) $18^{4}/7 \div 13$

40) $5^{1}/24 \div 6^{4}/14$

41) $8/15 + 9/20 + 3/25$

42) $11/12 - 3/8 - 1/3$

43) $18/35 - 2/14 + 5/21$

44) $36/45 + 6/15 - 7/18$

45) $25^{4}/13 + 6^{7}/26 - 15^{3}/4$

46) $36/51 \times 27/40 \times 17/18$

47) $3/28 \div 15/35 \div 13/21$

48) $6^{5}/12 \times 4^{1}/11 \div 8^{2}/9$

49) $13^{7}/8 \div 6^{3}/4 \times 12$

50) $23^{1}/3 \times 4^{1}/35 \div 5^{5}/8$

PROPORTIONS—
TELL IF EACH PROPORTION IS TRUE OR FALSE

1) $\dfrac{10}{15} = \dfrac{3}{5}$

2) $\dfrac{5}{9} = \dfrac{15}{27}$

3) $\dfrac{6}{5} = \dfrac{7}{3}$

4) $\dfrac{5}{14} = \dfrac{15}{42}$

5) $\dfrac{16}{5} = \dfrac{40}{8}$

6) $\dfrac{7}{3} = \dfrac{91}{39}$

7) $\dfrac{12}{18} = \dfrac{26}{39}$

8) $\dfrac{3}{17} = \dfrac{15}{200}$

9) $\dfrac{15}{9} = \dfrac{35}{21}$

10) $\dfrac{6}{8} = \dfrac{7}{9}$

11) $\dfrac{21}{12} = \dfrac{28}{16}$

12) $\dfrac{40}{25} = \dfrac{120}{75}$

13) $\dfrac{50}{1} = \dfrac{300}{6}$

14) $\dfrac{14}{15} = \dfrac{65}{75}$

15) $\dfrac{14}{20} = \dfrac{30}{45}$

16) $\dfrac{15}{25} = \dfrac{48}{240}$

17) $\dfrac{18}{15} = \dfrac{120}{100}$

18) $\dfrac{5}{8} = \dfrac{4}{7}$

19) $\dfrac{3}{3} = \dfrac{7}{7}$

20) $\dfrac{20}{35} = \dfrac{36}{63}$

21) $\dfrac{5}{91} = \dfrac{15}{273}$

22) $\dfrac{30}{64} = \dfrac{15}{32}$

23) $\dfrac{4}{9} = \dfrac{7}{11}$

24) $\dfrac{15}{36} = \dfrac{45}{108}$

25) $\dfrac{20}{14} = \dfrac{30}{18}$

26) $\dfrac{28}{35} = \dfrac{56}{70}$

27) $\dfrac{24}{18} = \dfrac{68}{51}$

28) $\dfrac{91}{39} = \dfrac{35}{15}$

29) $\dfrac{20}{8} = \dfrac{75}{30}$

30) $\dfrac{24}{30} = \dfrac{76}{95}$

31) $\dfrac{18}{15} = \dfrac{36}{30}$

32) $\dfrac{25}{18} = \dfrac{20}{15}$

33) $\dfrac{14}{21} = \dfrac{20}{30}$

34) $\dfrac{15}{19} = \dfrac{45}{57}$

35) $\dfrac{25}{35} = \dfrac{225}{315}$

36) $\dfrac{40}{144} = \dfrac{10}{36}$

37) $\dfrac{25}{175} = \dfrac{50}{350}$

38) $\dfrac{18}{27} = \dfrac{96}{144}$

39) $\dfrac{75}{80} = \dfrac{19}{20}$

40) $\dfrac{28}{130} = \dfrac{14}{65}$

41) $\dfrac{30}{3} = \dfrac{45}{12}$

42) $\dfrac{16}{25} = \dfrac{48}{75}$

43) $\dfrac{18}{7} = \dfrac{90}{40}$

44) $\dfrac{45}{18} = \dfrac{10}{4}$

45) $\dfrac{36}{144} = \dfrac{17}{68}$

46) $\dfrac{25}{200} = \dfrac{18}{144}$

47) $\dfrac{15}{9} = \dfrac{30}{18}$

48) $\dfrac{48}{49} = \dfrac{196}{200}$

49) $\dfrac{75}{40} = \dfrac{105}{56}$

50) $\dfrac{40}{1,000,000} = \dfrac{400}{100,000,000}$

PROPORTIONS—
TELL IF EACH PROPORTION IS TRUE OR FALSE

1) $\dfrac{3}{6} = \dfrac{6}{4}$

2) $\dfrac{5}{7} = \dfrac{8}{9}$

3) $\dfrac{12}{12} = \dfrac{4}{3}$

4) $\dfrac{16}{20} = \dfrac{28}{35}$

5) $\dfrac{15}{45} = \dfrac{8}{24}$

6) $\dfrac{21}{28} = \dfrac{42}{56}$

7) $\dfrac{3}{8} = \dfrac{15}{40}$

8) $\dfrac{18}{24} = \dfrac{24}{18}$

9) $\dfrac{13}{39} = \dfrac{7}{21}$

10) $\dfrac{4}{52} = \dfrac{7}{91}$

11) $\dfrac{.8}{1.4} = \dfrac{.08}{.14}$

12) $\dfrac{3}{4.2} = \dfrac{7}{8.4}$

13) $\dfrac{.15}{9} = \dfrac{15}{90}$

14) $\dfrac{3.2}{8} = \dfrac{.32}{80}$

15) $\dfrac{25}{.6} = \dfrac{100}{2.4}$

16) $\dfrac{.03}{.5} = \dfrac{.15}{2.5}$

17) $\dfrac{.003}{70} = \dfrac{.04}{9}$

18) $\dfrac{1.5}{.5} = \dfrac{1.05}{.35}$

19) $\dfrac{.08}{.0009} = \dfrac{16}{.18}$

20) $\dfrac{.24}{36} = \dfrac{.004}{.6}$

21) $\dfrac{3\frac{1}{2}}{5} = \dfrac{7}{10}$

22) $\dfrac{24}{16} = \dfrac{\frac{3}{4}}{\frac{1}{2}}$

23) $\dfrac{4\frac{1}{2}}{36} = \dfrac{9}{72}$

24) $\dfrac{\frac{1}{3}}{\frac{3}{5}} = \dfrac{\frac{2}{3}}{1\frac{3}{5}}$

25) $\dfrac{4}{\frac{3}{4}} = \dfrac{36}{5\frac{1}{2}}$

26) $\dfrac{4}{\frac{3}{5}} = \dfrac{36}{5\frac{2}{5}}$

27) $\dfrac{1\frac{3}{4}}{\frac{2}{3}} = \dfrac{15\frac{3}{4}}{6}$

28) $\dfrac{\frac{3}{8}}{6} = \dfrac{\frac{5}{8}}{8}$

29) $\dfrac{4\frac{4}{5}}{1\frac{1}{3}} = \dfrac{24}{6\frac{2}{3}}$

30) $\dfrac{1\frac{7}{8}}{\frac{5}{8}} = \dfrac{6}{3\frac{1}{8}}$

31) $\dfrac{9}{1.6} = \dfrac{18}{3.2}$

32) $\dfrac{.5}{\frac{3}{8}} = \dfrac{1}{\frac{3}{4}}$

33) $\dfrac{12}{2\frac{1}{2}} = \dfrac{18}{3\frac{1}{3}}$

34) $\dfrac{12}{.375} = \dfrac{24}{.75}$

35) $\dfrac{\frac{4}{5}}{15} = \dfrac{.4}{7\frac{1}{2}}$

36) $\dfrac{\frac{2}{3}}{.7} = \dfrac{8}{9}$

37) $\dfrac{14}{.091} = \dfrac{10}{.065}$

38) $\dfrac{\frac{3}{4}}{8} = \dfrac{\frac{1}{2}}{12}$

39) $\dfrac{\frac{5}{8}}{15} = \dfrac{4}{96}$

40) $\dfrac{\frac{1}{3}}{6} = \dfrac{2}{36}$

41) $\dfrac{.07}{42} = \dfrac{.06}{35}$

42) $\dfrac{24}{.015} = \dfrac{18}{.012}$

43) $\dfrac{\frac{7}{8}}{.875} = \dfrac{\frac{3}{5}}{.6}$

44) $\dfrac{6\frac{1}{2}}{3.9} = \dfrac{65}{39}$

45) $\dfrac{7}{.034} = \dfrac{3\frac{1}{2}}{.017}$

46) $\dfrac{24}{.8} = \dfrac{7\frac{1}{2}}{\frac{1}{4}}$

47) $\dfrac{.05}{400} = \dfrac{.025}{200}$

48) $\dfrac{15}{7\frac{1}{2}} = \dfrac{.07}{.035}$

49) $\dfrac{\frac{3}{4}}{9} = \dfrac{.6}{8}$

50) $\dfrac{.8}{40} = \dfrac{2\frac{1}{2}}{125}$

PROPORTIONS—SOLVE THE FOLLOWING

1) $\dfrac{3}{4} = \dfrac{x}{20}$

2) $\dfrac{13}{15} = \dfrac{39}{x}$

3) $\dfrac{5}{6} = \dfrac{x}{30}$

4) $\dfrac{x}{50} = \dfrac{3}{10}$

5) $\dfrac{7}{x} = \dfrac{63}{81}$

6) $\dfrac{x}{25} = \dfrac{16}{100}$

7) $\dfrac{5}{6} = \dfrac{25}{x}$

8) $\dfrac{45}{81} = \dfrac{x}{9}$

9) $\dfrac{75}{x} = \dfrac{15}{20}$

10) $\dfrac{x}{13} = \dfrac{42}{39}$

11) $\dfrac{16}{1} = \dfrac{x}{7}$

12) $\dfrac{37}{x} = \dfrac{43}{43}$

13) $\dfrac{x}{15} = \dfrac{52}{60}$

14) $\dfrac{5}{9} = \dfrac{45}{x}$

15) $\dfrac{17}{63} = \dfrac{x}{126}$

16) $\dfrac{7}{x} = \dfrac{91}{65}$

17) $\dfrac{x}{8} = \dfrac{15}{12}$

18) $\dfrac{16}{45} = \dfrac{48}{x}$

19) $\dfrac{37}{40} = \dfrac{x}{120}$

20) $\dfrac{44}{x} = \dfrac{2}{3}$

21) $\dfrac{x}{42} = \dfrac{14}{49}$

22) $\dfrac{144}{96} = \dfrac{12}{x}$

23) $\dfrac{25}{30} = \dfrac{x}{24}$

24) $\dfrac{96}{x} = \dfrac{16}{24}$

25) $\dfrac{x}{30} = \dfrac{95}{150}$

26) $\dfrac{6}{9} = \dfrac{16}{x}$

27) $\dfrac{x}{15} = \dfrac{9}{27}$

28) $\dfrac{17}{x} = \dfrac{51}{63}$

29) $\dfrac{x}{10} = \dfrac{144}{120}$

30) $\dfrac{36}{15} = \dfrac{1296}{x}$

31) $\dfrac{9}{18} = \dfrac{x}{54}$

32) $\dfrac{18}{x} = \dfrac{81}{45}$

33) $\dfrac{x}{3} = \dfrac{217}{93}$

34) $\dfrac{28}{50} = \dfrac{224}{x}$

35) $\dfrac{80}{120} = \dfrac{x}{90}$

36) $\dfrac{81}{x} = \dfrac{63}{42}$

37) $\dfrac{x}{12} = \dfrac{72}{288}$

38) $\dfrac{15}{23} = \dfrac{150}{x}$

39) $\dfrac{x}{24} = \dfrac{42}{28}$

40) $\dfrac{28}{x} = \dfrac{112}{432}$

41) $\dfrac{x}{20} = \dfrac{65}{100}$

42) $\dfrac{14}{23} = \dfrac{98}{x}$

43) $\dfrac{9}{10} = \dfrac{x}{100}$

44) $\dfrac{19}{x} = \dfrac{95}{100}$

45) $\dfrac{x}{25} = \dfrac{64}{100}$

46) $\dfrac{3}{4} = \dfrac{75}{x}$

47) $\dfrac{37}{50} = \dfrac{x}{100}$

48) $\dfrac{8}{x} = \dfrac{80}{100}$

49) $\dfrac{x}{2} = \dfrac{50}{100}$

50) $\dfrac{24}{35} = \dfrac{144}{x}$

PROPORTIONS—SOLVE THE FOLLOWING

1) $\dfrac{4}{5} = \dfrac{8}{x}$

2) $\dfrac{9}{10} = \dfrac{x}{100}$

3) $\dfrac{x}{5} = \dfrac{45}{25}$

4) $\dfrac{7}{x} = \dfrac{49}{63}$

5) $\dfrac{23}{14} = \dfrac{x}{28}$

6) $\dfrac{27}{48} = \dfrac{81}{x}$

7) $\dfrac{54}{x} = \dfrac{18}{15}$

8) $\dfrac{x}{25} = \dfrac{96}{150}$

9) $\dfrac{19}{x} = \dfrac{57}{90}$

10) $\dfrac{7}{8} = \dfrac{x}{64}$

11) $\dfrac{27}{17} = \dfrac{37}{x}$

12) $\dfrac{7}{x} = \dfrac{8}{9}$

13) $\dfrac{x}{15} = \dfrac{20}{18}$

14) $\dfrac{78}{34} = \dfrac{29}{x}$

15) $\dfrac{x}{16} = \dfrac{17}{12}$

16) $\dfrac{7}{3} = \dfrac{x}{2}$

17) $\dfrac{x}{7} = \dfrac{8}{9}$

18) $\dfrac{49}{21} = \dfrac{x}{9}$

19) $\dfrac{x}{23} = \dfrac{14}{100}$

20) $\dfrac{14}{21} = \dfrac{20}{x}$

21) $\dfrac{16}{x} = \dfrac{20}{25}$

22) $\dfrac{18}{27} = \dfrac{x}{22}$

23) $\dfrac{x}{2} = \dfrac{8}{64}$

24) $\dfrac{23}{x} = \dfrac{26}{15}$

25) $\dfrac{x}{27} = \dfrac{81}{18}$

26) $\dfrac{6}{9} = \dfrac{x}{17}$

27) $\dfrac{49}{x} = \dfrac{14}{24}$

28) $\dfrac{17}{34} = \dfrac{42}{x}$

29) $\dfrac{x}{40} = \dfrac{20}{50}$

30) $\dfrac{25}{35} = \dfrac{x}{65}$

31) $\dfrac{x}{13} = \dfrac{17}{25}$

32) $\dfrac{23}{x} = \dfrac{64}{47}$

33) $\dfrac{17}{83} = \dfrac{19}{x}$

34) $\dfrac{x}{19} = \dfrac{24}{16}$

35) $\dfrac{75}{160} = \dfrac{x}{110}$

36) $\dfrac{x}{8} = \dfrac{40}{16}$

37) $\dfrac{3}{5000} = \dfrac{x}{10}$

38) $\dfrac{22}{x} = \dfrac{55}{60}$

39) $\dfrac{12}{27} = \dfrac{32}{x}$

40) $\dfrac{x}{26} = \dfrac{15}{34}$

41) $\dfrac{14}{16} = \dfrac{x}{21}$

42) $\dfrac{x}{28} = \dfrac{18}{63}$

43) $\dfrac{7}{100} = \dfrac{x}{6}$

44) $\dfrac{16}{23} = \dfrac{45}{x}$

45) $\dfrac{x}{6} = \dfrac{9}{72}$

46) $\dfrac{150}{x} = \dfrac{100}{75}$

47) $\dfrac{320}{420} = \dfrac{x}{140}$

48) $\dfrac{200}{14} = \dfrac{7}{x}$

49) $\dfrac{x}{32} = \dfrac{20}{24}$

50) $\dfrac{16}{x} = \dfrac{18}{15}$

PROPORTIONS—SOLVE THE FOLLOWING

1) $\dfrac{3/8}{3} = \dfrac{x}{5/12}$

2) $\dfrac{x}{6/7} = \dfrac{7/8}{10}$

3) $\dfrac{2/3}{x} = \dfrac{1/2}{9}$

4) $\dfrac{7/8}{1/2} = \dfrac{3/4}{x}$

5) $\dfrac{7/8}{3/4} = \dfrac{x}{6/7}$

6) $\dfrac{x}{15/16} = \dfrac{8/9}{2/3}$

7) $\dfrac{25/27}{15/8} = \dfrac{x}{9/10}$

8) $\dfrac{4/27}{x} = \dfrac{16/81}{2/3}$

9) $\dfrac{9/10}{7/12} = \dfrac{9/14}{x}$

10) $\dfrac{15/16}{x} = \dfrac{9/10}{3/5}$

11) $\dfrac{x}{3/4} = \dfrac{1/3}{2/5}$

12) $\dfrac{8/24}{4/6} = \dfrac{x}{3/30}$

13) $\dfrac{4/5}{1/3} = \dfrac{x}{7/8}$

14) $\dfrac{5/8}{x} = \dfrac{1/4}{5/6}$

15) $\dfrac{3/8}{2/3} = \dfrac{x}{3/5}$

16) $\dfrac{5/12}{6} = \dfrac{2/15}{x}$

17) $\dfrac{6/42}{x} = \dfrac{8/21}{8/9}$

18) $\dfrac{x}{100/125} = \dfrac{75/225}{4/25}$

19) $\dfrac{4/9}{6/18} = \dfrac{x}{1/9}$

20) $\dfrac{30/45}{30/21} = \dfrac{81/100}{x}$

21) $\dfrac{20/48}{x} = \dfrac{25/42}{16/7}$

22) $\dfrac{x}{8/12} = \dfrac{15/8}{4/5}$

23) $\dfrac{12/16}{3/5} = \dfrac{x}{18/50}$

24) $\dfrac{6/49}{23/98} = \dfrac{7/10}{x}$

25) $\dfrac{20/75}{x} = \dfrac{4/9}{35/100}$

26) $\dfrac{x}{3\frac{1}{3}} = \dfrac{4/5}{1\frac{2}{3}}$

27) $\dfrac{5\frac{2}{5}}{1\frac{3}{27}} = \dfrac{x}{3}$

28) $\dfrac{10}{6\frac{3}{5}} = \dfrac{7/11}{x}$

29) $\dfrac{25}{x} = \dfrac{2\frac{2}{9}}{3\frac{1}{5}}$

30) $\dfrac{x}{6\frac{3}{4}} = \dfrac{8/9}{4\frac{1}{3}}$

31) $\dfrac{2/3}{x} = \dfrac{1\frac{1}{2}}{45}$

32) $\dfrac{3}{3\frac{1}{3}} = \dfrac{9/10}{x}$

33) $\dfrac{6\frac{2}{3}}{3\frac{1}{3}} = \dfrac{x}{5\frac{5}{12}}$

34) $\dfrac{4\frac{3}{4}}{8\frac{2}{3}} = \dfrac{19}{x}$

35) $\dfrac{2\frac{1}{4}}{x} = \dfrac{6\frac{3}{4}}{9\frac{3}{7}}$

36) $\dfrac{x}{2\frac{9}{11}} = \dfrac{4\frac{2}{5}}{3\frac{1}{3}}$

37) $\dfrac{7\frac{1}{2}}{3\frac{2}{5}} = \dfrac{x}{2\frac{2}{3}}$

38) $\dfrac{5\frac{3}{5}}{2\frac{1}{10}} = \dfrac{4\frac{2}{3}}{x}$

39) $\dfrac{x}{4\frac{1}{2}} = \dfrac{3\frac{1}{3}}{15}$

40) $\dfrac{4\frac{3}{8}}{3\frac{1}{3}} = \dfrac{x}{16/21}$

41) $\dfrac{6\frac{1}{8}}{2\frac{1}{3}} = \dfrac{7/8}{x}$

42) $\dfrac{2\frac{3}{7}}{x} = \dfrac{8\frac{1}{2}}{3\frac{1}{2}}$

43) $\dfrac{45/49}{1\frac{2}{7}} = \dfrac{x}{3\frac{1}{2}}$

44) $\dfrac{3\frac{1}{2}}{x} = \dfrac{2\frac{4}{5}}{4/5}$

45) $\dfrac{x}{8\frac{3}{10}} = \dfrac{2\frac{4}{5}}{16/25}$

46) $\dfrac{12\frac{1}{2}}{x} = \dfrac{2\frac{4}{5}}{3\frac{3}{5}}$

47) $\dfrac{4\frac{4}{9}}{x} = \dfrac{8\frac{1}{3}}{40\frac{1}{2}}$

48) $\dfrac{x}{12\frac{1}{10}} = \dfrac{40/77}{3\frac{2}{7}}$

49) $\dfrac{2\frac{6}{7}}{2\frac{1}{14}} = \dfrac{7\frac{3}{7}}{x}$

50) $\dfrac{3\frac{3}{4}}{15/16} = \dfrac{x}{8\frac{1}{3}}$

PROPORTIONS—SOLVE THE FOLLOWING

1) $\dfrac{x}{8} = \dfrac{.6}{1.2}$

2) $\dfrac{.9}{9} = \dfrac{x}{.09}$

3) $\dfrac{.2}{.06} = \dfrac{5}{x}$

4) $\dfrac{.008}{x} = \dfrac{.5}{7}$

5) $\dfrac{x}{6.9} = \dfrac{.8}{13.8}$

6) $\dfrac{5.4}{3.7} = \dfrac{x}{.74}$

7) $\dfrac{1}{2.7} = \dfrac{.8}{x}$

8) $\dfrac{9.6}{x} = \dfrac{1.6}{5}$

9) $\dfrac{x}{.656} = \dfrac{.9}{.3}$

10) $\dfrac{.7}{1.6} = \dfrac{x}{.4}$

11) $\dfrac{2.5}{2.03} = \dfrac{.5}{x}$

12) $\dfrac{.004}{x} = \dfrac{5}{.9}$

13) $\dfrac{x}{.9} = \dfrac{7.2}{.8}$

14) $\dfrac{.7}{.002} = \dfrac{x}{8}$

15) $\dfrac{3.4}{.7} = \dfrac{.85}{x}$

16) $\dfrac{.18}{x} = \dfrac{1.8}{.5}$

17) $\dfrac{x}{8.3} = \dfrac{.6}{.24}$

18) $\dfrac{.09}{24} = \dfrac{x}{8}$

19) $\dfrac{x}{.09} = \dfrac{.06}{.025}$

20) $\dfrac{.09}{x} = \dfrac{.024}{.72}$

21) $\dfrac{.0105}{.7} = \dfrac{.006}{x}$

22) $\dfrac{.23}{4.6} = \dfrac{x}{.006}$

23) $\dfrac{1.5}{.48} = \dfrac{.08}{x}$

24) $\dfrac{.78}{x} = \dfrac{13}{60}$

25) $\dfrac{x}{20} = \dfrac{.48}{1.5}$

26) $\dfrac{.28}{.63} = \dfrac{.3}{x}$

27) $\dfrac{x}{2.3} = \dfrac{.4}{.008}$

28) $\dfrac{2.8}{.42} = \dfrac{x}{.6}$

29) $\dfrac{2.16}{x} = \dfrac{8.1}{.3}$

30) $\dfrac{69.3}{210} = \dfrac{x}{.07}$

31) $\dfrac{x}{.006} = \dfrac{1.46}{2.4}$

32) $\dfrac{5.6}{2.1} = \dfrac{.256}{x}$

33) $\dfrac{.005}{.64} = \dfrac{.073}{x}$

34) $\dfrac{2.1}{7} = \dfrac{x}{.256}$

35) $\dfrac{.005}{x} = \dfrac{30}{384}$

36) $\dfrac{6.3}{x} = \dfrac{.018}{.019}$

37) $\dfrac{x}{64} = \dfrac{.2}{2.5}$

38) $\dfrac{.0096}{1.2} = \dfrac{x}{8}$

39) $\dfrac{.26}{5} = \dfrac{7.8}{x}$

40) $\dfrac{14}{x} = \dfrac{3.5}{.67}$

41) $\dfrac{x}{.076} = \dfrac{.84}{.0028}$

42) $\dfrac{.71}{x} = \dfrac{20}{300}$

43) $\dfrac{.7}{4.7} = \dfrac{x}{94}$

44) $\dfrac{.026}{.258} = \dfrac{.065}{x}$

45) $\dfrac{x}{7.3} = \dfrac{86}{5}$

46) $\dfrac{8.2}{42.4} = \dfrac{x}{636}$

47) $\dfrac{5}{2.9} = \dfrac{7.003}{x}$

48) $\dfrac{103}{x} = \dfrac{9.5}{7.6}$

49) $\dfrac{x}{13} = \dfrac{7.63}{6.5}$

50) $\dfrac{105}{3.5} = \dfrac{x}{28.1}$

PROPORTIONS—SOLVE THE FOLLOWING
ROUND MONEY TO NEAREST CENT

1) $\dfrac{3}{4} = \dfrac{n}{52}$

2) $\dfrac{12}{8} = \dfrac{6}{n}$

3) $\dfrac{12}{n} = \dfrac{8}{12}$

4) $\dfrac{n}{12} = \dfrac{10}{24}$

5) $\dfrac{9}{n} = \dfrac{18}{24}$

6) $\dfrac{4}{48} = \dfrac{t}{6}$

7) $\dfrac{.4}{6} = \dfrac{6}{t}$

8) $\dfrac{.4}{t} = \dfrac{25}{5}$

9) $\dfrac{t}{1.2} = \dfrac{8}{.06}$

10) $\dfrac{200}{.2} = \dfrac{.48}{t}$

11) $\dfrac{30}{40} = \dfrac{18}{m}$

12) $\dfrac{6}{\frac{1}{2}} = \dfrac{m}{14}$

13) $\dfrac{8}{m} = \dfrac{6}{\frac{3}{4}}$

14) $\dfrac{m}{4} = \dfrac{15}{2\frac{1}{2}}$

15) $\dfrac{10}{m} = \dfrac{\frac{5}{8}}{2\frac{1}{2}}$

16) $\dfrac{r}{16} = \dfrac{27}{18}$

17) $\dfrac{.8}{2} = \dfrac{12}{r}$

18) $\dfrac{8}{\frac{4}{5}} = \dfrac{r}{16}$

19) $\dfrac{36}{3} = \dfrac{9}{r}$

20) $\dfrac{.03}{r} = \dfrac{.4}{.2}$

21) $\dfrac{k}{6} = \dfrac{5}{48}$

22) $\dfrac{20}{.6} = \dfrac{k}{\frac{3}{5}}$

23) $\dfrac{45}{k} = \dfrac{1\frac{1}{2}}{\frac{4}{5}}$

24) $\dfrac{20}{.3} = \dfrac{.8}{k}$

25) $\dfrac{k}{13} = \dfrac{7}{100}$

26) $\dfrac{12}{16} = \dfrac{l}{24}$

27) $\dfrac{6}{l} = \dfrac{\frac{3}{8}}{3\frac{1}{2}}$

28) $\dfrac{l}{.16} = \dfrac{.9}{48}$

29) $\dfrac{3\frac{1}{2}}{.3} = \dfrac{14}{l}$

30) $\dfrac{8}{96} = \dfrac{l}{9}$

31) $\dfrac{.4}{27} = \dfrac{8}{c}$

32) $\dfrac{.12}{\frac{9}{10}} = \dfrac{c}{.6}$

33) $\dfrac{3}{c} = \dfrac{48}{.12}$

34) $\dfrac{c}{18} = \dfrac{\frac{5}{6}}{\frac{5}{8}}$

35) $\dfrac{.4}{.9} = \dfrac{.2}{c}$

36) $\dfrac{4\frac{1}{2}}{.2} = \dfrac{.18}{k}$

37) $\dfrac{\frac{3}{8}}{4} = \dfrac{a}{16}$

38) $\dfrac{\$9.00}{t} = \dfrac{.6}{5}$

39) $\dfrac{h}{2\frac{1}{2}} = \dfrac{1\frac{1}{9}}{25}$

40) $\dfrac{5}{4\frac{1}{2}} = \dfrac{y}{18}$

41) $\dfrac{t}{14} = \dfrac{3}{56}$

42) $\dfrac{.0004}{.03} = \dfrac{16}{e}$

43) $\dfrac{.09}{\frac{1}{2}} = \dfrac{r}{.7}$

44) $\dfrac{r}{\$25.00} = \dfrac{15}{8}$

45) $\dfrac{4}{24} = \dfrac{i}{4}$

46) $\dfrac{13}{91} = \dfrac{k}{.7}$

47) $\dfrac{a}{\frac{3}{4}} = \dfrac{16}{.75}$

48) $\dfrac{\frac{1}{2}}{t} = \dfrac{5}{\frac{1}{4}}$

49) $\dfrac{.18}{.054} = \dfrac{4}{h}$

50) $\dfrac{225}{1\frac{1}{8}} = \dfrac{y}{.005}$

PROPORTIONS—SOLVE THE FOLLOWING

1) $\dfrac{5}{7} = \dfrac{25}{x}$

2) $\dfrac{13}{x} = \dfrac{39}{45}$

3) $\dfrac{x}{144} = \dfrac{21}{24}$

4) $\dfrac{30}{51} = \dfrac{10}{x}$

5) $\dfrac{65}{91} = \dfrac{x}{7}$

6) $\dfrac{129}{x} = \dfrac{43}{49}$

7) $\dfrac{x}{14} = \dfrac{66}{42}$

8) $\dfrac{75}{105} = \dfrac{15}{x}$

9) $\dfrac{x}{13} = \dfrac{60}{78}$

10) $\dfrac{15}{50} = \dfrac{x}{100}$

11) $\dfrac{7}{x} = \dfrac{9}{15}$

12) $\dfrac{x}{16} = \dfrac{20}{25}$

13) $\dfrac{33}{40} = \dfrac{40}{x}$

14) $\dfrac{19}{20} = \dfrac{x}{50}$

15) $\dfrac{16}{x} = \dfrac{5}{17}$

16) $\dfrac{x}{43} = \dfrac{39}{55}$

17) $\dfrac{17}{23} = \dfrac{19}{x}$

18) $\dfrac{30}{52} = \dfrac{x}{23}$

19) $\dfrac{9}{x} = \dfrac{5}{8}$

20) $\dfrac{x}{13} = \dfrac{23}{35}$

21) $\dfrac{\frac{1}{2}}{\frac{3}{4}} = \dfrac{\frac{1}{4}}{x}$

22) $\dfrac{\frac{2}{3}}{\frac{5}{6}} = \dfrac{x}{\frac{7}{12}}$

23) $\dfrac{\frac{4}{5}}{x} = \dfrac{\frac{6}{20}}{\frac{7}{10}}$

24) $\dfrac{x}{8} = \dfrac{\frac{3}{4}}{\frac{5}{8}}$

25) $\dfrac{^{17}/_{20}}{\frac{3}{4}} = \dfrac{^{4}/_{20}}{x}$

26) $\dfrac{2\frac{1}{2}}{6\frac{1}{3}} = \dfrac{x}{4\frac{1}{4}}$

27) $\dfrac{1\frac{2}{3}}{x} = \dfrac{3\frac{1}{7}}{2\frac{6}{7}}$

28) $\dfrac{x}{1\frac{3}{7}} = \dfrac{3\frac{2}{3}}{2\frac{5}{14}}$

29) $\dfrac{2\frac{1}{5}}{7\frac{1}{2}} = \dfrac{6\frac{1}{3}}{x}$

30) $\dfrac{\frac{3}{4}}{^{5}/_{24}} = \dfrac{x}{2\frac{1}{3}}$

31) $\dfrac{1.2}{x} = \dfrac{.6}{3.8}$

32) $\dfrac{x}{10} = \dfrac{158}{15.8}$

33) $\dfrac{.34}{2.3} = \dfrac{6.8}{x}$

34) $\dfrac{1.3}{.05} = \dfrac{x}{.41}$

35) $\dfrac{2.1}{x} = \dfrac{8}{7.4}$

36) $\dfrac{x}{.56} = \dfrac{6.3}{.24}$

37) $\dfrac{.15}{.7} = \dfrac{2.1}{x}$

38) $\dfrac{3.5}{.49} = \dfrac{x}{7}$

39) $\dfrac{.008}{x} = \dfrac{2.5}{.9}$

40) $\dfrac{x}{.62} = \dfrac{4.75}{3.1}$

41) $\dfrac{.5}{\frac{1}{2}} = \dfrac{\frac{3}{4}}{x}$

42) $\dfrac{x}{1} = \dfrac{\frac{1}{2}}{.8}$

43) $\dfrac{1^{4}/_{15}}{2.5} = \dfrac{x}{1\frac{1}{19}}$

44) $\dfrac{\frac{1}{4}}{x} = \dfrac{.2}{^{3}/_{20}}$

45) $\dfrac{^{3}/_{5}}{.72} = \dfrac{.25}{x}$

46) $\dfrac{\frac{7}{8}}{^{1}/_{12}} = \dfrac{x}{.4}$

47) $\dfrac{\frac{7}{9}}{x} = \dfrac{1.5}{.5}$

48) $\dfrac{x}{^{3}/_{10}} = \dfrac{^{15}/_{100}}{.08}$

49) $\dfrac{.75}{1\frac{4}{5}} = \dfrac{^{3}/_{7}}{x}$

50) $\dfrac{.6}{.08} = \dfrac{x}{^{18}/_{45}}$

PERCENTS—
CHANGE THE FOLLOWING FRACTIONS INTO DECIMALS

1)	$\frac{1}{2}$	26)	$1\frac{1}{5}$
2)	$\frac{1}{4}$	27)	$\frac{3}{7}$
3)	$\frac{3}{4}$	28)	$\frac{15}{20}$
4)	$\frac{3}{5}$	29)	$3\frac{3}{100}$
5)	$\frac{3}{8}$	30)	$\frac{3}{500}$
6)	$\frac{7}{10}$	31)	$2\frac{1}{2}$
7)	$\frac{7}{100}$	32)	$\frac{1}{3}$
8)	$\frac{7}{8}$	33)	$4\frac{2}{5}$
9)	$\frac{7}{20}$	34)	$\frac{5}{6}$
10)	$\frac{7}{25}$	35)	$\frac{72}{90}$
11)	$\frac{5}{8}$	36)	$\frac{21}{8}$
12)	$\frac{19}{25}$	37)	$\frac{7}{12}$
13)	$\frac{7}{50}$	38)	$\frac{9}{11}$
14)	$\frac{7}{200}$	39)	$3\frac{1}{8}$
15)	$\frac{45}{50}$	40)	$\frac{48}{100}$
16)	$\frac{39}{52}$	41)	$\frac{19}{5}$
17)	$\frac{16}{40}$	42)	$\frac{8}{15}$
18)	$\frac{144}{160}$	43)	$\frac{15}{8}$
19)	$\frac{57}{76}$	44)	$4\frac{3}{11}$
20)	$\frac{70}{175}$	45)	$\frac{13}{40}$
21)	$\frac{9}{5}$	46)	$\frac{1}{10000}$
22)	$\frac{47}{100}$	47)	$4\frac{5}{15}$
23)	$\frac{17}{4}$	48)	$\frac{39}{40}$
24)	$\frac{35}{8}$	49)	$1\frac{7}{100}$
25)	$\frac{2}{3}$	50)	$\frac{43}{16}$

PERCENTS—
CHANGE THE FOLLOWING FRACTIONS INTO PERCENTS

1)	$\frac{1}{4}$	26)	$1\frac{1}{10}$
2)	$\frac{1}{2}$	27)	$\frac{5}{9}$
3)	$\frac{3}{4}$	28)	$2\frac{1}{2}$
4)	$\frac{1}{3}$	29)	$\frac{7}{11}$
5)	$\frac{2}{3}$	30)	$\frac{48}{60}$
6)	$\frac{1}{5}$	31)	$2\frac{3}{10}$
7)	$\frac{1}{6}$	32)	$\frac{15}{20}$
8)	$\frac{1}{8}$	33)	$1\frac{1}{100}$
9)	$\frac{3}{5}$	34)	$2\frac{9}{10}$
10)	$\frac{3}{10}$	35)	$\frac{51}{68}$
11)	$\frac{3}{20}$	36)	$\frac{3}{400}$
12)	$\frac{3}{8}$	37)	$\frac{15}{25}$
13)	$\frac{5}{6}$	38)	$\frac{7}{50}$
14)	$\frac{5}{8}$	39)	$1\frac{7}{3}$
15)	$\frac{4}{5}$	40)	$3\frac{3}{4}$
16)	$\frac{7}{8}$	41)	$\frac{23}{25}$
17)	$\frac{17}{20}$	42)	$2\frac{3}{5}$
18)	$\frac{17}{50}$	43)	$\frac{36}{60}$
19)	$\frac{7}{10}$	44)	1
20)	$\frac{4}{100}$	45)	$\frac{17}{200}$
21)	$\frac{19}{20}$	46)	$\frac{15}{300}$
22)	$\frac{13}{25}$	47)	$2\frac{7}{4}$
23)	$\frac{17}{40}$	48)	$\frac{21}{35}$
24)	$\frac{11}{50}$	49)	$\frac{39}{65}$
25)	$\frac{21}{25}$	50)	$1\frac{2}{7}$

PERCENTS—
CHANGE THE FOLLOWING DECIMALS INTO FRACTIONS

1)	.3	26)	.09
2)	.03	27)	.5
3)	.003	28)	1.55
4)	.8	29)	2.5
5)	.08	30)	.92
6)	.008	31)	4.48
7)	1.3	32)	1.003
8)	.13	33)	.024
9)	.131	34)	.24
10)	.48	35)	.0024
11)	4.8	36)	2.4
12)	.048	37)	.33
13)	.0048	38)	.67
14)	.16	39)	1.7
15)	.016	40)	.17
16)	1.6	41)	.017
17)	.1	42)	5.4
18)	.25	43)	5.25
19)	.02	44)	.4
20)	.75	45)	.04
21)	.6	46)	.0004
22)	.15	47)	.004
23)	1.5	48)	25.36
24)	.015	49)	100.25
25)	.9	50)	.1875

PERCENTS—
CHANGE THE FOLLOWING DECIMALS INTO FRACTIONS

1) .6	2) .16	3) .3
4) .83	5) .5	6) .45
7) .17	8) .46	9) .54
10) .13	11) 6.2	12) .47
13) .23	14) 8.72	15) .416
16) .945	17) 77.7	18) .583
19) .08	20) .61	21) .39
22) .126	23) 2.38	24) 4.92
25) .003	26) .339	27) 6.14
28) .073	29) .015	30) .972
31) 39.15	32) .876	33) .408
34) 7.84	35) .671	36) .274
37) .381	38) 8.37	39) 33.4
40) .148	41) .4136	42) .4136
43) .4136	44) .4136	45) 4.136
46) 8.437	47) .4583	48) 2.172
49) .0761	50) .2135	

PERCENTS—
CHANGE THE FOLLOWING DECIMALS INTO PERCENTS

1)	.5	26)	1
2)	.05	27)	.8
3)	.14	28)	.08
4)	.005	29)	1.8
5)	.3	30)	.18
6)	.03	31)	.018
7)	.003	32)	.118
8)	.4	33)	1.18
9)	.04	34)	.67
10)	.004	35)	.35
11)	1.4	36)	3.5
12)	.14	37)	.035
13)	1.04	38)	.0035
14)	.014	39)	9.2
15)	.64	40)	.92
16)	6.4	41)	.0092
17)	.064	42)	2
18)	.0064	43)	.2
19)	1.1	44)	2.02
20)	.011	45)	.202
21)	.7	46)	7.035
22)	.07	47)	.131
23)	.007	48)	.0455
24)	.1	49)	2.9
25)	.45	50)	.029

PERCENTS—
CHANGE THE FOLLOWING PERCENTS INTO FRACTIONS

1)	50%	26)	65%
2)	25%	27)	52%
3)	10%	28)	3%
4)	75%	29)	30%
5)	20%	30)	300%
6)	85%	31)	.3%
7)	36%	32)	72%
8)	7%	33)	64%
9)	70%	34)	95%
10)	8%	35)	5%
11)	80%	36)	90%
12)	15%	37)	9%
13)	150%	38)	190%
14)	44%	39)	77%
15)	60%	40)	7.7%
16)	6%	41)	$33\frac{1}{3}$%
17)	.6%	42)	$66\frac{2}{3}$%
18)	40%	43)	$12\frac{1}{2}$%
19)	4%	44)	$37\frac{1}{2}$%
20)	400%	45)	$16\frac{2}{3}$%
21)	.4%	46)	84%
22)	17%	47)	840%
23)	170%	48)	$83\frac{1}{3}$%
24)	57%	49)	$87\frac{1}{}$%
25)	78%	50)	155%

CHANGE THE FOLLOWING PERCENTS INTO DECIMALS

1)	50%	26)	8%
2)	5%	27)	100%
3)	35%	28)	10%
4)	3%	29)	1%
5)	30%	30)	.1%
6)	300%	31)	45%
7)	17%	32)	7%
8)	170%	33)	90%
9)	4%	34)	67%
10)	40%	35)	3.5%
11)	400%	36)	.35%
12)	6%	37)	4.1%
13)	60%	38)	175%
14)	.6%	39)	$1\frac{1}{2}$%
15)	600%	40)	$62\frac{1}{2}$%
16)	150%	41)	$3\frac{3}{4}$%
17)	15%	42)	$5\frac{1}{5}$%
18)	1.5%	43)	9.25%
19)	.15%	44)	$13\frac{3}{4}$%
20)	75%	45)	$15\frac{4}{5}$%
21)	7.5%	46)	$19\frac{1}{4}$%
22)	20%	47)	$9\frac{3}{5}$%
23)	2%	48)	120%
24)	25%	49)	625%
25)	80%	50)	$13\frac{3}{8}$%

PERCENTS—CONVERT THE FOLLOWING

	Fraction	Decimal	Percent			Fraction	Decimal	Percent
1)	¼			26)			.18	
2)	½			27)			.018	
3)	⅔			28)			1.4	
4)	¾			29)			.14	
5)	⅜			30)			.014	
6)	⅞			31)			.7	
7)	$^{11}/_{20}$			32)			.07	
8)	$^{17}/_{50}$			33)			1.07	
9)	$^{7}/_{100}$			34)			1.7	
10)	$^{3}/_{50}$			35)			.017	
11)	$1^{4}/_{5}$			36)				60%
12)	$1^{3}/_{25}$			37)				6%
13)	$3^{7}/_{100}$			38)				.6%
14)	$^{1}/_{50}$			39)				116%
15)	$1^{2}/_{5}$			40)				16%
16)	$^{3}/_{10}$			41)				1.6%
17)	$^{3}/_{100}$			42)				100%
18)	$1^{3}/_{10}$			43)				48%
19)	$^{3}/_{1000}$			44)				12%
20)	$4^{1}/_{20}$			45)				85%
21)		.9		46)				95%
22)		.09		47)				120%
23)		.8		48)				80%
24)		.08		49)				8%
25)		1.8		50)				.8%

PERCENTS—CONVERT THE FOLLOWING

	Fraction	Decimal	Percent			Fraction	Decimal	Percent
1)	1/5			26)			.011	
2)	7/25			27)			.11	
3)	13/52			28)			1	
4)	1 1/5			29)			.008	
5)	1/200			30)			.0018	
6)	7/40			31)				60%
7)	17/4			32)				6%
8)	2			33)				.6%
9)	6/7			34)				6 1/2 %
10)	10/3			35)				65%
11)	1 1/8			36)				6 3/4 %
12)	7/11			37)				67%
13)	33/40			38)				180%
14)	39/52			39)				115%
15)	15/9			40)				11 1/2 %
16)		.4		41)				11.25%
17)		.04		42)				62 1/2 %
18)		.004		43)				6.25%
19)		4.4		44)				625%
20)		4.04		45)				.06%
21)		.78		46)	3 1/8			
22)		.078		47)		4.2		
23)		.9		48)				.75%
24)		.09		49)		.042		
25)		1.1		50)	1/16			

PERCENTS—CONVERT THE FOLLOWING

	Fraction	Decimal	Percent		Fraction	Decimal	Percent
1)	¼			26)		.24	
2)	⁴⁄₅			27)		.6	
3)	¹⁵⁄₃₀			28)		.06	
4)	¹⁹⁄₂₀			29)		1.6	
5)	³⁄₁₀			30)		.16	
6)	¹³⁄₂₅			31)			9%
7)	¹³⁄₂₀			32)			90%
8)	¹³⁄₅₀			33)			75%
9)	³⁄₈			34)			12%
10)	⁷⁄₅			35)			120%
11)	1⁴⁄₅			36)			7%
12)	⁵⁄₆			37)			70%
13)	³⁄₇			38)			700%
14)	¹⁄₁₀			39)			17%
15)	1¹⁄₁₀			40)			170%
16)		.11		41)			35%
17)		.85		42)			34%
18)		.2		43)			85%
19)		.02		44)			150%
20)		2.02		45)			15%
21)		.44		46)		1.34	
22)		.64		47)			100%
23)		.04		48)	³⁄₁₁		
24)		.19		49)		1.11	
25)		1.9		50)			3.5%

PERCENTS—CONVERT THE FOLLOWING

	Fraction	Decimal	Percent		Fraction	Decimal	Percent
1)	$\frac{1}{2}$			26)		.008	
2)	$\frac{3}{4}$			27)		.1	
3)	$\frac{7}{20}$			28)		.01	
4)	$\frac{3}{5}$			29)		1.01	
5)	$\frac{17}{50}$			30)		.375	
6)	$\frac{5}{8}$			31)			3%
7)	$\frac{2}{3}$			32)			30%
8)	$\frac{37}{50}$			33)			45%
9)	$\frac{1}{6}$			34)			8%
10)	$\frac{1}{8}$			35)			55%
11)	$1\frac{3}{5}$			36)			40%
12)	$\frac{9}{4}$			37)			4%
13)	$\frac{7}{200}$			38)			.4%
14)	$\frac{1}{20}$			39)			400%
15)	$1\frac{5}{6}$			40)			125%
16)		.7		41)			12.5%
17)		.07		42)			72%
18)		.35		43)			59%
19)		3.5		44)			140%
20)		.035		45)			14%
21)		.9		46)		.03	
22)		.09		47)	$1\frac{7}{8}$		
23)		1.9		48)			95%
24)		.8		49)		1.1	
25)		.08		50)	$\frac{13}{4}$		

PERCENTS—CONVERT THE FOLLOWING

	Fraction	Decimal	Percent			Fraction	Decimal	Percent
1)	$\frac{1}{5}$			26)			.52	
2)	$\frac{1}{3}$			27)			.06	
3)	$\frac{15}{20}$			28)			.6	
4)	$\frac{9}{10}$			29)			1.2	
5)	$\frac{9}{100}$			30)			.12	
6)	$\frac{9}{1000}$			31)			.012	
7)	$\frac{17}{25}$			32)			.84	
8)	$\frac{17}{20}$			33)			.084	
9)	$\frac{17}{50}$			34)			1.07	
10)	$\frac{5}{8}$			35)			1.007	
11)	$1\frac{1}{2}$			36)				20%
12)	$1\frac{3}{4}$			37)				2%
13)	$\frac{1}{8}$			38)				200%
14)	$3\frac{3}{5}$			39)				40%
15)	$\frac{5}{6}$			40)				75%
16)	$\frac{2}{25}$			41)				92%
17)	$3\frac{1}{10}$			42)				14.4%
18)	$\frac{31}{100}$			43)				10.5%
19)	$\frac{31}{1000}$			44)				25%
20)	$5\frac{23}{1000}$			45)				250%
21)		.1		46)				2.5%
22)		.01		47)				8%
23)		.001		48)				80%
24)		1		49)				$12\frac{1}{2}$%
25)		.48		50)				$11\frac{3}{4}$%

PERCENTS—CONVERT THE FOLLOWING

	Fraction	Decimal	Percent		Fraction	Decimal	Percent
1)		.7		26)			62½%
2)			75%	27)		.875	
3)	3/50			28)	1/8		
4)		.07		29)	26/65		
5)			60%	30)			80%
6)		.28		31)	1⅔		
7)	5/8			32)		3.3	
8)		1.3		33)	1¹³/50		
9)	5/9			34)			400%
10)			135%	35)		.137	
11)		.85		36)			12¾%
12)	5/15			37)	3½		
13)		.16		38)			14.1%
14)			18%	39)		.75	
15)	6/10			40)	6/16		
16)			4%	41)			24%
17)		.014		42)		.015	
18)	7/16			43)	7/15		
19)			5.5%	44)		.905	
20)		1.01		45)			36%
21)			5¼%	46)	5/11		
22)	7/400			47)			6.4%
23)			9⅔%	48)		.08	
24)		.17		49)			9⅕%
25)	8/5			50)	1⅞		

PERCENTS—SOLVE THE FOLLOWING

1) What is 35% of 40?

2) What is 48% of 990?

3) What is 56% of 80?

4) 65% of 55 is what?

5) What is 32% of 67?

6) 78% of 85 is what?

7) 43% of 88 is what?

8) What is 90% of 90?

9) 7% of 7000 is what?

10) 83% of 522 is what?

11) What is 45% of 6?

12) 8% of 72 is what?

13) 850% of 72 is what?

14) What is 19% of 19?

15) What is 100% of 48?

16) 43% of 13 is what?

17) 95% of 1,200 is what?

18) 5% of 64 is what?

19) What is 3% of 55?

20) What is 125% of 6?

21) 70% of 210 is what?

22) 13% of 85 is what?

23) 6% of 4 is what?

24) What is 18% of 443?

25) What is 57% of 16?

26) 37% of 530 is what?

27) 1,236% of 90 is what?

28) What is 88% of 313?

29) What is 11% of 66?

30) What is 62% of 70?

31) 97% of 215 is what?

32) 2,500% of 90 is what?

33) What is 74% of 167?

34) What is 500% of 75?

35) 41% of 2,536 is what?

36) 5% of 760 is what?

37) 27% of 6 is what?

38) What is 58% of 371?

39) What is 795% of 864?

40) 3% of 800 is what?

41) What is 22% of 153?

42) 45% of 6,439 is what?

43) What is 99% of 9?

44) What is 71% of 1,000?

45) 447% of 53 is what?

46) 7,250% of 65 is what?

47) 87% of 629 is what?

48) What is 111% of 333?

49) What is 17% of 804?

50) 27% of 4,538 is what?

PERCENTS—SOLVE THE FOLLOWING

1) What is 45% of 75?

2) 63% of 125 is what?

3) 81% of 400 is what?

4) 169% of 7 is what?

5) What is 9% of 274?

6) What is 62% of 62?

7) 58% of 229 is what?

8) What is 5% of 5?

9) 4,350% of 41 is what?

10) 77% of 264 is what?

11) 42.3% of 28 is what?

12) What is 4.8% of 72?

13) What is 25% of 7.6?

14) 83% of 9.8 is what?

15) What is .9% of 81?

16) What is 1.1% of 8?

17) 7.52% of 12 is what?

18) What is 80% of 6.54?

19) 97% of .38 is what?

20) 6.75% of 2.6 is what?

21) What is .58% of 17?

22) What is 12.5% of 654?

23) What is 6.8% of .13?

24) 17% of 4.32 is what?

25) 200% of .8 is what?

26) What is 4.4% of 8.5?

27) What is 1.9% of 4,250?

28) 67.3% of 28 is what?

29) 93% of 6.7 is what?

30) What is .75% of 400?

31) $12\frac{1}{2}$% of 80 is what?

32) 40% of $6\frac{1}{4}$ is what?

33) $7\frac{1}{8}$% of 50 is what?

34) What is 29% of $35\frac{1}{10}$?

35) What is $45\frac{1}{5}$% of 25?

36) $18\frac{3}{4}$% of 26 is what?

37) $5\frac{7}{12}$% of 90 is what?

38) What is 50% of $\frac{1}{5}$?

39) What is 8% of $17\frac{3}{8}$?

40) 15% of $24\frac{1}{2}$ is what?

41) What is $7\frac{3}{4}$% of $\frac{4}{5}$?

42) What is 95% of $4\frac{7}{10}$?

43) 62% of $4\frac{9}{20}$ is what?

44) $82\frac{7}{8}$% of 120 is what?

45) What is $\frac{1}{2}$% of $\frac{1}{4}$?

46) What is 45% of $5\frac{1}{4}$?

47) $52\frac{1}{8}$% of 200 is what?

48) What is $33\frac{1}{3}$% of 600?

49) What is $16\frac{2}{3}$% of 120?

50) 70% of $\frac{1}{6}$ is what?

PERCENTS—SOLVE THE FOLLOWING

1) 20 is _____ % of 50?

2) What percent of 50 is 30?

3) 10 = _____ % of 50?

4) What percent of 50 is 33?

5) 2 is _____ % of 50?

6) 13 = _____ % of 20?

7) 21 = _____ % of 20?

8) 12 is what % of 20?

9) What % of 20 is 1?

10) 15 = _____ % of 20?

11) 30 is _____ % of 25?

12) What percent of 25 = 13?

13) 2 = _____ % of 25?

14) 17 is _____ % of 25?

15) What percent of 25 is 20?

16) 20 = _____ % of 80?

17) What percent of 80 = 60?

18) 120 = _____ % of 80?

19) 30 is what percent of 80?

20) What percent of 80 is 4?

21) 42 = _____ % of 56?

22) What percent of 68 = 51?

23) 27 = _____ % of 36?

24) 72 is _____ % of 96?

25) 57 = _____ % of 76?

26) 24 is what percent of 60?

27) 3 = _____ % of 60?

28) 13 = _____ % of 52?

29) What percent of 80 = 64?

30) 44 is _____ % of 200?

31) 8 = _____ % of 20?

32) 19 is what percent of 5?

33) 34 = _____ % of 85?

34) 72 = _____ % of 80?

35) 35 = _____ % of 700?

36) What percent of 35 = 14?

37) 4 = _____ % of 5?

38) 5 = _____ % of 4?

39) What percent of 360 is 18?

40) 300 is what percent of 30,000?

41) 50 is what percent of 125?

42) 32 = _____ % of 20?

43) 3 is what percent of 25?

44) 25 is what percent of 4?

45) 60 = _____ % of 400?

46) 2 = _____ % of 5?

47) 41 is _____ % of 50?

48) What % of 800 = 24?

49) 75 is what percent of 100?

50) What percent of 120 is 48?

PERCENTS—SOLVE THE FOLLOWING

1) What is 22% of 29?

2) 74% of 360 is what?

3) 29% of 65 is what?

4) What is 243% of 2?

5) What is 8% of 751?

6) 46% of 219 is what?

7) What is 1,235% of 23?

8) 97% of 97 is what?

9) 82% of 9 is what?

10) What is 650% of 148?

11) 6.5% of 24 is what?

12) What is 35% of 3.52?

13) What is 9.21% of 60?

14) 67.3% of 8 is what?

15) 12.1% of 250 is what?

16) What is 3% of .36?

17) What is .6% of 240?

18) What is 28.1% of 56?

19) 7.82% of 30 is what?

20) 93% of .45 is what?

21) What is 8.4% of 4.2?

22) What is 4.9% of .04?

23) 7.1% of 62.8 is what?

24) What is .06% of 35?

25) 4.75% of 5 is what?

26) 8.8% of 9.5 is what?

27) What is 3.7% of .045?

28) What is .9% of 4.2?

29) What is 400% of .04?

30) 2.643% of 1 is what?

31) What is $12\frac{1}{4}$% of 50?

32) What is $8\frac{1}{2}$% of 45?

33) 35% of $3\frac{3}{8}$ is what?

34) $4\frac{1}{5}$% of 25 is what?

35) What is 25% of $\frac{7}{10}$?

36) What is $6\frac{1}{10}$% of 758?

37) $18\frac{3}{4}$% of 40 is what?

38) 65% of $5\frac{5}{16}$ is what?

39) What is 25% of $\frac{1}{4}$?

40) What is $16\frac{2}{3}$% of 100?

41) What is $5\frac{1}{4}$% of $\frac{1}{8}$?

42) $12\frac{3}{5}$% of $2\frac{1}{2}$ is what?

43) $58\frac{3}{10}$% of $4\frac{1}{5}$ is what?

44) $3\frac{1}{25}$% of $15\frac{1}{40}$ is what?

45) What is $8\frac{5}{8}$% of 40?

46) What is $35\frac{1}{4}$% of 64?

47) What is $3\frac{1}{3}$% of 600?

48) 12% of $4\frac{1}{6}$ is what?

49) $18\frac{3}{5}$% of $5\frac{1}{9}$ is what?

50) What is $8\frac{1}{6}$% of 1,200?

PERCENTS—SOLVE THE FOLLOWING

1) $47 =$ _____ % of 50?

2) What percent of 20 $=$ 19?

3) 30 is what % of 40?

4) $2 =$ _____ % of 25?

5) What percent of 40 is 16?

6) $40 =$ _____ % of 200?

7) 7 is what percent of 20?

8) What percent of 150 is 90?

9) $4 =$ _____ % of 25?

10) 76 is what percent of 95?

11) $1.5 =$ _____ % of 6?

12) What percent of 20 is 2.5?

13) 3 is what percent of 8?

14) $.14 =$ _____ % of .7?

15) What percent of 8 is 5?

16) $.625 =$ _____ % of 1?

17) 2.4 is _____ % of 6?

18) .24 is _____ % of 6?

19) 4.8 is what percent of 5?

20) $14 =$ _____ % of 25?

21) $1.4 =$ _____ % of 25?

22) $.14 =$ _____ % of 25?

23) What percent of 4.8 $=$ .12?

24) What percent of 4.8 $=$ 12?

25) 7.5 is what percent of 45?

26) $.04 =$ _____ % of .2?

27) $9.3 =$ _____ % of 50?

28) .7 is _____ % of 25?

29) $.7 =$ _____ % of 2.5?

30) .002 is what % of 8?

31) $5 =$ _____ % of 8?

32) What percent of 8 $=$ 7?

33) $7\frac{1}{2}$ is what percent of 30?

34) $17 =$ _____ % of 51?

35) $3\frac{1}{3}$ is what percent of 30?

36) What percent of 6 $=$ $1\frac{1}{5}$?

37) $5\frac{1}{2}$ is what % of 22?

38) $3\frac{1}{2}$ is _____ % of 35?

39) What % of 50 $=$ $22\frac{1}{2}$?

40) $34 =$ _____ % of 51?

41) $12\frac{1}{2}$ is what percent of 20?

42) $12\frac{1}{4} =$ _____ % of 25?

43) What percent of 25 $=$ $14\frac{3}{4}$?

44) $28 =$ _____ % of 42?

45) 24 is what percent of 64?

46) $4 =$ _____ % of 600?

47) $9\frac{1}{2} =$ _____ % of 76?

48) $6\frac{1}{4} =$ _____ % of $18\frac{3}{4}$?

49) What % of $26\frac{2}{5}$ is $6\frac{3}{5}$?

50) $4\frac{1}{3}$ is what percent of 26?

PERCENTS—SOLVE THE FOLLOWING

1) 4 is what percent of 20?

2) 9 = ____ % of 50?

3) 13 = ____ % of 20?

4) 30 = ____ % of 25?

5) 24 = ____ % of 30?

6) What percent of 50 is 43?

7) What percent of 25 is 23?

8) ____ % of 36 = 24?

9) ____ % of 24 = 36?

10) What percent of 60 = 48?

11) 27 is ____ % of 30?

12) 19 = ____ % of 5?

13) 35 = ____ % of 140?

14) 24 = ____ % of 64?

15) What percent of 56 is 35?

16) What percent of 72 is 56?

17) 50 = what percent of 40?

18) 40 = what percent of 50?

19) 13 is ____ % of 50?

20) 18 is ____ % of 40?

21) What percent of 54 is 36?

22) 18 = ____ % of 27?

23) 36 = ____ % of 108?

24) 75 is ____ % of 50?

25) 26 = ____ % of 65?

26) 34 = ____ % of 85?

27) 38 = ____ % of 95?

28) 98 = ____ % of 245?

29) What percent of 24 is 20?

30) 9 is what percent of 45?

31) 3 is what percent of 16?

32) What percent of 56 = 48?

33) What percent of 85 = 68?

34) ____ % of 25 = 40?

35) ____ % of 30 = 25?

36) 45 = ____ % of 60?

37) 90 = ____ % of 60?

38) 25 = ____ % of 45?

39) What percent of 36 = 144?

40) What percent of 50 = 41?

41) ____ % of 360 = 24?

42) ____ % of 288 = 72?

43) 35 = ____ % of 25?

44) 42 = ____ % of 28?

45) 25 = ____ % of 1,000?

46) 144 = ____ % of 18?

47) What percent of 65 = 91?

48) What percent of 24 = $3\frac{3}{5}$?

49) What percent of 36 = 2.7?

50) What percent of 60 = .12?

PERCENTS—SOLVE THE FOLLOWING

1) 40 is 25% of what?

2) 75 is 20% of what?

3) 120 is 30% of what?

4) 45% of what is 900?

5) 70% of what is 2,100?

6) 65 is 40% of what?

7) 150 is 75% of what?

8) 93 is 50% of what?

9) 13% of what is 2,600?

10) 125% of what is 100?

11) 1,500 is 80% of what?

12) 72% of what is 216?

13) 144 is 24% of what?

14) 4% of what is 352?

15) 32% of what is 512?

16) 77% of what is 1,309?

17) 60 is 500% of what?

18) 42 is 14% of what?

19) 99 is 30% of what?

20) 28% of what is 7?

21) 64% of what is 48?

22) 35 is 40% of what?

23) 5 is 8% of what?

24) 81 is 27% of what?

25) 35% of what is 168?

26) 15% of what is 192?

27) 11% of what is 99?

28) 665 is 500% of what?

29) 144 is 12% of what?

30) 320 is 80% of what?

31) 3% of what is 135?

32) 72% of what is 1,440?

33) 484 is 22% of what?

34) 54 is 150% of what?

35) 360% of what is 450?

36) 39 is 13% of what?

37) 721 is 700% of what?

38) 52% of what is 1,300?

39) 28 is 14% of what?

40) 630 is 9% of what?

41) 55% of what is 3,025?

42) 2% of what is 176?

43) 775 is 155% of what?

44) 1,000 is 100% of what?

45) 29% of what is 87?

46) 270% of what is 810?

47) 850 is 5% of what?

48) 35% of what is 315?

49) 64 is 16% of what?

50) 950% of what is 285?

PERCENTS—SOLVE THE FOLLOWING

1)	60% of what is 240?	26)	10.75% of what is 5.16?
2)	5% of what is 175?	27)	95.5% of what is 43.93?
3)	22 is 11% of what?	28)	58.2% of what is 71.586?
4)	120 is 40% of what?	29)	71 is 35.5% of what?
5)	64 is 16% of what?	30)	136 is .68% of what?
6)	700% of what is 63?	31)	66 is $6\frac{3}{5}$% of what?
7)	35% of what is 2,415?	32)	$\frac{1}{4}$% of what is 360?
8)	100% of what is 59?	33)	225 is $33\frac{1}{3}$% of what?
9)	84 is 28% of what?	34)	98 is $8\frac{1}{6}$% of what?
10)	54 is 75% of what?	35)	318 is $21\frac{1}{5}$% of what?
11)	12.5% of what is 68?	36)	$66\frac{2}{3}$% of what is 114?
12)	10% of what is 9.5?	37)	$24\frac{1}{2}$% of what is 147?
13)	252 is 4.5% of what?	38)	280 is $3\frac{8}{9}$% of what?
14)	80 is .5% of what?	39)	$17\frac{3}{4}$% of what is 284?
15)	6.3 is 7.2% of what?	40)	216 is $5\frac{1}{7}$% of what?
16)	4.9% of what is 147?	41)	$28\frac{7}{12}$% of what is 686?
17)	.08% of what is 48?	42)	$52\frac{1}{2}$ is 20% of what?
18)	1.5% of what is 192?	43)	112 is $11\frac{1}{5}$% of what?
19)	45 is .15% of what?	44)	1,704 is $21\frac{3}{10}$% of what?
20)	2.75 is 5.5% of what?	45)	$\frac{1}{2}$% of what is $62\frac{1}{2}$?
21)	38 is 1.9% of what?	46)	$16\frac{2}{3}$% of what is 750?
22)	3.2% of what is 25.6?	47)	1,284 is $85\frac{3}{5}$% of what?
23)	6.25% of what is 125?	48)	235 is $29\frac{3}{8}$% of what?
24)	2.48 is 31% of what?	49)	$25\frac{1}{4}$% of what is 808?
25)	520 is 1.3% of what?	50)	1,295 is $30\frac{5}{6}$% of what?

PERCENTS—SOLVE THE FOLLOWING

1) 56% of what is 4,088?
2) 12% of what is 216?
3) 9% of what is 207?
4) 3,337 is 47% of what?
5) 4,900 is 140% of what?
6) 75% of what is 12?
7) 92% of what is 37.72?
8) 20.47 is 23% of what?
9) 227.25 is 225% of what?
10) 49% of what is 2,744?
11) 8.5% of what is 629?
12) 35.4% of wht is 23.364?
13) 26.25 is .21% of what?
14) 8.4364 is 18.34% of what?
15) 75.2% of what is 30.08?
16) .8% of what is 7.992?
17) 5.67 is 37.8% of what?
18) 3.875 is 12.5% of what?
19) .27% of what is 2,241?
20) 1.1% of what is 3.927?
21) 99.9% of what is 31.968?
22) 50.72 is 8% of what?
23) 4,128 is 1.72% of what?
24) 2.2% of what is .902?
25) 172% of what is 4.3?
26) 47.8% of what is 144.356?
27) 338.96 is 8.92% of what?
28) .806 is 1.3% of what?
29) 1.65% of what is 9.075?
30) 8.7% of what is 36.627?
31) 55 is $5\frac{1}{2}$% of what?
32) 17,324 is $24\frac{2}{5}$% of what?
33) $16\frac{2}{3}$% of what is 550?
34) $9\frac{1}{4}$% of what is 111?
35) $20\frac{1}{6}$% of what is 363?
36) 550 is $30\frac{5}{9}$% of what?
37) 1,516 is $31\frac{7}{12}$% of what?
38) $19\frac{9}{16}$% of what is 626?
39) $\frac{1}{8}$% of what is 65?
40) 13,916 is $14\frac{1}{5}$% of what?
41) 450 is $\frac{2}{5}$% of what?
42) $3\frac{1}{7}$% of what is 110?
43) $33\frac{1}{3}$% of what is 81?
44) 175 is $83\frac{1}{3}$% of what?
45) $22\frac{1}{2}$ is 20% of what?
46) $\frac{1}{15}$% of what is 3?
47) $4\frac{1}{8}$% of what is 132?
48) $7\frac{3}{4}$% of what is 372?
49) 294 is $29\frac{2}{5}$% of what?
50) $\frac{3}{10}$ is $\frac{3}{10}$% of what?

PERCENTS—SOLVE THE FOLLOWING

1) 50% of 60 is ?

2) 42 is ____ % of 84?

3) 24 is 50% of ____ ?

4) ____ = 50% of 90?

5) ____ % of 80 = 20?

6) 75% of 40 = ____ ?

7) 20% of ____ = 7?

8) 8 is ____ % of 80?

9) 75 is 100% of ____ ?

10) 30% of 360 is ____ ?

11) 24 = ____ % of 96?

12) 30 = 15% of ____ ?

13) 85% of 300 = ____ ?

14) 24 is 20% of ____ ?

15) 39 is ____ % of 52?

16) ____ is 40% of 120?

17) 26 is ____ % of 52?

18) 25% of ____ is 24?

19) 72 is ____ % of 120?

20) 36 is 25% of ____ ?

21) 7% of 1000 = ____ ?

22) 34 is ____ % of 136?

23) 13 is ____ % of 52?

24) 80% of 120 = ____ ?

25) 72% of 500 is ____ ?

26) 102 = ____ % of 136?

27) 10 = 40% of ____ ?

28) 10% of 40 = ____ ?

29) 72 is 50% of ____ ?

30) ____ % of 20 is 30?

31) 20% of ____ is 12?

32) ____ is 20% of 300?

33) ____ % of 960 is 96?

34) 60% of 60 = ____ ?

35) 96 is 75% of ____ ?

36) 13% of 100 = ____ ?

37) 8 is ____ % of 20?

38) 45 = ____ % of 60?

39) 75% of ____ is 12?

40) 12% of $1200 = ____ ?

41) 15 is 25% of ____ ?

42) 68 is ____ % of 136?

43) 30% of $70.00 = ____ ?

44) 16 is 80% of ____ ?

45) 48 is 80% of ____ ?

46) 10% of $2,500.00 = ____ ?

47) ____ % of 60 is 24?

48) ____ = 75% of 80?

49) 20% of $75,000.00 = ____ ?

50) 52 is ____ % of 65?

PERCENTS—SOLVE THE FOLLOWING

1) 20 is ___ % of 50?

2) 40% of 45 is ___?

3) 25 is 75% of ___?

4) 17 is ___ % of 68?

5) 52 is 80% of ___?

6) ___ is 90% of 250?

7) ___ % of 51 is 17?

8) 30% of ___ = 21?

9) 25% of 248 is ___?

10) 21 is 60% of ___?

11) ___ is 95% of 500?

12) 13 is ___ % of 25?

13) 13 is ___ % of 20?

14) 35 is 10% of ___?

15) 16 is 40% of ___?

16) ___ is 35% of 1000?

17) 14 is ___ % of 16?

18) 45% of 160 = ___?

19) $37\frac{1}{2}$% of ___ = 15?

20) 35 is ___ % of 40?

21) 6% of 84 = ___?

22) 25% of 52 is ___?

23) 18 is ___ % of 144?

24) 56 is 80% of ___?

25) 25% of ___ is 75?

26) 40% of ___ is 300?

27) ___ is 50% of 12.5?

28) 24 is 80% of ___?

29) 45 is ___ % of 60?

30) What % of 72 is 45?

31) 90% of 600 is ___?

32) 9% of 600 is ___?

33) 34 is 85% of ___?

34) 51 is ___ % of 85?

35) ___ is 95% of 130?

36) 80% of ___ is 52?

37) 9 is ___ % of 54?

38) 65% of ___ is 91?

39) 30 is ___ % of 36?

40) What % of 400 is 20?

41) 12% of $55.00 is ___?

42) $12.50 is ___ % of $50.00?

43) $62.50 is ___ % of $100?

44) $5\frac{1}{2}$% of $750 = ___?

45) 55% of $750 = ___?

46) $28.68 is 80% of ___?

47) 37.5% of ___ is $51.00?

48) $20.40 is ___ % of $30.60?

49) 8.3% of $5,765.30 = ___?

50) $12\frac{3}{4}$% of $40,000.00 = ___?

PERCENTS—SOLVE THE FOLLOWING

1) 40% of 200 = ____?

2) What % of 80 is 30?

3) 15 is 60% of ____?

4) What is 25% of 84?

5) 80% of ____ = 52?

6) 63 is 90% of what number?

7) 150% of 66 is ____?

8) 25 is 25% of ____?

9) 13 is what % of 25?

10) 30% of 450 is ____?

11) 48 is 50% of what number?

12) 13 = what % of 50?

13) 86.4 is 36% of ____?

14) $\frac{1}{2}$ = ____% of 2?

15) $4\frac{1}{2}$ is 10% of what number?

16) 17 = what % of 20?

17) 3.25% of $500.00 = ____?

18) 84 is 66⅔% of ____?

19) 350% of $40.50 is ____?

20) 13 = what % of 10?

21) What is 18% of 650?

22) $3\frac{1}{2}$ = ____% of 28?

23) 35 = 62½% of what number?

24) 37½% of $88.96 = ____?

25) 75 = ____% of 225?

26) 40 = 20% of what number?

27) 8½% of $500.00 = ____?

28) 18 = ____% of 150?

29) 2% of ____ = 6000?

30) 85% of $5000 = ____?

31) 13 is what % of 20?

32) 4.5 is 20% of ____?

33) What is 5% of $120.00?

34) $7\frac{1}{2}$ is 25% of ____?

35) 45 is 62½ % of ____?

36) 1.5 = what % of 50?

37) 7% of $750.00 = ____?

38) .7% of $750.00 = ____?

39) 1.3 is what % of 20?

40) 30 = 2% of ____?

41) What is 125% of 36?

42) 24.6 is 37½% of ____?

43) 5.20 = what % of 26?

44) $50.40 is 40% of ____?

45) 4¼% of $8400.00 = ____?

46) .13 = what % of 20?

47) 250 is 125% of ____?

48) .5% of 120 = what number?

49) .005 = ____% of .08?

50) What is 9¼% of $2000.00?

PERCENTS—SOLVE THE FOLLOWING

1) 30 is 60% of what number?

2) 45% of 300 is what?

3) 42 is what percent of 56?

4) What is 25% of 92?

5) 40 is what % of 50?

6) 25% of what number is 17?

7) What is 50% of 128?

8) What % of 80 is 16?

9) 54 is 90% of what number?

10) 12 is what % of 30?

11) 25% of 400 is what number?

12) 2.5% of 400 is what number?

13) 1.3 is what % of 5.2?

14) 12 is 37.5% of what number?

15) 600 is what % of 150?

16) 9.5% of $300.00 is what?

17) 1.5 is 25% of what number?

18) 35% of $125.70 equals what?

19) $12.50 is what % of $50?

20) 62.5% of what number equals 25?

21) What is 30% of $900.50?

22) 87.5 = what % of 175?

23) .28 = 80% of what number?

24) $21.60 is what % of $36.00?

25) 75% of $300.42 = what?

26) 1.5 = 5% of what number?

27) What is 62.5% of 3.2?

28) .3 = what % of 50?

29) 3.8 = 95% of what number?

30) 1.5% of 360 is what number?

31) 40% of what number = 28?

32) $7\frac{1}{2}$% of $2000.00 = what?

33) 16 = what % of 128?

34) 80 = $62\frac{1}{2}$% of what number?

35) 16 = 80% of what number?

36) $7\frac{3}{4}$% of $2000.00 = what?

37) 17 is what % of 51?

38) $\frac{3}{8}$ is 30% of what?

39) 75 = what % of 90?

40) 7% of $39,150 = what?

41) 80 is $2\frac{1}{2}$% of what number?

42) $9\frac{1}{2}$% of $75,300 = what?

43) 15 = what % of 120?

44) $7\frac{1}{4}$% of $2000.00 = what?

45) What % of 56 is 21?

46) 34 is $66\frac{2}{3}$% of what number?

47) 5% of $98.50 = what?

48) 9.5% of what = $6080?

49) What % of 57 is 38?

50) $.24 = $37\frac{1}{2}$% of what?

ESTIMATION—PICK THE LETTER
OF THE BEST ESTIMATION FOR THE FOLLOWING

1) $47 + 75 + 61 =$ a) 130 b) 170 c) 190 d) 210

2) $479 - 121 =$ a) 36 b) 300 c) 360 d) 400

3) $8 \times 300 =$ a) 24 b) 240 c) 2,400 d) 24,000

4) $16 \times 25 =$ a) 40 b) 400 c) 480 d) 1,000

5) $25 \times 300 =$ a) 3000 b) 4500 c) 7500 d) 90,000

6) $150 \times 6 =$ a) 300 b) 600 c) 9000 d) 1200

7) $75 \times 12 =$ a) 600 b) 900 c) 1200 d) 1500

8) $25 \overline{\smash{\big)}\ 775} =$ a) 10 b) 30 c) 50 d) 200

9) $9 \overline{\smash{\big)}\ 7281} =$ a) 80 b) 8 c) 8000 d) 800

10) $38 \times 7 =$ a) 200 b) 280 c) 360 d) 450

11) $35 \times 35 =$ a) 1000 b) 1600 c) 2000 d) 2500

12) $200 \times 300 =$ a) 6,000 b) 12,000 c) 30,000 d) 60,000

13) $78 \times 50 =$ a) 4,000 b) 40 c) 400 d) 40,000

14) $150 \times 17 =$ a) 1,500 b) 2,000 c) 3,000 d) 5,500

15) $68 + 72 + 39 =$ a) 180 b) 150 c) 120 d) 240

16) $415 + 885 + 989 =$ a) 1500 b) 1900 c) 2300 d) 2700

17) $50 \times 19 =$ a) 750 b) 950 c) 1250 d) 1700

18) $65 \times 40 =$ a) 2600 b) 2900 c) 3200 d) 3500

19) $150 \times 150 =$ a) 200 b) 225 c) 2,250 d) 22,500

20) $35 \times 600 =$ a) 21,000 b) 28,000 c) 221,000 d) 228,000

21) $400 \times 400 =$ a) 160 b) 1,600 c) 16,000 d) 160,000

22) $75 \times 18 =$ a) 1000 b) 15,000 c) 1,500 d) 1,750

23) $5000 \times 31 =$ a) 15,000 b) 155,000 c) 1,500,000 d) 15,500,000

24) $8 \overline{\smash{\big)}\ 96040} =$ a) 7,300 b) 13,000 c) 1,200 d) 12,000

25) $7 \overline{\smash{\big)}\ 356172} =$ a) 5,500 b) 50,100 c) 50,900 d) 500,800

ESTIMATION—PICK THE LETTER
OF THE BEST ESTIMATION FOR THE FOLLOWING

1) $3.4 + 2.9 + 8.1 =$ a) 12   b) 15   c) 18   d) 21

2) $.9 + 23.2 + 5.7 =$ a) 18   b) 22   c) 25   d) 30

3) $\$25 - \$3.17 =$ a) $.80   b) \$2.20   c) \$20.00   d) \$22.00

4) $\$50 - \$27.41 =$ a) \$30.00   b) \$23.00   c) \$13.00   d) \$2.50

5) $20 \times 2.5 =$ a) 25   b) 40   c) 50   d) 70

6) $3.5 \times 91 =$ a) 270   b) 310   c) 360   d) 410

7) $1500 \times .25 =$ a) 50   b) 180   c) 290   d) 400

8) $\$95,000 \times .1 =$ a) \$9500   b) \$950   c) \$95.00   d) \$9.50

9) $12 \overline{)\,.18} =$ a) 1.5   b) .15   c) .015   d) .0015

10) $.8 \overline{)\,32.44} =$ a) 40   b) 4   c) 4000   d) 400

11) $.003 \overline{)\,2736} =$ a) 900   b) 90,000   c) 9,000   d) 900,000

12) $\$25.50 + \$7.95 + \$17.15 =$ a) \$40.00   b) \$50.00   c) \$80.00   d) \$120.00

13) $\$2.90 + \$1.45 + \$3.61 =$ a) \$5.00   b) \$6.00   c) \$7.00   d) \$8.00

14) $\$2.13 + \$7.69 + \$5.95 =$ a) \$14.00   b) \$16.00   c) \$18.00   d) \$20.00

15) $\$20 - \$8.85 =$ a) \$12.00   b) \$11.00   c) \$13.00   d) \$1.20

16) $\$50 - \$17.89 =$ a) \$32.00   b) \$23.00   c) \$33.00   d) \$24.00

17) $\$2500.00 \times 19 =$ a) \$50.00   b) \$50,000.00   c) \$5,000.00   d) \$500,000.00

18) $\$7850.00 \times .008 =$ a) \$650.00   b) \$700.00   c) \$750.00   d) \$70.00

19) $\$3599.00 \times .12 =$ a) \$45.00   b) \$300.00   c) \$350.00   d) \$400.00

20) $\$360.00 \times .625 =$ a) \$175.00   b) \$225.00   c) \$300.00   d) \$330.00

21) $\$8979.00 \times .2 =$ a) \$90.00   b) \$180.00   c) \$900.00   d) \$1800.00

22) $8 \overline{)\,\$7260.00} =$ a) \$95.00   b) \$120.00   c) \$900.00   d) \$980.00

23) $.13 \overline{)\,\$2639.00} =$ a) \$203.00   b) \$230.00   c) \$2030.00   d) \$20,000.00

24) $25 \overline{)\,\$497361.17} =$ a) \$250.00   b) \$2000.00   c) \$2500.00   d) \$20,000.00

25) $.09 \overline{)\,\$3599.00} =$ a) \$390.00   b) \$4000.00   c) \$40,000.00   d) \$3900.00

ESTIMATION—PICK THE LETTER
OF THE BEST ESTIMATE FOR THE FOLLOWING

1) 50% of 240 = a) 12   b) 120   c) 180   d) 200

2) 5% of 240 = a) 12   b) 24   c) 120   d) 150

3) 10% of 240 = a) 12   b) 24   c) 120   d) 180

4) 25% of 240 = a) 24   b) 48   c) 60   d) 100

5) 60% of 240 = a) 48   b) 60   c) 120   d) 1440

6) 80% of 560 = a) 300   b) 500   c) 1000   d) 250

7) 20% of 493 = a) 10   b) 50   c) 100   d) 150

8) 40% of 2479 = a) 1000   b) 2000   c) 1500   d) 100

9) 75% of 3064 = a) 500   b) 1200   c) 1800   d) 2300

10) 66⅔% of 5100 = a) 4000   b) 3400   c) 2700   d) 2000

11) 150% of 600 = a) 90   b) 300   c) 600   d) 900

12) 100% of 500 = a) 5   b) 50   c) 500   d) 5000

13) 30% of 80 = a) 10   b) 15   c) 20   d) 24

14) 12% of 895 = a) 50   b) 90   c) 120   d) 240

15) 39% of 119 = a) 50   b) 60   c) 6   d) 80

16) 82% of 249 = a) 20   b) 120   c) 150   d) 200

17) 126% of 791 = a) 15   b) 120   c) 600   d) 1000

18) 52% of 1515 = a) 350   b) 600   c) 750   d) 900

19) 9% of 2147 = a) 140   b) 210   c) 300   d) 1200

20) 26% of 78 = a) 2   b) 20   c) 15   d) 30

21) 9% of $8989 = a) $300.00   b) $700.00   c) $900.00   d) $1200.00

22) 40% of $39.95 = a) $3.00   b) $10.00   c) $16.00   d) $20.00

23) 25% of $158.55 = a) $40.00   b) $60.00   c) $80.00   d) $10.00

24) 20% of $29.95 = a) $1.00   b) $3.00   c) $6.00   d) $10.00

25) 30% of $295.75 = a) $9.00   b) $30.00   c) $60.00   d) $90.00

ESTIMATION—PICK THE LETTER
OF THE BEST ESTIMATE FOR THE FOLLOWING

1) $\frac{1}{2}$ of $945.17 = a) $300   b) $450   c) $30   d) $42

2) $\frac{2}{3}$ of $895.35 = a) $100   b) $500   c) $600   d) $1000

3) $\frac{1}{4}$ of 3,000,000 = a) 1,000,000   b) 2,000,000   c) 750,000   d) 70,000

4) 9.5% of $407.31 = a) $40   b) $400   c) $70   d) $120

5) 24% of $140.00 = a) $20   b) $30   c) $35   d) $45

6) 53% of $1754 = a) $63   b) $95   c) $630   d) $860

7) .3 $\times$ $75.00 = a) $2.50   b) $25   c) $60.00   d) $37

8) .01 $\times$ $75,000.00 = a) $750   b) $7.50   c) $75.00   d) $7500.00

9) .75 $\times$ $8,500 = a) $550   b) $6500   c) $5500   d) $650

10) $9.50 + $7 + $35.40 = a) $10   b) $30   c) $40   d) $50

11) $40.59 + $215 + $9.71 = a) $265   b) $315   c) $175   d) $365

12) $3.95 + $36 + $1.91 = a) $25   b) $40   c) $50   d) $63.00

13) $300 − $91.35 = a) $22   b) $200   c) $185   d) $95

14) $20 − $3.50 − $9.00 = a) $7.00   b) $10   c) $.80   d) $12.41

15) $20 − $31.75 + $15 = a) $26   b) $3.00   c) $45   d) $14.00

16) 75% of $950 = a) $230   b) $560   c) $750   d) $900

17) $33\frac{1}{3}$% of $9.75 = a) $1.00   b) $3.00   c) $600   d) $.90

18) 80% of $75 = a) $70   b) $60   c) $50   d) $40

19) 7.4 + 17.76 + 13 = a) 18.12   b) 14.92   c) 12.7   d) 40

20) .3 $\times$ .02 $\times$ .04 = a) .24   b) .00024   c) .024   d) .0024

21) .1 $\times$ .1 $\times$ .1 = a) .1   b) .01   c) .001   d) .0001

22) $65.75 + $9 + $26.30 = a) $85   b) $100   c) $125   d) $9.50

23) 30% of $180,000.00 = a) $90,000   b) $70,000   c) $6,000   d) $60,000

24) 5% of $8500 = a) $4200   b) $850   c) $630   d) $420

25) $\frac{3}{5}$% of $600 = a) $36   b) $48   c) $60   d) $6.00

MONEY—ADD OR SUBTRACT THE FOLLOWING

1) $20.47 + $3.16 + $7

2) $.75 + $.57 + $.91

3) $20 − $4.78

4) $20 − $9.59

5) $20 − $.53

6) $6.71 + $.97 + $8

7) $.07 + $.70 + $7.00

8) $20 − $2.19

9) $20 − $19.40

10) $3.21 + $90.87 + $6.54

11) $50 − $21.49

12) $74.65 − $15.65

13) $51 + $9.71 + $.78

14) $123.54 + $16.78 + $9.90

15) $7 + $9 + $.80 + $.56

16) $100 − $4.91

17) $10 − $.78

18) $4 + $.76 + $3.21 + $9

19) $.50 + $5.00 + $.55 + $5

20) $1000 − $897.62

MULTIPLY & DIVIDE THE FOLLOWING— ROUND MONEY TO THE NEAREST CENT

21) $49.76 × .05

22) $49.76 × .5

23) $49.76 × .005

24) $32.32 × .875

25) $1000 × .075

26) $450.50 × .06

27) $34.71 × .009

28) $25.12 × .23

29) $48.87 × .0019

30) $696.58 × .0004

31) $.75 × .9

32) $41.67 × .06

33) $2057.18 × .025

34) $634.78 × .043

35) $7941.68 × .870

36) 9 ⟌ $364.57

37) 7 ⟌ $113.28

38) 5 ⟌ $93.71

39) 3 ⟌ $412.82

40) 8 ⟌ $420.50

41) 25 ⟌ $750.45

42) .32 ⟌ $65

43) .007 ⟌ $21.40

44) .85 ⟌ $341.47

45) .9 ⟌ $451.43

46) .18 ⟌ $36.50

47) .13 ⟌ $40.38

48) .95 ⟌ $450.50

49) 75 ⟌ $75150.37

50) .35 ⟌ $701052.19

MONEY—MULTIPLY AND DIVIDE THE FOLLOWING—
ROUND MONEY TO THE NEAREST CENT

1) $43.19
   × .5

2) $43.19
   × .05

3) $28.67
   × .06

4) $28.67
   × .007

5) $59.89
   × .09

6) $59.89
   × .009

7) $706.34
   × .003

8) $218.52
   × .48

9) $9.89
   × .07

10) $8500
   × .0003

11) $605.78
   × .35

12) $792.04
   × .68

13) $113.35
   × .079

14) $9897.01
   × .042

15) $6050.71
   × .108

16) $32.78
   × .7

17) $59.69
   × .69

18) $400.88
   × 1.5

19) $795.13
   × .68

20) $795.13
   × .97

21) 3 ⟌ $41.12

22) 5 ⟌ $315.09

23) 7 ⟌ $1492.66

24) 9 ⟌ $71.14

25) .09 ⟌ $71.14

26) .004 ⟌ $32.33

27) 2 ⟌ $148.99

28) .6 ⟌ $3672.40

29) .008 ⟌ $300

30) 9 ⟌ $918.70

31) .24 ⟌ $41.49

32) 15 ⟌ $75.98

33) .48 ⟌ $18.00

34) .035 ⟌ $100.00

35) 25 ⟌ $1504.70

36) .79 ⟌ $617.10

37) .8 ⟌ $411.17

38) .84 ⟌ $400

39) 12 ⟌ $364.88

40) 7.5 ⟌ $6000

41) $409.71
   × .015

42) .015 ⟌ 6.15

43) .75 ⟌ $6.66

44) $805.91
   × .037

45) $6050.40
   × .089

46) 9.6 ⟌ $19.20

47) .35 ⟌ $701.03

48) $5091.18
   × .075

49) $5091.18
   × .0075

50) 3.3 ⟌ $66.77

MONEY—SOLVE THE FOLLOWING
ROUND TO THE NEAREST CENT (IF NECESSARY)

1) $2.75 + $3.25

2) $2.70 − $.87

3) $27.00 − $8

4) $35 + $3.50 + $.35

5) $70 − $3.90

6) $70 − $39.00

7) $70 − $.39

8) $57.36 + $.27

9) $57.36 + $2.70

10) $57.36 + $27

11) $250 − $7.50

12) $250 − $75.00

13) $250 − $.75

14) $700 − $631.73

15) $50.27 + $41.73 + $9

16) $65.35 + $4.04 + $.37

17) $3 + $.07 + $.61

18) $25 − $3.94

19) $25 − $18.72

20) $25 − $24.04

21) $75.45
   ×   .4

22) $75.45
   ×   .04

23) $8,000.00
   ×   .13

24) $80,000.00
   ×   2.7

25) $125.55
   ×   .9

26) $125.55
   ×   .009

27) $450.36
   ×   .4

28) $450.36
   ×   .04

29) $63.63
   ×   .07

30) $63.63
   ×   .0008

31)   4 ⟌ $64.20

32)   3 ⟌ $111.81

33) .05 ⟌ $75.77

34) 75 ⟌ $60.00

35) .002 ⟌ $95

36) 36 ⟌ $144.00

37)   9 ⟌ $53.25

38)   7 ⟌ $425.65

39)   8 ⟌ $60.44

40)   6 ⟌ $547.25

41) 40% of $75.81

42) 4% of $75.81

43) 60% of $45.35

44) 10% of $324.17

45) 12% of $765.71

46) 9.5% of $50.00

47) 7.25% of $3000.00

48) 150% of $900.00

49) 1.25% of $3575.00

50) 60% of $95.85

MONEY—SOLVE THE FOLLOWING
ROUND TO THE NEAREST CENT (IF NECESSARY)

1) $20 + $3.52

2) $20 − $3.52

3) $20 − $7.00

4) $20 − $.70

5) $20 − $.07

6) $4.19 + $.35 + $5

7) $6 + $3.24 + $1.76

8) $41.71 − $36.58

9) $50 − $9.46

10) $100 − $24.37 + $17.76

11) $25 − $20.75

12) $10 − $3.12

13) $10 − $.84

14) $10 − $9.21

15) $7.50 + $25

16) $75 + $2.50

17) $.75 + $.25

18) $50 − $4.11

19) $.35 + $4 + $6.75

20) $6.70 − $.95

21) $75.50
    ×   .5

22) $75.50
    ×   .05

23) $75.50
    ×   .005

24) $80.00
    ×   .14

25) $3.50
    ×   .09

26) $3.50
    ×   .9

27) $750.00
    ×   .09

28) $3000.00
    ×   .095

29) $100,000.00
    ×   .12

30) $875.45
    ×   .006

31) $8 \overline{)\$120.48}$

32) $.08 \overline{)\$120.48}$

33) $.005 \overline{)\$40}$

34) $15 \overline{)\$1.20}$

35) $7 \overline{)\$6342.77}$

36) $9 \overline{)\$721.86}$

37) $6 \overline{)\$36.11}$

38) $.04 \overline{)\$2463.31}$

39) $75 \overline{)\$3.45}$

40) $3 \overline{)\$4551.50}$

41) 50% of $95.00

42) 5% of $95.00

43) .5% of $95.00

44) 30% of $60.50

45) 3% of $60.50

46) .50% of $325.00

47) 17% of $120.00

48) 25% of $84.48

49) 75% of $60.72

50) 12.5% of $200.00

MONEY—FIND THE DISCOUNT AND SALE PRICE
OF FOLLOWING—ROUND DISCOUNT TO THE NEAREST CENT
IF NECESSARY

	Regular Price	% Discount		Regular Price	% Discount
1)	$80.00	25%	26)	$799.50	10%
2)	$60.00	15%	27)	$79.95	20%
3)	$25.50	10%	28)	$82.68	25%
4)	$44.00	20%	29)	$41.40	5%
5)	$65.00	5%	30)	$37.75	15%
6)	$35.00	8%	31)	$7950.00	12%
7)	$20.00	12%	32)	$6500.00	11%
8)	$75.00	25%	33)	$7200.00	20%
9)	$120.00	4%	34)	$4675.00	25%
10)	$20,000.00	3.5%	35)	$7500.00	10%
11)	$45.50	8%	36)	$4800.00	30%
12)	$29.99	10%	37)	$7000.00	5%
13)	$18.50	25%	38)	$10,200.00	4%
14)	$32.75	30%	39)	$15,300.00	8%
15)	$24.95	20%	40)	$12,000.00	10%
16)	$60.00	40%	41)	$15,000.00	15%
17)	$55.75	50%	42)	$35.37	10%
18)	$78.49	20%	43)	$65.21	8%
19)	$60.50	7%	44)	$48.41	40%
20)	$42.00	15%	45)	$48.41	50%
21)	$95.00	10%	46)	$48.41	10%
22)	$43.43	25%	47)	$36.75	20%
23)	$600.00	9.5%	48)	$42.42	30%
24)	$850.00	8.5%	49)	$42.42	3%
25)	$850.00	8%	50)	$74.39	50%

MONEY—FIND THE TWO MISSING ITEMS FOR EACH PROBLEM

	Regular Price	% Discount	Dollar Discount	Sale Price
1)	$40.00	20%	?	?
2)	$60.00	25%	?	?
3)	$43.00	60%	?	?
4)	$52.00	10%	?	?
5)	$30.00	15%	?	?
6)	$45.00	20%	?	?
7)	$20.00	40%	?	?
8)	$80.00	15%	?	?
9)	$25.00	25%	?	?
10)	$28.80	30%	?	?
11)	$40.00	?	$10.00	?
12)	$50.00	?	$5.00	?
13)	$60.00	?	$20.00	?
14)	$45.00	?	$18.00	?
15)	$30.00	?	$6.00	?
16)	$75.00	?	$22.50	?
17)	$90.00	?	$7.20	?
18)	$450.00	?	$54.00	?
19)	$7250.00	?	$1087.50	?
20)	$48.54	?	$24.27	?
21)	$60.00	?	?	$48.00
22)	$40.00	?	?	$36.00
23)	$50.00	?	?	$42.00
24)	$75.00	?	?	$60.00
25)	$56.00	?	?	$42.00
26)	$30.00	?	?	$28.50
27)	$144.00	?	?	$108.00
28)	$75.50	?	?	$67.95
29)	$80.00	?	?	$70.40
30)	$45.75	?	?	$27.45
31)	?	?	$8.00	$72.00
32)	?	?	$12.00	$28.00
33)	?	?	$9.00	$41.00
34)	?	?	$24.00	$36.00
35)	?	?	$1.60	$18.40
36)	?	?	$4.50	$25.50
37)	?	?	$12.50	$12.50
38)	?	?	$18.00	$36.00
39)	?	?	$7.10	$28.40
40)	?	?	$900.00	$6600.00
41)	$50.00	35%	?	?
42)	$144.00	?	$18.00	?
43)	?	?	$21.00	$39.00
44)	$450.00	?	?	$270.00
45)	$75.70	40%	?	?
46)	$55.85	?	?	$33.51
47)	$120.60	15%	?	?
48)	?	?	$212.68	$638.04
49)	$360.00	?	$120.00	?
50)	$6000.00	?	?	$1700.00

MONEY—FIND THE MISSING ANSWER

	Sale	% Commission	$ Commission		Sale	% Commission	$ Commission
1)	$40.00	10%	?	26)	$60.00	?	$15.00
2)	$75.00	20%	?	27)	$75.00	?	$7.50
3)	$60.00	15%	?	28)	$35.00	?	$14.00
4)	$25.00	13%	?	29)	$50.00	?	$6.50
5)	$95.00	25%	?	30)	$750.00	?	$30.00
6)	$350.00	5%	?	31)	$420.00	?	$21.00
7)	$50.00	23%	?	32)	$5,600.00	?	$140.00
8)	$120.00	30%	?	33)	$9,140.00	?	$914.00
9)	$20.00	20%	?	34)	$80,000.00	?	$4800.00
10)	$45.00	40%	?	35)	$144,000.00	?	$18,000.00
11)	$12,500.00	7%	?	36)	?	20%	$17.00
12)	$7,340.00	9%	?	37)	?	10%	$17.50
13)	$15,255.00	8%	?	38)	?	5%	$32.00
14)	$6,545.00	5%	?	39)	?	15%	$9.00
15)	$8,417.00	6%	?	40)	?	25%	$24.50
16)	$9,999.00	4%	?	41)	?	6%	$5,400.00
17)	$5,549.00	10%	?	42)	?	8%	$3,200.00
18)	$6,399.00	3%	?	43)	?	5%	$120.00
19)	$8,995.00	2%	?	44)	?	7%	$35.00
20)	$10,649.00	5%	?	45)	?	5½%	$1100.00
21)	$80,000.00	6%	?	46)	$5000.00	8½%	?
22)	$120,000.00	5.5%	?	47)	$5000.00	8¾%	?
23)	$95,000.00	4%	?	48)	$699.95	12%	?
24)	$75,500.00	6%	?	49)	$520.00	?	$65.00
25)	$90,450.00	6½%	?	50)	?	12½%	$500.00

MONEY—
FIND THE SIMPLE INTEREST IN THE FOLLOWING PROBLEMS

	Principal	Rate	Time		Principal	Rate	Time
1)	$400.00	10%	1 year	26)	$75,000.00	13%	15 years
2)	$500.00	8%	2 years	27)	$45,000.00	11.8%	30 years
3)	$650.00	9%	2½ years	28)	$60,000.00	12.25%	25 years
4)	$1000.00	5%	3 years	29)	$54,000.00	9%	20 years
5)	$1200.00	6%	6 months	30)	$250,000.00	8¾%	25 years
6)	$2000.00	7%	9 months	31)	$700.00	5½%	1 year 6 months
7)	$7500.00	12%	36 months	32)	$2500.00	6½%	2½ years
8)	$8000.00	11%	40 months	33)	$500.00	8¾%	2 years
9)	$9500.00	9%	48 months	34)	$750.00	9%	9 months
10)	$7780.00	13%	3 years 4 months	35)	$1000.00	10%	1 year 3 months
11)	$4200.00	7%	24 months	36)	$2000.00	9.7%	24 months
12)	$1500.00	15%	15 months	37)	$3000.00	8%	45 months
13)	$4800.00	6%	2 years 6 months	38)	$6000.00	9¼%	8 years
14)	$5400.00	8½%	3 years	39)	$3500.00	11%	2½ years
15)	$5400.00	8%	36 months	40)	$3600.00	11%	30 months
16)	$5400.00	8¾%	3 years	41)	$2000.00	5½%	9 months
17)	$6000.00	10%	4 months	42)	$400.00	6%	4 months
18)	$21,350.00	12%	6 years	43)	$800.00	6%	8 months
19)	$40,000.00	15%	6 months	44)	$6500.00	13%	21 months
20)	$3,600.00	9½%	1 year	45)	$4400.00	12.5%	36 months
21)	$4,500.00	8½%	2 years	46)	$3250.00	11.5%	48 months
22)	$80,000.00	7½%	15 years	47)	$5875.00	9¼%	24 months
23)	$55,000.00	6%	30 years	48)	$7200.00	8%	36 months
24)	$120,000.00	12.5%	25 years	49)	$9540.00	10%	48 months
25)	$90,000.00	10%	30 years	50)	$3675.00	10¾%	30 months

MONEY—SOLVE THE FOLLOWING. ROUND TO NEAREST CENT

1) $3 + $4.17 + $5.23

2) $8\overline{)\$64.72}$

3) $50 - $37.34

4) $50.30
   $\times$ .5

5) $7.24 + $3.56 + $15

6) 10% of $350.00

7) $20 - $9.71

8) $54.71
   $\times$ .07

9) $4 + $5 + $6.50

10) 25% of $75.20

11) $12\overline{)\$360.48}$

12) $10 - $7.59

13) $651.71
    $\times$ .12

14) 150% of $150.00

15) 20% of $7450.00

16) $10 - $2.43

17) $.05\overline{)\$25.00}$

18) $30 + $31.71 + $9.47

19) $15\overline{)\$6000.60}$

20) 5% of $950.00

21) $10 - $.84

22) $20.43 + $50 - $65.17

23) $20 - $15.17 + $4.21

24) $120\overline{)\$480.60}$

25) $30 - $17.21 - $12.39

26) 15% of $4000.00

27) 1.5% of $4000.00

28) $413.51
    $\times$ .05

29) $30 - $40.21 + $15.07

30) $7\overline{)\$55.43}$

31) 7½% of $800.00

32) $723.47
    $\times$ .11

33) $50 - $61.71 + $11.72

34) 7¾% of $8000.00

35) $9\overline{)\$3154.57}$

FIND THE FOLLOWING COMMISSIONS

36) $700.00 sale at 12%

37) $450.00 sale at 15%

38) $950.00 sale at 5%

39) $8450.00 sale at 7%

40) $68,500.00 sale at 6%

FIND THE FOLLOWING SIMPLE INTEREST

41) $500.00 at 5% for 2 years

42) $750.00 at 8% for 24 months

43) $2500.00 at 7½% for 36 months

44) $2000.00 at 12% for 30 months

45) $6000.00 at 12½% for 9 months

FIND THE FOLLOWING DISCOUNTS AND SALE PRICE

	Regular Price	% Discount
46)	$45.00	25%
47)	$33.00	20%
48)	$400.00	10%
49)	$5600.00	15%
50)	$25,000.00	10½%

MONEY—SOLVE THE FOLLOWING.
ROUND TO THE NEAREST CENT

1) $20 − $1.72

2) $20 + $1.72

3) $20 + $17.20

4) $24.21 − $22

5) $24.21 − $.22

6) $3.51 + $14 + $9.49

7) $5.89 + $.77 + $3.34

8) $10 − $7.43

9) $10 − $.74

10) $10 + $74.30

11) $75.51
    × .7

12) $75.51
    × .06

13) $75.51
    × .005

14) $475.50
    × .12

15) $600.50
    × .75

16) 13 $526.50

17) .13 $526.50

18) 7 $843.56

19) 4 $4875.50

20) 3 $4214.12

21) 20% of $360.00

22) 2% of $360.00

23) 15% of $360.00

24) 75% of $360.00

25) 150% of $360.00

26) $34.71 − $45.67 + $17

27) 10% of $32.99

28) $945.50
    × .08

29) 17 $515.19

30) 15% of $75,000.00

31) $75 − $24.71 − $49.34

32) $7260.00
    × .13

33) 25% of $950.50

34) 13 $91653.98

35) 9½% of $75,000.00

FIND THE FOLLOWING
COMMISSIONS

36) 15% on a $120.00 sale

37) 18% on a $425.50 sale

38) 20% on a $75.25 sale

39) 6% on a $84,500.00 sale

40) 12% on a $7,999.50 sale

FIND THE SIMPLE INTEREST ON:

41) $800.00 at 7% for 2 years

42) $1000.00 at 5% for 36 months

43) $2500.00 at 5½% for 24 months

44) $6500.00 at 11% for 30 months

45) $75,000.00 at 12½% for 30 years

FIND THE DOLLAR DISCOUNT
AND SALE PRICE
FOR THE FOLLOWING

	Regular Price	% Discount
46)	$144.00	25%
47)	$46.00	5%
48)	$250.00	15%
49)	$475.00	20%
50)	$75.50	40%

INTEGERS—ADD THE FOLLOWING

1) $-7 + 4$ 2) $-9 + -3$

3) $-18 + 9$ 4) $-4 + 15$

5) $-63 + -18$ 6) $-27 + 6$

7) $27 + 14$ 8) $-36 + -46$

9) $137 + -9$ 10) $-84 + -125$

11) $-9 + 28$ 12) $83 + -19$

13) $-35 + 0$ 14) $19 + -103$

15) $-14 + -195$ 16) $-604 + 318$

17) $-413 + -98$ 18) $827 + -36$

19) $-801 + 38$ 20) $64 + -64$

21) $-8 + 5 + 9$ 22) $-4 + 0 + -8$

23) $9 + -4 + -5$ 24) $-7 + -6 + -4$

25) $3 + -6 + -5$ 26) $-4 + -2 + 7$

27) $-8 + 5 + 9$ 28) $-7 + 4 + 0$

29) $1 + 8 + -4$ 30) $-4 + 4 + -4$

31) $18 + -7 + 5$ 32) $-6 + 24 + -13$

33) $-25 + -18 + -9$ 34) $-16 + 24 + -14$

35) $0 + -85 + -14$ 36) $-38 + 146 + 9$

37) $-143 + 16 + -8$ 38) $304 + -214 + -118$

39) $48 + -113 + -36$ 40) $65 + 213 + -65$

41) $-19 + 227 + 8$ 42) $-67 + -18 + 113$

43) $29 + -18 + 367$ 44) $-9 + 147 + -28$

45) $-79 + 0 + -117$ 46) $-36 + -84 + -147$

47) $69 + -23 + -85$ 48) $817 + -4 + -85$

49) $64 + -75 + -19$ 50) $84 + -73 + -11$

INTEGERS—ADD THE FOLLOWING

1) $-8 + 9$

2) $-6 + -5$

3) $-11 + 15$

4) $-13 + 25$

5) $15 + 28$

6) $-26 + -53$

7) $-29 + -48$

8) $34 + -17$

9) $-77 + 45$

10) $97 + 86$

11) $-157 + -243$

12) $583 + -64$

13) $-235 + 486$

14) $293 + 843$

15) $-285 + 186$

16) $480 + -186$

17) $2946 + 284$

18) $-2864 + 5063$

19) $-4935 + -2581$

20) $483 + -742$

21) $-15 + -15 + -15$

22) $-38 + 43 + -5$

23) $63 + 48 + -63$

24) $-29 + -46 + -48$

25) $47 + -19 + 31$

26) $979 + -201 + 961$

27) $-68 + -57 + -70$

28) $345 + -54 + -300$

29) $72 + -641 + 85$

30) $-210 + 869 + -87$

31) $59 + 47 + 56 + 27$

32) $-324 + -18 + 106 + -9$

33) $76 + -6 + 39 + -40$

34) $66 + -72 + 83 + 92$

35) $300 + -465 + 39 + -486$

36) $183 + -48 + -89 + -634$

37) $-426 + -92 + -8 + -53$

38) $748 + -615 + -409 + 672$

39) $-361 + 958 + 47 + 610$

40) $-2146 + 718 + 496 + -3154$

41) $-15 + 28 + 37 + -8 + -15$

42) $43 + 86 + 54 + -28 + 67$

43) $-285 + -17 + 164 + -25 + 59$

44) $713 + -258 + -917 + -68 + -42$

45) $385 + -99 + 652 + -21 + -46$

46) $-294 + 856 + -346 + 41 + -493$

47) $40 + -385 + -410 + 38 + 76$

48) $864 + -158 + -346 + -256 + 283$

49) $350 + -17 + -39 + -26 + -183$

50) $493 + 263 + 46 + -1053 + -381$

INTEGERS—SUBTRACT THE FOLLOWING

1) $-5 - -7$

2) $-11 - 4$

3) $5 - -7$

4) $-11 - -4$

5) $-5 - 7$

6) $11 - 4$

7) $5 - 7$

8) $11 - -4$

9) $-6 - -17$

10) $14 - 21$

11) $-6 - 17$

12) $14 - -21$

13) $6 - 17$

14) $-14 - 21$

15) $6 - -17$

16) $-14 - -21$

17) $-35 - 49$

18) $-91 - -72$

19) $-61 - -84$

20) $73 - 106$

21) $-21 - 4 - -18$

22) $-25 - 4 - -18$

23) $-30 - 9 - 47$

24) $46 - 35 - 14$

25) $28 - -36 - -52$

26) $46 - -35 - 14$

27) $-19 - -73 - 36$

28) $-46 - -35 - 14$

29) $-40 - -57 - 17$

30) $46 - -35 - -14$

31) $-63 - -54 - 45$

32) $3 - 9 - -12$

33) $-42 - 56 - -70$

34) $48 - 59 - 63$

35) $-91 - -103 - 5$

36) $-8 - -92 - -37$

37) $47 - -51 - 91$

38) $53 - -47 - 96$

39) $66 - 77 - -88$

40) $100 - -125 - 275$

41) $-35 - -62 - 47 - -21$

42) $-5 - -31 - -43 - -78$

43) $26 - -49 - 37 - 38$

44) $-25 - -38 - 75 - -72$

45) $-29 - -4 - 61 - -8 - 95$

46) $-2 - -4 - 6 - -8 - 10 - -12$

47) $41 - -39 - -47 - 67 - 33 - -28$

48) $-31 - -37 - 41 - -43 - 47 - -53$

49) $1 - 4 - -9 - 16 - -25 - 36 - 49$

50) $-83 - -89 - -97 - 101 - -103$

INTEGERS—SUBTRACT THE FOLLOWING

1) $8 - 10$

2) $13 - 9$

3) $-8 - 10$

4) $13 - -9$

5) $-8 - -10$

6) $-13 - 9$

7) $-8 - 5$

8) $-13 - -9$

9) $8 - -5$

10) $15 - 21$

11) $6 - 7$

12) $-15 - 21$

13) $6 - -7$

14) $-15 - -21$

15) $5 - 12$

16) $15 - -21$

17) $-5 - 12$

18) $-17 - -47$

19) $-5 - -12$

20) $-16 - 33$

21) $-14 - 15 - -17$

22) $-21 - -11 - 16$

23) $-14 - -15 - -17$

24) $21 - -11 - -16$

25) $14 - 15 - 17$

26) $-21 - 11 - -16$

27) $14 - 15 - -17$

28) $-21 - -11 - -16$

29) $-19 - 18 - -10$

30) $-24 - 19 - -33$

31) $-41 - -54 - 13$

32) $-39 - -52 - -13$

33) $-29 - 35 - 45$

34) $-33 - 34 - -35$

35) $-29 - -35 - -45$

36) $-40 - -36 - 47$

37) $-45 - 31 - -54$

38) $-85 - 19 - -62$

39) $-53 - -81 - 27$

40) $-34 - 45 - -68$

41) $-27 - -35 - 43 - -51$

42) $-4 - -33 - -47 - 59$

43) $-32 - 45 - 54 - 65$

44) $28 - -35 - 59 - -73$

45) $29 - -37 - -43 - -9$

46) $6 - -31 - 4 - -43$

47) $-30 - -40 - -70 - 100$

48) $-52 - -63 - -63 - 52$

49) $-47 - -65 - -35 - 53$

50) $25 - -71 - 49 - 7 - 50$

INTEGERS—MULTIPLY THE FOLLOWING

1) -3×-9

2) 8×7

3) -9×5

4) 8×-6

5) -10×-5

6) -9×8

7) 7×7

8) -6×-6

9) -11×8

10) 4×-7

11) -54×3

12) -61×-8

13) 28×-9

14) 72×5

15) -79×-2

16) -27×-11

17) -63×92

18) 32×-59

19) 98×20

20) -76×-32

21) $-3 \times -2 \times -8$

22) $-7 \times 5 \times -3$

23) $-5 \times 6 \times 9$

24) $-9 \times 8 \times 7$

25) $4 \times -8 \times -6$

26) $-3 \times -9 \times -4$

27) $2 \times 9 \times 7$

28) $-4 \times -8 \times 7$

29) $-3 \times 3 \times -9$

30) $-7 \times 7 \times 8$

31) $-4 \times 7 \times -8 \times 3$

32) $6 \times -9 \times 7 \times 6$

33) $-7 \times -3 \times -2 \times -8$

34) $-4 \times 5 \times -6 \times -7$

35) $-3 \times 3 \times -4 \times 4$

36) $6 \times -6 \times 6 \times 6$

37) $-7 \times -1 \times -3 \times -5$

38) $4 \times 5 \times 3 \times 2$

39) $-8 \times -5 \times 4 \times 2$

40) $-7 \times 8 \times -5 \times -4$

41) $-6 \times -2 \times -3 \times -1 \times -3$

42) $4 \times -8 \times 5 \times -3 \times 2$

43) $-5 \times -5 \times -5 \times -5 \times -5$

44) $-2 \times -5 \times -8 \times 2 \times 3$

45) $4 \times 8 \times 3 \times 5 \times 2$

46) $-7 \times -3 \times -4 \times 5 \times -9$

47) $9 \times 9 \times 8 \times 2 \times 3$

48) $5 \times 4 \times -6 \times 3 \times 4$

49) $-7 \times 2 \times 1 \times -4 \times 5$

50) $9 \times -8 \times -6 \times -7 \times 2$

INTEGERS—DIVIDE THE FOLLOWING

1) $56 \div -7$ 2) $-60 \div 5$

3) $-56 \div 8$ 4) $-60 \div -15$

5) $-56 \div -14$ 6) $-60 \div 4$

7) $56 \div -28$ 8) $60 \div -20$

9) $-56 \div -7$ 10) $-60 \div -30$

11) $-56 \div 4$ 12) $-60 \div 2$

13) $56 \div -2$ 14) $60 \div -3$

15) $56 \div 8$ 16) $-60 \div -60$

17) $65 \div -13$ 18) $-60 \div 6$

19) $-57 \div -3$ 20) $60 \div 10$

21) $91 \div 7$ 22) $-60 \div -12$

23) $87 \div -29$ 24) $-45 \div -15$

25) $-98 \div -14$ 26) $-75 \div 25$

27) $-84 \div 7$ 28) $-90 \div 6$

29) $-48 \div -16$ 30) $-57 \div 19$

31) $-192 \div -3$ 32) $480 \div -6$

33) $-575 \div 25$ 34) $-600 \div -8$

35) $400 \div -2$ 36) $300 \div -75$

37) $-800 \div -8 \div 25$ 38) $-600 \div -15 \div -2$

39) $-50 \div -25 \div 2$ 40) $91 \div -7 \div 13$

41) $-40 \div 5 \times -8$ 42) $-60 \div 15 \div 4$

43) $-54 \div 2 \div -3$ 44) $-48 \div -12 \times -3$

45) $-225 \div 25 \div 3$ 46) $-18 \times 9 \div -27$

47) $-50 \times 30 \div -15$ 48) $-400 \div -25 \div -2$

49) $-6750 \div -25 \div 9$ 50) $-18225 \div 9 \div 45$

INTEGERS—USE $<$, $>$ or $=$ TO COMPARE THE FOLLOWING

1) -4 ( ) 3

2) -9 ( ) -6

3) 0 ( ) -4

4) -7 ( ) -8

5) 9 ( ) 7

6) -3 ( ) 3

7) 24 ( ) -40

8) 5 ( ) -5

9) -14 ( ) 0

10) -36 ( ) -24

11) 17 ( ) -21

12) -13 ( ) 16

13) 0 ( ) 6

14) -14 ( ) 13

15) 8 ( ) -6

16) -8 ( ) -8

17) -5 ( ) -11

18) 37 ( ) -15

19) 29 ( ) -32

20) -8 ( ) 9

21) -5 + 4 ( ) -2

22) -9 + -2 ( ) -11

23) 9 ( ) -2 + 7

24) -5 ( ) 4 + 1

25) -14 + 3 ( ) -6

26) -8 ( ) -6 + 2

27) -14 ( ) -8 + -6

28) -12 × -4 ( ) -48

29) -4 × -3 ( ) 0

30) -9 × 2 ( ) 18

ARRANGE FROM SMALLEST TO LARGEST

31) -7, 5, -4, 0

32) 9, -4, -1, 6

33) -2, -7, -1, -8

34) 6, -5, -4, -8

35) -5, -1, 7, 0

36) 14, -8, -5, 5

37) -11, -7, -15, 3

38) 6, -7, 4, -8

39) -3, -6, 5, -4

40) 9, 14, -5, -9

41) -3, -5, 3, 5

42) -9, -3, 3, 9

43) 12, -8, -3, 4

44) 6, -2, -5, -7

45) 7, -5, -12, 8

46) 3, -8, -2, -7

47) 21, -11, 0, -1

48) -2, -6, 7, -4

49) 8, -4, -1, 5

50) -6, 6, 3, -3

INTEGERS—ADD AND SUBTRACT THE FOLLOWING

1) $-8 + -16$

2) $-4 + -8$

3) $-16 + 20$

4) $8 + -17$

5) $-8 + -3 + -7$

6) $-6 + -8 + 14$

7) $43 + -36 + 8$

8) $19 + -16 + -23$

9) $-84 + -3 + 8 + -8$

10) $-41 + -8 + -15 + 20$

11) $-6 - -8$

12) $-6 - 8$

13) $6 - -8$

14) $6 - 8$

15) $-6 - 4 - -3$

16) $-3 - -4 - 6$

17) $8 - 16 - 24$

18) $19 - 6 - -8$

19) $-18 - -16 - -53$

20) $-58 - 84 - -23$

21) $-5 + 3 - 4$

22) $-8 - 6 + 15$

23) $-15 - 6 + 43$

24) $-8 + -16 - 4$

25) $31 - -61 + 42$

26) $-16 - 16 - 16$

27) $-48 - -63 + -16$

28) $28 - 43 + 83$

29) $69 - 43 + -81$

30) $-43 + -86 - 48$

31) $-6 + -8 + -4 - 3$

32) $-3 - -8 + 10 - 9$

33) $-6 + 15 - 8 - -6$

34) $-15 + 4 - 16 - -6$

35) $-8 - 16 - 24 + 48$

36) $-19 + -11 - -16 + 23$

37) $28 - 46 + -41 - 20$

38) $-16 + -20 - 16 - -14$

39) $-63 + 48 - 5 - 64$

40) $-68 + 41 - 8 + -15$

41) $-8 - 6 - 15 - -16 + 20$

42) $-8 + -16 - 48 + 62 - -15$

43) $-16 + 8 - 24 + -16 - 23$

44) $-15 + 20 - 16 + 48 - -13$

45) $14 + 83 + 64 + 82 + 53$

46) $-16 + -15 - -63 + 48 - 100$

47) $84 - 42 - -51 + 37 - 18$

48) $-62 + 48 - -14 + 16 - 4$

49) $39 - 14 - 83 - 16 - 38$

50) $-39 - -34 + 38 - 36 + -31$

INTEGERS—MULTIPLY AND DIVIDE THE FOLLOWING

1) 24×-3

2) $42 \div -3$

3) $24 \div -3$

4) 42×-3

5) -24×3

6) $-42 \div -7$

7) $-24 \div 3$

8) $42 \div -6$

9) -24×-3

10) -42×-7

11) $-24 \div -3$

12) $-42 \div -14$

13) 48×5

14) $55 \div 11$

15) $-72 \div 12$

16) $36 \div -18$

17) 68×-10

18) -5×-14

19) $87 \div -3$

20) $-72 \div -18$

21) $-4 \times -6 \times 5$

22) $-84 \div 21$

23) $-65 \div -13$

24) $-96 \div -24$

25) -36×-12

26) $45 \times -2 \times -3$

27) $-36 \div -12$

28) $-44 \div -4$

29) 36×-12

30) $-120 \times -5 \times 3$

31) $-36 \div 12$

32) $-120 \div -24$

33) -45×15

34) $-120 \div 15$

35) $-45 \div -15$

36) $-25 \times -3 \times -6$

37) 48×-16

38) $45 \times -20 \times 2$

39) $-48 \div -16$

40) $-91 \div -7$

41) $-12 \times 5 \times -8$

42) $-240 \div 15$

43) $-9 \times -8 \times -9$

44) $-36 \times -100 \times -5$

45) $144 \div -18$

46) $-48 \times -5 \div -12$

47) $-144 \div -16$

48) $-36 \div -12 \times -9$

49) $-12 \times -10 \div -24$

50) $-144 \div -9 \times -25$

INTEGERS—
ADD, SUBTRACT, MULTIPLY OR DIVIDE THE FOLLOWING

1) $-8 + 4$

2) $-9 + -7$

3) $-5 + -6 + -7$

4) $9 + -3 + -2$

5) $-8 + -2 + 0$

6) $12 + -5 + 14$

7) $-4 + -8 + -6$

8) $9 + -3 + -11$

9) $-7 + 8 + -3$

10) $-24 + 7 + 12$

11) $-5 - -8$

12) $14 - -6$

13) $-7 - 9 - -3$

14) $13 - -5 - 2$

15) $-9 - 10 - 4$

16) $-16 - 18 - -4$

17) $-1 - 7 - -4$

18) $17 - -5 - 0$

19) $-318 - 4 - -91$

20) $17 - -17 - 17$

21) -8×-6

22) -7×9

23) $-4 \times -3 \times 5$

24) $6 \times -7 \times 9$

25) $-15 \times 3 \times -5$

26) $18 \times -2 \times 6$

27) $-10 \times 10 \times 10$

28) $-4 \times -9 \times -14$

29) $-25 \times -8 \times -15$

30) $21 \times -18 \times 28$

31) $-18 \div -3$

32) $-72 \div 6$

33) $-24 \div -3 \div -4$

34) $-100 \div 5 \div 20$

35) $-81 \div -3 \div 9$

36) $-64 \div 4 \div 2$

37) $180 \div -6 \div 3$

38) $450 \div 15 \div -3$

39) $-372 \div 3 \div -4$

40) $-560 \div -8 \div 35$

41) $-8 + -4 - -5$

42) $-6 + 9 - 12$

43) $15 - -9 + -5$

44) $-8 \times -5 \div -2$

45) $-16 \div 4 \times -15$

46) $-32 \times 4 \div 16$

47) $24 \div 6 \times -5$

48) $-240 \div -3 \times -8$

49) $-6 \times -5 + 4 - -9$

50) $-49 \div 7 \times 2 - -5$

INTEGERS—
ADD, SUBTRACT, MULTIPLY, OR DIVIDE THE FOLLOWING

1) $-6 + -8$

2) $-12 + 7$

3) $-4 + -12 + 8$

4) $18 + 23 + -15$

5) $-6 + 8 + -15$

6) $15 + -8 + -23$

7) $-24 + -7 + -15$

8) $28 + 52 + -81$

9) $-16 + -8 + 43 + -39$

10) $-153 + 43 + 282 + -18$

11) $-8 - -3$

12) $-9 - 16$

13) $16 - -23$

14) $14 - 83$

15) $-6 - -4 - 8$

16) $16 - 42 - 83$

17) $-8 - -5 - -9$

18) $-21 - 49 - 32$

19) $-18 - -41 - 86 - -15$

20) $76 - 23 - -123 - 28$

21) -7×8

22) -9×-4

23) -5×3

24) 10×7

25) $-5 \times -3 \times 4$

26) $-4 \times -7 \times -3$

27) $9 \times 3 \times -5$

28) $-15 \times 2 \times 5$

29) $-3 \times -4 \times -3 \times -4$

30) $-5 \times -7 \times 6 \times 2$

31) $-64 \div 8$

32) $81 \div 9$

33) $-144 \div -12$

34) $-288 \div 6$

35) $440 \div 11 \div -2$

36) $-144 \div 2 \div -8$

37) $-1296 \div -36 \div -9$

38) $500 \div -5 \div -20$

39) $-1000 \div 10 \div -10 \div 10$

40) $640 \div -16 \div 2 \div -5$

41) $-8 + -16 - -3$

42) $-8 \times -16 \div -4$

43) $-8 \times 3 + -4$

44) $-5 + -8 - -16$

45) $-4 \times -5 + -8$

46) $-6 - -6 \times 5$

47) $-64 \div -8 + -16$

48) $-63 \div -9 + -48 \div -6$

49) $-6 + -8 + -16 - -14$

50) $-100 \div -10 + -3 \times -4$

RATIONALS—ADD AND SIMPLIFY EACH

1) $\frac{3}{4} + -\frac{2}{3}$

2) $7.3 + -9$

3) $3\frac{1}{2} + -1$

4) $7.3 + -.9$

5) $-3\frac{1}{2} + 2\frac{1}{2}$

6) $-6.18 + 3.4$

7) $-5\frac{1}{2} + -3\frac{1}{2}$

8) $-9.46 + -8.5$

9) $4\frac{1}{3} + 3\frac{5}{6}$

10) $2.1 + -8$

11) $-4\frac{1}{5} + -7\frac{1}{4}$

12) $4.25 + -6.1$

13) $-9 + 3\frac{3}{7}$

14) $-40.1 + -39.97$

15) $5\frac{1}{8} + -4\frac{2}{3}$

16) $-6.1 + -8.8$

17) $-6\frac{7}{12} + -7\frac{5}{12}$

18) $.7 + -6.3$

19) $-9\frac{4}{5} + 7\frac{5}{6}$

20) $9.483 + -.59$

21) $-4\frac{1}{2} + -5\frac{1}{3} + 7\frac{5}{6}$

22) $-13.1 + 1.87 + -7.3$

23) $4\frac{3}{5} + -9\frac{1}{5} + 2\frac{3}{4}$

24) $-.91 + 3 + 2.8$

25) $-6\frac{2}{3} + -7\frac{1}{4} + -8\frac{5}{6}$

26) $-.4 + 32.3 + -9$

27) $-20 + 7\frac{3}{4} + 9\frac{5}{8}$

28) $-30.3 + -2.91 + 24.8$

29) $4\frac{1}{2} + -5 + -6\frac{1}{3}$

30) $-.41 + .8 + -1.9$

31) $3\frac{2}{5} + -9\frac{1}{8} + -4\frac{3}{4}$

32) $-3.8 + -.493 + -5$

33) $6\frac{1}{2} + -7\frac{1}{3} + 8\frac{1}{4}$

34) $-25 + -6.31 + 7.4$

35) $-2\frac{1}{9} + 3\frac{5}{6} + -4\frac{1}{3}$

36) $-1.9 + -3.48 + 20$

37) $7\frac{4}{7} + -3\frac{3}{14} + -5\frac{19}{21}$

38) $4 + -2.1 + -1.971$

39) $-7\frac{3}{4} + 9 + -6\frac{1}{2}$

40) $-6.1 + -.819 + 24.73$

41) $-8\frac{1}{2} + 3\frac{3}{4} + -2\frac{5}{12} + -6\frac{2}{3}$

42) $-2.91 + 3 + 24.7 + -36.148$

43) $-4\frac{5}{8} + 3 + -\frac{5}{6} + -7\frac{5}{12}$

44) $5 + -2.19 + -71.8 + 29.74$

45) $-9\frac{1}{2} + 14.13 + 3\frac{3}{4} + -6.3$

46) $-21 + -3.19 + 1\frac{4}{5} + 2\frac{3}{8}$

47) $-2.07 + 1.7 + -\frac{13}{25} + -7\frac{1}{2}$

48) $-5\frac{1}{4} + -.414 + 1\frac{3}{8} + -4$

49) $-2.97 + .87 + .6 + 1\frac{5}{8}$

50) $4\frac{1}{8} + -7.2 + -.86 + 5\frac{3}{4}$

RATIONALS—SUBTRACT AND SIMPLIFY EACH

1) $\frac{3}{8} - -\frac{2}{3}$

2) $-\frac{1}{4} - \frac{1}{8}$

3) $\frac{3}{5} - \frac{5}{6}$

4) $\frac{11}{12} - -\frac{3}{4}$

5) $-\frac{7}{16} - -\frac{7}{10}$

6) $\frac{5}{32} - -\frac{5}{8}$

7) $-\frac{17}{60} - \frac{5}{12}$

8) $\frac{13}{24} - \frac{7}{9}$

9) $-\frac{19}{36} - \frac{23}{30}$

10) $\frac{25}{26} - -\frac{4}{39}$

11) $3\frac{1}{6} - 5\frac{5}{9}$

12) $-7\frac{3}{7} - 4\frac{5}{21}$

13) $25 - -3\frac{7}{12}$

14) $63\frac{9}{20} - 14$

15) $73\frac{3}{28} - -4\frac{3}{14}$

16) $-12\frac{5}{72} - -\frac{4}{9}$

17) $-9\frac{31}{32} - 4\frac{7}{16}$

18) $16\frac{6}{27} - -3\frac{2}{45}$

19) $-8\frac{6}{11} - 4\frac{2}{3}$

20) $-5\frac{4}{15} - -6\frac{11}{20}$

21) $28\frac{1}{9} - -28\frac{1}{9}$

22) $0 - -6\frac{3}{7}$

23) $-68\frac{13}{40} - 5\frac{3}{16}$

24) $9\frac{7}{48} - 10$

25) $-9\frac{3}{14} - -4\frac{5}{42}$

26) $4.05 - -2.66$

27) $-8.4 - 6.2$

28) $-9.08 - -4.6$

29) $36 - -1.82$

30) $-4.73 - -6.54$

31) $-38.7 - 9.8$

32) $273.1 - -4.76$

33) $-22.7 - 9.5$

34) $59.72 - -4.836$

35) $-6.47 - -8.5$

36) $107.3 - 157.8$

37) $-30.58 - -16$

38) $1004.7 - -5.87$

39) $-84.27 - 93.8$

40) $-2.75 - .009$

41) $-8.71 - -4.09$

42) $783 - -.147$

43) $46.78 - 59.84$

44) $-13.7 - 28.682$

45) $894.1 - -25.87$

46) $-.008 - -.09$

47) $67.4 - 38.6$

48) $-76.41 - 18.5$

49) $63.4 - -19.88$

50) $-647.1 - 8.479$

RATIONALS—MULTIPLY AND SIMPLIFY EACH

1) $-\frac{12}{15} \times \frac{7}{8}$

2) $-\frac{18}{35} \times -\frac{21}{24}$

3) $\frac{5}{36} \times -\frac{9}{25}$

4) $-\frac{39}{42} \times 0$

5) $6 \times -\frac{21}{30}$

6) $-\frac{7}{18} \times -\frac{27}{35}$

7) $-\frac{1}{3} \times -\frac{9}{10} \times \frac{5}{6}$

8) $\frac{11}{20} \times \frac{5}{33} \times -\frac{6}{7}$

9) $-\frac{3}{8} \times -\frac{5}{9} \times -\frac{16}{24}$

10) $3\frac{2}{3} \times -4\frac{1}{5}$

11) $-9\frac{5}{8} \times -1\frac{1}{11}$

12) $0 \times -16\frac{3}{10}$

13) $-5 \times -6\frac{1}{15}$

14) $-7\frac{1}{4} \times 5\frac{1}{7}$

15) $12\frac{5}{6} \times 2\frac{8}{14}$

16) $-2\frac{1}{3} \times -\frac{6}{49} \times -14$

17) $-14\frac{2}{5} \times 0 \times -6\frac{1}{8}$

18) $-\frac{35}{36} \times \frac{18}{25} \times -8\frac{1}{3}$

19) $-3\frac{1}{5} \times -4\frac{3}{8} \times 2\frac{3}{7}$

20) $-8\frac{1}{6} \times \frac{13}{14} \times 3\frac{1}{5}$

21) $14\frac{2}{3} \times -4\frac{9}{10} \times 30$

22) $\frac{17}{28} \times -2\frac{1}{3} \times -24$

23) $25\frac{3}{5} \times 3\frac{1}{8} \times -1\frac{3}{4}$

24) $-9\frac{1}{6} \times 36 \times 0$

25) $-3\frac{4}{7} \times -6\frac{3}{8} \times -\frac{2}{3}$

26) 4.7×-2.3

27) -48.1×-0.6

28) -423×1.8

29) $-.48 \times -.06$

30) 5.23×-1.5

31) $-.004 \times .09$

32) -6.47×0

33) 4.8×-93

34) -2.003×1.6

35) $4.7 \times 5.8 \times -2.1$

36) $-9.03 \times 8 \times -4.15$

37) $4.97 \times -.07 \times 3.5$

38) $-84.5 \times -12.2 \times -8$

39) $14.7 \times 0 \times -8.7$

40) $-.083 \times 4.5 \times -9.2$

41) $-87 \times .43 \times 56.1$

42) $400.3 \times -4.2 \times -8$

43) $66.4 \times .08 \times -14.8$

44) $-25.7 \times -3.46 \times -7.1$

45) $-4.2 \times -.8 \times 6 \times -4.1$

46) $-8.03 \times -.5 \times -1.3 \times -4$

47) $6.4 \times -8.1 \times .7 \times -.6$

48) $15 \times 6.3 \times 8 \times -4.7$

49) -4.007×-3.15

50) $67.85 \times -.047$

RATIONALS—DIVIDE AND SIMPLIFY EACH

1) $\frac{5}{6} \div \frac{1}{3}$

2) $-.8 \div 4$

3) $\frac{4}{8} \div -\frac{4}{5}$

4) $-8 \div -.04$

5) $-\frac{3}{4} \div \frac{2}{3}$

6) $-.8 \div 5$

7) $-\frac{4}{9} \div -\frac{5}{6}$

8) $.8 \div -.05$

9) $-3\frac{1}{2} \div -14$

10) $-2.4 \div -12$

11) $-4\frac{1}{2} \div -4\frac{2}{4}$

12) $-.04 \div 8$

13) $-30 \div \frac{5}{6}$

14) $-12.3 \div .3$

15) $-4\frac{1}{5} \div -\frac{7}{25}$

16) $4.5 \div -90$

17) $24 \div -\frac{3}{4}$

18) $-2.5 \div -50$

19) $-30 \div -\frac{7}{10}$

20) $1 \div -.0008$

21) $48 \div -\frac{2}{3}$

22) $-.15 \div 8$

23) $-\frac{9}{10} \div -\frac{3}{4}$

24) $-.15 \div -.8$

25) $-2\frac{1}{2} \div -20$

26) $-15 \div .008$

27) $-3\frac{1}{3} \div \frac{5}{8}$

28) $4.5 \div -15$

29) $-\frac{5}{6} \div 3$

30) $.52 \div 13$

31) $-24 \div -\frac{8}{9}$

32) $-6.4 \div -.0016$

33) $-\frac{15}{16} \div -\frac{5}{8}$

34) $.005 \div -4$

35) $4\frac{1}{3} \div -3\frac{1}{4}$

36) $-42.56 \div 14$

37) $-144 \div \frac{8}{11}$

38) $-.0034 \div -1.7$

39) $4\frac{1}{2} \div -1\frac{1}{2}$

40) $.6 \div -40$

41) $-8\frac{1}{3} \div 4\frac{1}{6} \div -\frac{2}{5}$

42) $-.06 \div -3 \times -.5$

43) $24 \div -\frac{2}{3} \times -1\frac{1}{8}$

44) $-6\frac{3}{4} \div -9 \div 1\frac{1}{4}$

45) $-4\frac{4}{5} \times -\frac{3}{8} \div -3\frac{1}{8}$

46) $-45 \times -.02 \div -5$

47) $-800 \div .05 \times -.0024$

48) $-.06 \times .05 \div -.04$

49) $-4.8 \div \frac{1}{2} \times -\frac{2}{3}$

50) $1\frac{1}{5} \div .4 \times 1\frac{4}{5}$

RATIONALS—USE >, < or = TO COMPARE THE FOLLOWING

1) $\frac{3}{4}$ 1   2) $-\frac{7}{8}$ 1

3) $-\frac{3}{4}$ 1   4) $\frac{7}{8}$ 1

5) $\frac{3}{4}$ $\frac{2}{3}$ 6) $-\frac{5}{6}$ $-\frac{7}{9}$

7) $-\frac{3}{4}$ $-\frac{2}{3}$ 8) $\frac{5}{6}$ $\frac{7}{9}$

9) $\frac{3}{5}$ $\frac{1}{2}$ 10) $-\frac{4}{5}$ $-\frac{16}{20}$

11) $-\frac{3}{5}$ $-\frac{1}{2}$ 12) $\frac{5}{7}$ $\frac{7}{5}$

13) $\frac{3}{5}$ $-\frac{1}{2}$ 14) $-\frac{15}{20}$ $-\frac{9}{12}$

15) $-1\frac{1}{3}$ $-1\frac{1}{4}$ 16) $-1\frac{2}{5}$ $-\frac{7}{5}$

17) $1\frac{1}{3}$ $1\frac{1}{4}$ 18) $\frac{4}{3}$ $1\frac{2}{3}$

19) $-\frac{3}{7}$ $-\frac{2}{5}$ 20) $-\frac{16}{18}$ $-\frac{7}{9}$

21) $1\frac{2}{3}$ $1\frac{3}{5}$ 22) $5\frac{1}{8}$ $-5\frac{1}{2}$

23) $-4\frac{1}{2}$ $-4\frac{11}{20}$ 24) $-\frac{8}{15}$ $-\frac{32}{60}$

25) $-5\frac{4}{9}$ $-5\frac{5}{12}$ 26) $1\frac{3}{8}$ $1\frac{3}{4}$

27) $4\frac{1}{8}$ $4\frac{3}{16}$ 28) $-1\frac{1}{12}$ $-\frac{16}{18}$

29) $-20\frac{7}{8}$ $-20\frac{5}{6}$ 30) $-3\frac{3}{20}$ $-3\frac{6}{50}$

LIST IN ORDER FROM THE SMALLEST TO THE LARGEST

31) $\frac{4}{5}, 1\frac{1}{2}, -\frac{2}{3}, -1\frac{1}{4}$

32) $-\frac{5}{7}, \frac{5}{7}, -\frac{5}{9}, \frac{5}{9}$

33) $-\frac{3}{4}, 0, -1, 1\frac{1}{2}$

34) $\frac{4}{5}, \frac{2}{3}, \frac{3}{4}, \frac{1}{2}$

35) $-\frac{4}{5}, -\frac{2}{3}, -\frac{3}{4}, -\frac{1}{2}$

36) $-\frac{1}{8}, -\frac{1}{3}, \frac{1}{4}, 0$

37) $1\frac{1}{5}, -\frac{5}{6}, -\frac{8}{10}, \frac{2}{5}$

38) $-\frac{3}{8}, -\frac{2}{5}, -\frac{3}{7}, -\frac{4}{9}$

39) $1\frac{1}{3}, -2, -1\frac{1}{2}, \frac{4}{5}$

40) $-1\frac{1}{2}, -\frac{5}{4}, -\frac{7}{2}, -\frac{5}{6}$

41) $-4\frac{1}{4}, -3\frac{1}{3}, -4, -3\frac{3}{4}$

42) $-5\frac{1}{5}, -4\frac{3}{4}, -5\frac{1}{10}, -4\frac{4}{5}$

43) $-\frac{3}{8}, -1, -\frac{5}{4}, -\frac{5}{3}$

44) $3\frac{1}{4}, 2\frac{3}{8}, -\frac{3}{5}, 2\frac{5}{6}$

45) $-7\frac{1}{2}, 7\frac{1}{2}, -3\frac{3}{4}, 3\frac{3}{4}$

46) $\frac{4}{9}, \frac{4}{7}, \frac{4}{12}, \frac{4}{18}$

47) $-\frac{2}{5}, \frac{3}{4}, -\frac{3}{8}, \frac{5}{3}$

48) $-1, \frac{4}{5}, -\frac{4}{5}, 0$

49) $-6\frac{1}{2}, 6\frac{1}{3}, -6\frac{1}{4}, 6\frac{1}{5}$

50) $-\frac{5}{4}, -\frac{7}{3}, -\frac{3}{2}, -\frac{8}{5}$

RATIONALS—USE >, < or = TO COMPARE THE FOLLOWING

1) 4.8 ( ) 3.6

2) 9.07 ( ) 9.6

3) 9 ( ) 8.99

4) 2.34 ( ) 2.333

5) 7.003 ( ) 7.1

6) .33 ( ) .330

7) -2.7 ( ) -2.6

8) 0 ( ) -0.4

9) 1.5 ( ) -1.5

10) -35 ( ) -3.5

11) .009 ( ) .1

12) .63 ( ) -.629

13) -1.84 ( ) -2

14) 1.84 ( ) 2

15) -4.85 ( ) -5.1

16) -.004 ( ) -.04

17) 6.2 ( ) 6.200

18) 24.3 ( ) -25

19) -33.3 ( ) -3.33

20) -5 ( ) -4.99

21) 6.83 ( ) -7

22) .075 ( ) .08

23) -.03 ( ) -.029

24) -8.4 ( ) -8.41

25) -1.5 ( ) -1.05

26) 7.77 ( ) 7.077

27) -9.2 ( ) -10

28) 66.31 ( ) -67

29) .47 ( ) 4.7

30) -8.20 ( ) -8.200

LIST FROM SMALLEST TO LARGEST

31) -3.6, -3.59, 3.6, 3.59

32) 7.4, 8, 8.7, 7.37

33) -8.2, -5, -12, -9

34) 4.3, 0, -2.8, -5

35) 4.27, 4.72, 2.47, 7.24

36) -4.9, -4.85, -5, -4.8

37) -.09, -.81, -.18, -1

38) .94, 1.1, 1.03, .935

39) -.7, -7, .07, -.07

40) -3.84, -3.09, -3.9, -3.1

41) 6.3, 6.29, 6.31, 6.305

42) -4.092, -4.089, -4.1, -4.09

43) .09, -1.1, 0, -1.5

44) 6.7, 6.66, 6.752, 6.72

45) -4.6, -5.2, -5, -5.15

46) -8, -.79, -7.9, -.8

47) .075, .8, .08, .81

48) -2.38, 1.7, 1.38, -1.7

49) -3.007, -3.101, -3, -3.2

50) .99, .9, 9, .09

RATIONALS—USE >, < or = TO COMPARE THE FOLLOWING

1)	$\frac{5}{8}$	$\frac{7}{9}$		16)	$-\frac{6}{7}$	-.67
2)	$-\frac{3}{4}$	$\frac{7}{10}$		17)	$-15\frac{1}{2}$	2.3
3)	$-\frac{4}{5}$	$-\frac{3}{4}$		18)	.88	$\frac{79}{100}$
4)	$-\frac{4}{9}$	$\frac{6}{7}$		19)	1.6	$\frac{7}{9}$
5)	$-4\frac{3}{8}$	$-4\frac{5}{9}$		20)	$\frac{43}{45}$	.895
6)	1.8	2.1		21)	-6.3	$-6\frac{5}{6}$
7)	.089	.09		22)	$-\frac{7}{8}$	.875
8)	16.3	-1.63		23)	2.8	$-2\frac{1}{2}$
9)	-.15	.15		24)	.23	$\frac{1}{4}$
10)	-2.399	-2.5		25)	2.36	$2\frac{9}{25}$
11)	-.75	$-\frac{3}{4}$		26)	$\frac{16}{20}$	-.8
12)	$-\frac{5}{6}$	.95		27)	-.9	-1
13)	$-\frac{4}{7}$	.8		28)	13.6	$-20\frac{3}{9}$
14)	6.9	$6\frac{9}{10}$		29)	$-\frac{4}{6}$	.66
15)	$\frac{4}{9}$	.4		30)	$\frac{7}{10}$	.9

LIST FROM SMALLEST TO LARGEST

31) $-\frac{1}{4}$, $\frac{1}{2}$, $-\frac{1}{2}$, $\frac{1}{4}$

32) $\frac{3}{8}$, 0, $-\frac{5}{6}$, 1

33) $-\frac{5}{8}$, $-\frac{3}{4}$, $-\frac{4}{3}$, $-\frac{5}{6}$

34) $\frac{3}{4}$, $\frac{5}{8}$, $-\frac{3}{5}$, $\frac{1}{2}$

35) $\frac{9}{8}$, $\frac{8}{9}$, $-\frac{5}{6}$, $-\frac{6}{5}$

36) -1.6, 1.6, -.8, .8

37) -.09, -.9, -9, -.009

38) 16.3, -14.5, 0, 20.38

39) 3.33, .333, -3.33, 33.3

40) .009, -.111, .238, -1.6

41) $\frac{3}{4}$, .6, $\frac{1}{2}$, .8

42) -.3, $-\frac{5}{8}$, $-\frac{1}{2}$, -.75

43) -1.6, $-1\frac{1}{2}$, -.16, 0

44) $\frac{23}{25}$, .8, 1.2, -15

45) $\frac{6}{5}$, $\frac{9}{10}$, 1.3, .78

46) $1\frac{3}{4}$, 1.89, -1.63, $-1\frac{2}{3}$

47) $\frac{2}{3}$, .66, .67, $\frac{665}{1000}$

48) $-\frac{1}{2}$, .8, -.75, $\frac{3}{4}$

49) $-\frac{5}{7}$, -.7, $-\frac{8}{9}$, -.8

50) 16.3, 1.63, $16\frac{1}{4}$, $1\frac{3}{5}$

RATIONALS—CHANGE EACH FRACTION INTO A DECIMAL

1) $\frac{1}{8}$

2) $-\frac{3}{32}$

3) $-\frac{8}{9}$

4) $\frac{3}{4}$

5) $-\frac{8}{15}$

6) $\frac{16}{20}$

7) $-\frac{1}{12}$

8) $\frac{5}{16}$

9) $-\frac{8}{3}$

10) $-\frac{8}{7}$

11) $\frac{3}{15}$

12) $-\frac{7}{12}$

13) $\frac{18}{11}$

14) $\frac{15}{8}$

15) $-\frac{2}{3}$

16) $-\frac{5}{6}$

17) $-\frac{23}{25}$

18) $-\frac{14}{20}$

19) $-\frac{7}{8}$

20) $\frac{3}{5}$

21) $-\frac{5}{8}$

22) $-\frac{5}{36}$

23) $\frac{3}{7}$

24) $-\frac{10}{11}$

25) $\frac{9}{16}$

CHANGE EACH DECIMAL INTO A FRACTION

26) $-.3$

27) $.303$

28) $-.6$

29) $.81$

30) $-.143$

31) 2.6

32) -3.81

33) -41.2

34) 6.03

35) -783.6

36) 7.9148

37) -4.2

38) 7.202002

39) -7.009

40) 9.0093

41) -2.915

42) 7.113

43) $-.14603$

44) $.2104$

45) $.001425$

46) 6.14183

47) 2.4143

48) -6.83

49) $-.00052$

50) 15.0043

RATIONALS—ADD OR SUBTRACT THE FOLLOWING AND EXPRESS IN SIMPLEST FORM

1) $\frac{5}{9} + \frac{-5}{6}$

2) $-\frac{11}{12} - \frac{5}{8}$

3) $-\frac{7}{15} + -\frac{9}{20}$

4) $\frac{21}{35} - -\frac{3}{14}$

5) $-\frac{28}{45} - \frac{13}{18}$

6) $\frac{3}{4} + -\frac{5}{7} - \frac{1}{14}$

7) $-\frac{4}{21} - \frac{4}{9} - -\frac{2}{3}$

8) $4\frac{3}{10} - 8\frac{4}{5}$

9) $- 6\frac{3}{28} + 4\frac{6}{7}$

10) $-9\frac{11}{16} - 5\frac{5}{6}$

11) $-18\frac{5}{22} - -9\frac{1}{4}$

12) $8\frac{7}{8} + -9\frac{5}{7}$

13) $5\frac{6}{25} + -3\frac{1}{30} - \frac{7}{15}$

14) $-9\frac{17}{72} - -\frac{8}{9} + 4\frac{13}{24}$

15) $-8\frac{1}{12} + -4\frac{2}{3} - 6\frac{5}{36}$

16) $7\frac{7}{10} - 9\frac{3}{16} - -5\frac{19}{40}$

17) $-4\frac{8}{49} + 11\frac{3}{35} - 8\frac{5}{7}$

18) $9\frac{25}{48} - 68 + -4\frac{17}{32}$

19) $-3\frac{9}{20} - -5\frac{13}{30} + 8\frac{3}{40}$

20) $14\frac{3}{56} + -5\frac{5}{8} + 8\frac{3}{4}$

21) $4.72 + -8.9$

22) $-6.053 - 9.2$

23) $-28.3 - -9.84$

24) $800 + -4.75$

25) $60 - -8.53$

26) $-67.08 + 3.495$

27) $-8.4 + 3.6 + -2.8$

28) $16.7 - 12 - -4.3$

29) $-84.52 + 9.6 + -12.78$

30) $253.1 - -4.82 - 46$

31) $89.03 - 6.7 + -4.8$

32) $4.07 + -.04 - 8.8$

33) $-9.9 - -65 + 8.41$

34) $-55.4 - 9.78 + -67.1$

35) $64.785 + 381 + -4.07$

36) $-3.77 - 3.7 - -7.47$

37) $-.08 + -.008 - -.8$

38) $89.4 - 98.4 + -8.4$

39) $101.1 + 11.1 - -1.11$

40) $-6.29 - -4.8 - .005$

41) $3\frac{3}{8} + -1.4$

42) $-4.6 - -\frac{3}{5}$

43) $.007 + -\frac{1}{2}$

44) $-25\frac{1}{4} - -25.25$

45) $6.06 + -9\frac{7}{10}$

46) $5.7 + 3\frac{7}{20} + -4.28$

47) $8\frac{1}{3} - 9.13 + -4\frac{1}{3}$

48) $-6\frac{8}{25} - 4.15 - -12$

49) $- 4\frac{3}{40} - -5\frac{7}{20} + 9.09$

50) $5.43 - 8.7 - -6\frac{7}{50}$

RATIONALS—ADD OR SUBTRACT THE FOLLOWING AND EXPRESS IN SIMPLEST FORM

1) $-4 + 1\frac{1}{3}$

2) $-6 + 2\frac{3}{7}$

3) $4 + -3.11$

4) $-6 + 2.43$

5) $-4\frac{1}{2} + -1\frac{3}{4}$

6) $1.6 - 8.18$

7) $-\frac{3}{8} + 2\frac{1}{6}$

8) $1.6 - -8.18$

9) $13.1 + -.91$

10) $7\frac{3}{5} - 3\frac{3}{4}$

11) $13.1 + -91$

12) $7\frac{3}{5} - -3\frac{3}{4}$

13) $1\frac{9}{10} + -2\frac{1}{2}$

14) $8 + -.617$

15) $1\frac{9}{10} - -2\frac{1}{2}$

16) $8 - -.617$

17) $1\frac{9}{10} - 2\frac{1}{2}$

18) $-8 + 6.17$

19) $-4.48 + 6.3$

20) $-15\frac{2}{5} + -8\frac{5}{6}$

21) $-4.48 - 6.3$

22) $-15\frac{2}{5} - -8\frac{5}{6}$

23) $-4.48 - -6.3$

24) $15\frac{2}{5} + -8\frac{5}{6}$

25) $15\frac{4}{9} - 8\frac{2}{3}$

26) $-7.1 + .42$

27) $15\frac{4}{9} - -8\frac{2}{3}$

28) $71 + -.42$

29) $-9 - -7\frac{3}{5}$

30) $.71 - 4.2$

31) $-.8 + 4 - 3.02$

32) $-6\frac{3}{7} + 1\frac{1}{14} - -4\frac{1}{3}$

33) $-8 + .4 - -30.2$

34) $-26\frac{3}{8} - -41\frac{7}{8} + -15\frac{1}{2}$

35) $8\frac{1}{3} - -3\frac{3}{4} + -9\frac{5}{6}$

36) $-.94 - 1.8 + -3.84$

37) $-12\frac{3}{8} + 1\frac{2}{9} - \frac{3}{4}$

38) $4 - 1.87 - -15.3$

39) $-.973 - -3.6 + -1.05$

40) $-21\frac{3}{4} + 17\frac{5}{6} + -2\frac{4}{5}$

41) $-3\frac{1}{2} + 4.17 + -1\frac{3}{4}$

42) $-3\frac{3}{25} + -.6 - -7\frac{1}{5}$

43) $2.07 - -1\frac{3}{5} + -4.48$

44) $.875 + -12\frac{3}{8} + 11\frac{1}{2}$

45) $2\frac{4}{5} + -.817 - -4$

46) $14.1 + -3\frac{7}{10} + .89$

47) $23\frac{3}{5} - -9.67 - 3\frac{1}{8}$

48) $-\frac{4}{50} - -2\frac{1}{4} - 5\frac{4}{5}$

49) $9 - -4\frac{13}{20} + -13.65$

50) $3.3 - 6\frac{1}{8} - -2\frac{1}{2}$

RATIONALS—ADD OR SUBTRACT THE FOLLOWING AND EXPRESS IN SIMPLEST FORM

1) $\frac{3}{4} + \frac{7}{8}$

2) $-\frac{5}{6} + \frac{1}{2}$

3) $\frac{9}{10} + -\frac{5}{6}$

4) $-\frac{4}{5} + -\frac{3}{4}$

5) $1\frac{5}{6} + -3\frac{1}{9}$

6) $\frac{4}{9} - \frac{5}{6}$

7) $-\frac{3}{5} - \frac{13}{15}$

8) $-\frac{9}{10} - -\frac{1}{2}$

9) $-3\frac{1}{2} - 5\frac{2}{3}$

10) $4\frac{3}{8} - -5\frac{1}{5}$

11) $-\frac{1}{2} + \frac{3}{4} - \frac{3}{5}$

12) $\frac{9}{10} + \frac{11}{12} - -\frac{5}{6}$

13) $-3\frac{1}{2} - 1\frac{2}{3} + 8\frac{3}{4}$

14) $-2\frac{1}{2} + 6\frac{2}{5} - -2\frac{2}{3}$

15) $-1\frac{5}{7} + 2\frac{2}{3} - 1\frac{1}{9}$

16) $6\frac{3}{5} + 20\frac{1}{4} + -15\frac{7}{10}$

17) $2\frac{1}{2} - 6\frac{3}{4} + 5\frac{7}{8} - -3\frac{2}{3}$

18) $-5\frac{1}{5} + 6\frac{2}{3} + -4\frac{3}{10} - -2\frac{5}{6}$

19) $7\frac{1}{3} + -6\frac{2}{5} + -8\frac{7}{12} + 5\frac{3}{10}$

20) $-4\frac{2}{9} + 5\frac{8}{24} + -4\frac{3}{8} + -2\frac{5}{6}$

21) $-1.6 + 4.8$

22) $-3.6 + 9.35$

23) $4.63 + 9.483$

24) $-2.318 + 5.8634$

25) $-2.853 + -.29$

26) $2.634 - 15.8$

27) $20.83 - -6.348$

28) $-2.3 - 5.834$

29) $-6.83 - -5.2953$

30) $-2.43 - 61.2$

31) $3.2 - 6.8 - 3.25$

32) $9.8 - -4.6 + -6.815$

33) $15 - 1.6 + -14.8$

34) $18.32 - 20.6 + -15.818$

35) $20.306 - 18.61 + 13.2951$

36) $-63.1 - 6.31 + -631$

37) $2.3 - 8.3 - -6.81 + 4.3$

38) $2.3 - 9.31 + 5.36 + -2$

39) $43.818 - 2.8 - -6.314 - 48.9$

40) $-16.8 + -2.6 - -5.810 + -6.9341$

41) $6.3 - 2\frac{1}{2}$

42) $-18\frac{5}{8} - -2.3$

43) $14.3 + 3\frac{3}{5}$

44) $-6\frac{7}{10} + -2.85$

45) $20.3 - -3\frac{3}{4} + 8.3$

46) $7\frac{3}{16} + -8.43 - 5\frac{3}{8}$

47) $-6\frac{5}{6} + 4.2 - 3\frac{1}{5}$

48) $-2\frac{2}{3} + 9\frac{3}{4} - -6.3$

49) $7.3 + 4\frac{19}{20} + -5.23 + -7\frac{3}{10}$

50) $-2\frac{5}{12} + 2.8 + -3\frac{2}{3} - 6\frac{7}{15}$

RATIONALS—MULTIPLY OR DIVIDE THE FOLLOWING AND EXPRESS IN SIMPLEST FORM

1) $\frac{4}{9} \times -\frac{5}{12}$

2) $-\frac{9}{10} \div \frac{4}{15}$

3) $-\frac{18}{25} \div -\frac{7}{30}$

4) $-\frac{10}{21} \times \frac{7}{8}$

5) $\frac{35}{45} \times -\frac{27}{60}$

6) $-\frac{24}{49} \div \frac{9}{14}$

7) $-\frac{16}{81} \times -\frac{36}{42} \times \frac{3}{8}$

8) $\frac{9}{20} \div -\frac{7}{15} \div \frac{12}{25}$

9) $4\frac{1}{5} \div -2\frac{1}{10}$

10) $-3\frac{1}{2} \times -1\frac{1}{21}$

11) $6\frac{3}{4} \times 4\frac{2}{9}$

12) $-15 \div -9\frac{1}{6}$

13) $-3\frac{2}{3} \times -4\frac{1}{2} \times -8\frac{1}{4}$

14) $7\frac{7}{8} \div 9 \div -\frac{3}{4}$

15) $-3\frac{6}{7} \div -\frac{9}{14} \times 2\frac{1}{6}$

16) $6\frac{1}{9} \div -12 \times 7\frac{1}{5}$

17) $-12\frac{3}{5} \times -4\frac{2}{9} \div -2\frac{1}{9}$

18) $24 \times -3\frac{1}{8} \times 4\frac{1}{5}$

19) $-14\frac{2}{3} \div 6\frac{1}{6} \times -3\frac{1}{4}$

20) $-60 \times 2\frac{3}{5} \div 3\frac{5}{9}$

21) 4.03×-2.6

22) $-8.8 \div -.05$

23) $.072 \div -3.6$

24) 6.95×47

25) -37.9×48.2

26) $4.8 \times -2.3 \times 6$

27) $-12.8 \div -.04 \div .2$

28) $-8.75 \times -.13 \times -9$

29) $-42.5 \div .005 \div -1.7$

30) $-6.5 \times -9.2 \times 4.8$

31) $28.2 \div -.08 \times 5$

32) $-8.64 \times -4.9 \div -1.4$

33) $75.5 \div -5 \times 3.6$

34) $-300.3 \div .003 \times .052$

35) $-35.36 \div 27.2 \times -16$

36) $48.3 \times 2.7 \div -1.8$

37) $-4.08 \times -.08 \div 1,600$

38) $87.5 \times .15 \times -4.7$

39) $-12.4 \div -40 \times -6.5$

40) $850 \times -5.6 \div 3.2$

41) $-4\frac{1}{4} \times 2.5$

42) $-9.75 \div -2\frac{1}{2}$

43) $8\frac{1}{8} \times -4.63$

44) $-5.03 \times 3\frac{4}{5}$

45) $8\frac{5}{16} \div -.05$

46) $9.6 \times -\frac{3}{25} \div -.004$

47) $-63 \div .07 \times 5\frac{3}{4}$

48) $-56.2 \times 4.2 \div -\frac{7}{10}$

49) $-13.5 \div -1\frac{1}{4} \times 6.7$

50) $-4\frac{1}{6} \times 7\frac{1}{5} \div -1.5$

RATIONALS—MULTIPLY AND DIVIDE THE FOLLOWING AND EXPRESS IN SIMPLEST FORM

1) $\frac{2}{3} \times \frac{5}{6}$

2) $\frac{7}{8} \times -\frac{10}{14}$

3) $-\frac{3}{10} \times \frac{15}{9}$

4) $-\frac{20}{27} \times -\frac{9}{40}$

5) $\frac{16}{25} \times -\frac{20}{48}$

6) $-\frac{2}{3} \div \frac{3}{4}$

7) $-\frac{5}{6} \div -\frac{15}{16}$

8) $\frac{25}{55} \div 1\frac{8}{11}$

9) $-3\frac{1}{2} \div 1\frac{3}{4}$

10) $-5\frac{2}{3} \div 1\frac{3}{5}$

11) $\frac{2}{3} \times -\frac{5}{6} \div \frac{3}{8}$

12) $\frac{7}{9} \div -\frac{3}{7} \times \frac{7}{10}$

13) $36 \div -\frac{4}{6} \times \frac{9}{10}$

14) $-\frac{2}{5} \times 10 \times -\frac{25}{28}$

15) $-\frac{36}{50} \div \frac{9}{10} \times -\frac{4}{7}$

16) $-\frac{14}{15} \times \frac{9}{13} \div 2\frac{2}{26}$

17) $-1\frac{1}{3} \times 2\frac{1}{4} \times 5\frac{2}{5}$

18) $-2\frac{1}{3} \div 7 \times 8\frac{1}{3}$

19) $-\frac{9}{10} \times 3\frac{1}{3} \div 3 \times -4\frac{1}{4}$

20) $7\frac{1}{2} \times -1\frac{4}{15} \div \frac{38}{43} \times 2\frac{1}{2}$

21) $8.3 \times -.6$

22) 2.28×7.3

23) $-4.6 \times -.005$

24) -6.8×4

25) -7.83×1.3

26) $-8.6 \div 4$

27) $-3.4 \div .08$

28) $-.0008 \div -.05$

29) $16.53 \div 2.9$

30) $.0537 \div .015$

31) $4.5 \times -1.2 \div .72$

32) $-6.3 \div .105 \times -1.3$

33) $-3.2 \times 4.8 \times -2.92$

34) $.144 \div .06 \div -.03$

35) $-.15 \div -60 \times -.03$

36) $-2.4 \div -10 \div 100$

37) $-7.2 \div .6 \times -1.5$

38) $-3.85 \times .2 \div .05$

39) $.217 \div 56 \times -22.4 \div 7$

40) $-.21 \div 5 \times -.7 \div 4.9$

41) $\frac{1}{2} \times .5 \times -\frac{3}{4} \times -.75$

42) $.9 \div .06 \times -\frac{3}{5} \div .05$

43) $-\frac{3}{4} \div -\frac{5}{6} \times .8 \div -\frac{3}{10}$

44) $-2\frac{1}{5} \div .08 \times -.6$

45) $-2\frac{3}{7} \times 4\frac{1}{2} \div 2.4$

46) $-25 \div 100 \times -\frac{5}{6}$

47) $-5\frac{1}{5} \times .6 \div .8$

48) $\frac{3}{7} \times -\frac{8}{9} \div 1.4$

49) $-2\frac{1}{2} \times 3\frac{1}{3} \div .7 \times .2$

50) $3\frac{5}{12} \div .3 \times .4 \div \frac{8}{20}$

RATIONALS—ADD, SUBTRACT, MULTIPLY OR DIVIDE THE FOLLOWING AND EXPRESS IN SIMPLEST FORM

1) $-4\frac{1}{5} + -3\frac{1}{3}$

2) $-6.4 + .008$

3) $8\frac{3}{4} + -14\frac{1}{8}$

4) $-5.28 + 8.6$

5) $-4\frac{3}{7} + -9\frac{1}{5}$

6) $7.45 - -6.564$

7) $-14\frac{4}{9} - 5\frac{5}{6}$

8) $-8.07 - -14.7$

9) $8\frac{1}{12} - 10\frac{7}{8}$

10) $-63.7 - -4.86$

11) $-6\frac{1}{8} \times -5\frac{1}{7}$

12) 4.87×-2.6

13) $-9.07 \times .085$

14) $12\frac{3}{5} \times 2\frac{1}{7}$

15) -49.8×-6.05

16) $-4\frac{1}{6} \div -2\frac{2}{3}$

17) $3.52 \div -4.4$

18) $-16\frac{1}{5} \div 18$

19) -66.4×9.72

20) $-4\frac{4}{9} \div -2\frac{2}{9}$

21) $4.5 + -6.72 + -9$

22) $3\frac{1}{5} + -4\frac{1}{10} + 2\frac{1}{4}$

23) $-9.8 + -3 + -.06$

24) $8\frac{3}{16} + -4\frac{7}{8} + 5\frac{1}{2}$

25) $-69.4 + -.067 + 9.8$

26) $-4\frac{2}{5} - 7\frac{1}{2} - -3\frac{1}{3}$

27) $9.48 - -6 - 8.752$

28) $-8\frac{3}{8} - 2\frac{5}{16} - -4\frac{5}{24}$

29) $19.8 - -4.52 - 7.9$

30) $-90 - 15\frac{7}{10} - -8\frac{4}{15}$

31) $8.75 \times 3.6 \times -9.8$

32) $-8\frac{5}{9} \times 3\frac{2}{11} \times -18$

33) $-8.8 \times -4.32 \times -1.7$

34) $-25 \times -6\frac{2}{5} \times 2\frac{1}{8}$

35) $4.83 \times 6.07 \times -8.2$

36) $5\frac{4}{7} \div 2\frac{1}{14} \div -13$

37) $-8.16 \div -3.2 \div -.05$

38) $-9\frac{3}{5} \div -3\frac{1}{3} \div 4\frac{2}{3}$

39) $9.36 \div -.08 \div -20$

40) $-16\frac{16}{25} \div -\frac{8}{15} \div -30$

41) $6\frac{1}{4} + 3.25 + -8\frac{1}{8}$

42) $7.05 - -3\frac{1}{5} + -2\frac{1}{10}$

43) $\frac{5}{8} - 3.4 + \frac{3}{5}$

44) $-8.72 - 9 + -8\frac{17}{50}$

45) $6.85 \times -4.3 \div -\frac{1}{25}$

46) $-6\frac{3}{10} \div -2\frac{1}{3} \times -4.62$

47) $\frac{3}{20} + -\frac{4}{5} \times 6.2 - 8$

48) $2\frac{3}{11} \times -33 - 6\frac{1}{4}$

49) $-2.76 \div 1\frac{1}{5} + -1.15$

50) $(67\frac{3}{16} - -4\frac{7}{8}) \div -72.0625$

RATIONALS—ADD, SUBTRACT, MULTIPLY OR DIVIDE
THE FOLLOWING AND EXPRESS IN SIMPLEST FORM

1) $-24 + 8$

2) $-24 - 8$

3) -24×8

4) $-24 \div 8$

5) $-24 - -8$

6) $24 \div -8$

7) $2.4 - 8$

8) $2.4 \div 8$

9) $-2.4 \times -.08$

10) $-2.4 - -8$

11) $-.24 + 8$

12) $-2.4 + -.08$

13) $8 \div -\frac{3}{4}$

14) $-8 \div \frac{3}{4}$

15) $-8 - -\frac{3}{4}$

16) $-8 \times -\frac{3}{4}$

17) $1\frac{3}{5} \div \frac{2}{5}$

18) $1\frac{3}{4} - \frac{5}{6}$

19) $-.35 - -.7$

20) $-.35 \div 7$

21) $-.7 + -.35$

22) $-.035 \times -.007$

23) $-\frac{5}{9} \times -\frac{3}{4}$

24) $-\frac{7}{8} \div 3\frac{1}{2}$

25) $4\frac{2}{3} + -1\frac{7}{8}$

26) $5\frac{2}{9} - -2\frac{5}{6}$

27) $-4.5 \div .0009$

28) $-4.5 + .09$

29) $.556 - -4.7$

30) $-.36 \times -2.4$

31) $1\frac{1}{2} + \frac{3}{8} + -2\frac{3}{4}$

32) $-\frac{3}{8} \div 1\frac{1}{4} \times -\frac{2}{5}$

33) $-\frac{7}{8} + 1\frac{2}{3} + -\frac{5}{12}$

34) $\frac{25}{49} \times -\frac{7}{15} \times -\frac{14}{10}$

35) $-.05 \div .8$

36) $-4.4 + -78 - -4.91$

37) $-500 \times -.12 \times .06$

38) $.12 \div -24$

39) $4\frac{1}{2} + -\frac{3}{5} + 3\frac{2}{3}$

40) $4\frac{1}{2} \div -9 \times -\frac{2}{5}$

41) $-\frac{3}{4} + .9$

42) $-1\frac{3}{5} \div 3.2$

43) $29.7 - -1\frac{3}{8}$

44) $\frac{3}{4} \times -.72$

45) $-\frac{4}{5} \times 8.5 \times -1\frac{1}{2}$

46) $-\frac{5}{8} + -8.2 - -2\frac{3}{4}$

47) $-.3045 \div -\frac{3}{20}$

48) $1\frac{7}{8} + -275.2 + 3\frac{4}{25}$

49) $24.12 \times -1\frac{1}{5} \div .005$

50) $-14.4 \div 1\frac{4}{5} \times -2.5$

RATIONALS—ADD, SUBTRACT, MULTIPLY OR DIVIDE
THE FOLLOWING AND EXPRESS IN SIMPLEST FORM

1) $18 + -.6$

2) $-\frac{3}{4} + \frac{2}{3}$

3) $18 - -.6$

4) $-\frac{3}{4} \times \frac{2}{3}$

5) $18 \times -.6$

6) $-\frac{3}{4} - \frac{2}{3}$

7) $-1.8 \div 6$

8) $-\frac{3}{4} \div \frac{2}{3}$

9) $.18 + -.6$

10) $-\frac{3}{4} - -\frac{2}{3}$

11) $-1.8 - -6$

12) $-\frac{3}{4} \div -\frac{2}{3}$

13) $-.18 \times -.06$

14) $\frac{5}{8} + -1\frac{1}{3}$

15) $-.018 \div -.6$

16) $-\frac{5}{8} \div 1\frac{1}{3}$

17) $-.18 \div -.2$

18) $-\frac{3}{5} + -\frac{7}{8}$

19) $-.4 \times -1.5 \times -.06$

20) $-1\frac{1}{2} \times -\frac{3}{4}$

21) $-1.8 + -18 + .24$

22) $-5 + 2\frac{1}{3}$

23) $-50 \div -.0008$

24) $-6 \div -1\frac{1}{9}$

25) $-2.3 - -1.91 + -3$

26) $-8\frac{1}{5} - -3\frac{3}{4}$

27) $-.18 \times .5 \times -.04$

28) $-9\frac{1}{3} \times 1\frac{1}{14}$

29) $18 + -.93 - 1.9$

30) $-2\frac{3}{4} + 1\frac{4}{5}$

31) $-.056 \div 140$

32) $-6\frac{1}{2} \div 5\frac{1}{5} \times -\frac{2}{5}$

33) $-.8 - -3 + -2.31$

34) $-3\frac{1}{3} - -8 + -2\frac{3}{4}$

35) $-.09 \times -.06 \times 300$

36) $18 \div -\frac{2}{3} \times 1\frac{1}{3}$

37) $-.06 + -34.1 + -.8$

38) $-5\frac{3}{8} + -1\frac{1}{12} + 4\frac{3}{4}$

39) $2.4 \div -.144$

40) $-1\frac{1}{4} \times -6 \times -1\frac{1}{3}$

41) $1\frac{1}{5} + -2\frac{3}{4} + 1.9$

42) $-4\frac{1}{2} \times -.5$

43) $6.3 + -14\frac{3}{4}$

44) $-1.8 \div -\frac{3}{4}$

45) $-1\frac{4}{5} \times .8$

46) $-6\frac{1}{2} - -1.07 + -3\frac{3}{8}$

47) $\frac{5}{6} + -\frac{3}{4} + .7$

48) $7\frac{1}{2} \times -4.8 \div -.5$

49) $-1\frac{1}{3} \times .75$

50) $-\frac{5}{8} + -1\frac{1}{4} - -7.36$

EXPONENTS—WRITE THE STANDARD NUMERAL FOR EACH

1) 2^3

2) 3^4

3) 10^3

4) 1^8

5) 15^0

6) 23^1

7) 7^2

8) 4^5

9) 2^8

10) 5^3

11) 3^5

12) 19^2

13) 3^3

14) 6^4

15) 2^2

16) 13^2

17) 1^5

18) 7^3

19) 10^0

20) 4^4

21) 30^4

22) 8^2

23) 10^9

24) 10^1

25) 43^0

26) 9^3

27) 3^7

28) 12^2

29) 2^5

30) 14^2

31) 10^5

32) 16^2

33) 9^4

34) 4^3

35) 25^3

36) 10^4

37) 15^2

38) 11^3

39) 5^4

40) 24^2

41) 10^8

42) 8^4

43) 100^3

44) 7^4

45) 13^3

46) 5^5

47) 20^3

48) 36^2

49) 9^6

50) 12^4

EXPONENTS—WRITE THE STANDARD NUMERAL FOR EACH

1) 2^4

2) 3^2

3) 5^2

4) 8^3

5) 9^2

6) $(-6)^4$

7) -4^4

8) $(-2)^7$

9) -3^5

10) 2^3

11) $(-4)^3$

12) -15^2

13) $(-3)^4$

14) -5^0

15) $(-21)^2$

16) 11^2

17) -7^2

18) $(-10)^6$

19) -6^5

20) $(-10)^5$

21) 3^{-5}

22) 9^{-3}

23) 23^{-2}

24) 5^{-3}

25) 4^{-5}

26) $\frac{1}{2}^6$

27) $(\frac{1}{24})^2$

28) $\frac{1}{5}^{-1}$

29) $(\frac{1}{6})^{-2}$

30) 1^{-8}

31) $\frac{1}{2}^{-5}$

32) $(\frac{1}{10})^7$

33) $(\frac{1}{12})^{-2}$

34) $\frac{1}{3}^6$

35) $\frac{1}{3}^{-3}$

36) $(\frac{1}{22})^2$

37) $(\frac{1}{20})^{-3}$

38) $\frac{1}{14}^{-3}$

39) 9^{-5}

40) $\frac{1}{13}^{-2}$

41) $(-\frac{1}{4})^2$

42) $(-8)^{-2}$

43) $\frac{1}{6}^{-3}$

44) $-\frac{1}{10}^0$

45) $\frac{1}{-7}^{-1}$

46) $(\frac{1}{9})^{-3}$

47) $\frac{1}{-8}^{-5}$

48) $(-\frac{1}{12})^{-3}$

49) $\frac{1}{-10}^{-2}$

50) $(-\frac{1}{11})^4$

EXPONENTS—WRITE THE SIMPLEST EXPONENTIAL NOTATION FOR EACH

1) $2^3 \cdot 2^4$

2) $3^5 \cdot 3^7$

3) $4^0 \cdot 4^2 \cdot 4^3$

4) $5^1 \cdot 5^5 \cdot 5^6$

5) $10^5 \cdot 10^7 \cdot 10^8$

6) $6^3 \cdot 6^4 \cdot 6^3 \cdot 6^2$

7) $9^2 \cdot 9^5 \cdot 9^{10} \cdot 9^6$

8) $8^3 \cdot 8^5 \cdot 8^6 \cdot 8^4$

9) $15^0 \cdot 15^1 \cdot 15^3 \cdot 15^8$

10) $20^3 \cdot 20^8 \cdot 20^6 \cdot 20^{10}$

11) $\dfrac{10^5}{10^3}$

12) $\dfrac{10^8}{10^0}$

13) $\dfrac{2^6}{2^2}$

14) $\dfrac{3^{10}}{3^1}$

15) $\dfrac{5^{15}}{5^3}$

16) $\dfrac{8^2}{8^6}$

17) $\dfrac{7^0}{7^6}$

18) $\dfrac{9^3}{9^{10}}$

19) $\dfrac{20^{10}}{20^3}$

20) $\dfrac{5^7}{5^{20}}$

21) $(2^3)^4$

22) $(3^2)^5$

23) $(5^4)^6$

24) $(4^3)^3$

25) $(6^1)^7$

26) $(8^0)^9$

27) $(2^2)^8$

28) $(7^5)^6$

29) $((3^2)^3)^4$

30) $((16^3)^1)^5$

31) $\dfrac{5^2 \cdot 5^3}{5^4}$

32) $\dfrac{6^3 \cdot 6^5}{6^2}$

33) $\dfrac{8^3 \cdot 8^5}{8^2 \cdot 8^3}$

34) $\dfrac{9^0 \cdot 9^5}{9^2 \cdot 9^7}$

35) $\dfrac{10^7 \quad 10^2 \quad 10^5}{10^3 \quad 10^5 \quad 10^6}$

36) $\dfrac{2^3 \cdot 2^4 \cdot 2^8}{2^6 \cdot 2^7 \cdot 2^4}$

37) $\dfrac{(5^2)^3 \cdot 5^6}{(5^2)^4}$

38) $\dfrac{(2^3 \cdot 2^4)^2}{2^3 \quad 2^4 \quad 2^8}$

39) $\dfrac{(4^2)^5 \cdot (4^2 \cdot 4^3)^3}{(4^2 \quad 4^3 \quad 4^1)^4}$

40) $\dfrac{(8^2)^3 \cdot (8^4)^3}{8^2 \cdot (8^3)^4 \cdot 8^3}$

41) $2^{-3} \cdot 2^4 \cdot 2^{-5}$

42) $\dfrac{3^{-4}}{3^5}$

43) $(5^{-3})^5$

44) $\dfrac{6^{-2} \cdot 6^5}{6^{-3} \cdot 6^{-4}}$

45) $\dfrac{9^2 \cdot 9^3 \cdot 9^{-8}}{9^{-2} \cdot 9^{-5} \cdot 9^3}$

46) $(4^{-2})^{-3} \cdot 4^2 \cdot 4^{-3}$

47) $\dfrac{1}{4^2 \cdot 4^{-3} \cdot (4^2)^{-3}}$

48) $\dfrac{6^2 \cdot 6^{-3}}{(6^{-2})^2 \cdot 6^{-3}}$

49) $\dfrac{(10^0)^3 \cdot 10^5}{(10^{-2} \cdot 10^{-3})^3}$

50) $\dfrac{(9^{-2})^{-3} \cdot (9^{-2})^{-4}}{9^5 \cdot 9^3 \cdot 9^4}$

EXPONENTS—FIND THE SQUARE ROOT OF THE FOLLOWING

1) $\sqrt{16}$ 2) $\sqrt{144}$

3) $\sqrt{81}$ 4) $\sqrt{49}$

5) $\sqrt{225}$ 6) $\sqrt{121}$

7) $\sqrt{36}$ 8) $\sqrt{196}$

9) $\sqrt{289}$ 10) $\sqrt{400}$

11) $\sqrt{169}$ 12) $\sqrt{25}$

13) $\sqrt{10,000}$ 14) $\sqrt{100}$

15) $\sqrt{64}$ 16) $\sqrt{289}$

17) $\sqrt{361}$ 18) $\sqrt{484}$

19) $\sqrt{529}$ 20) $\sqrt{256}$

21) $\sqrt{324}$ 22) $\sqrt{8100}$

23) $\sqrt{841}$ 24) $\sqrt{1681}$

25) $\sqrt{1521}$ 26) $\sqrt{441}$

27) $\sqrt{9216}$ 28) $\sqrt{7056}$

29) $\sqrt{676}$ 30) $\sqrt{9604}$

31) $\sqrt{9025}$ 32) $\sqrt{3721}$

33) $\sqrt{3249}$ 34) $\sqrt{1296}$

35) $\sqrt{7569}$ 36) $\sqrt{784}$

37) $\sqrt{2116}$ 38) $\sqrt{6561}$

39) $\sqrt{9801}$ 40) $\sqrt{2809}$

41) $\sqrt{5476}$ 42) $\sqrt{2304}$

43) $\sqrt{6241}$ 44) $\sqrt{8464}$

45) $\sqrt{1936}$ 46) $\sqrt{2601}$

47) $\sqrt{5929}$ 48) $\sqrt{7921}$

49) $\sqrt{961}$ 50) $\sqrt{1369}$

EXPONENTS—FIND THE SQUARE ROOT OF THE FOLLOWING
ROUND OFF TO THE NEAREST TENTH

1) $\sqrt{2}$ 2) $\sqrt{17}$ 3) $\sqrt{8}$

4) $\sqrt{27}$ 5) $\sqrt{39}$ 6) $\sqrt{50}$

7) $\sqrt{65}$ 8) $\sqrt{75}$ 9) $\sqrt{90}$

10) $\sqrt{105}$ 11) $\sqrt{131}$ 12) $\sqrt{150}$

13) $\sqrt{175}$ 14) $\sqrt{200}$ 15) $\sqrt{235}$

ROUND OFF TO THE NEAREST HUNDREDTH

16) $\sqrt{2}$ 17) $\sqrt{19}$ 18) $\sqrt{10}$

19) $\sqrt{40}$ 20) $\sqrt{52}$ 21) $\sqrt{68}$

22) $\sqrt{82}$ 23) $\sqrt{29}$ 24) $\sqrt{108}$

25) $\sqrt{135}$ 26) $\sqrt{156}$ 27) $\sqrt{180}$

28) $\sqrt{205}$ 29) $\sqrt{243}$ 30) $\sqrt{265}$

ROUND OFF TO THE NEAREST THOUSANDTH

31) $\sqrt{2}$ 32) $\sqrt{20}$

33) $\sqrt{12}$ 34) $\sqrt{33}$

35) $\sqrt{45}$ 36) $\sqrt{56}$

37) $\sqrt{70}$ 38) $\sqrt{85}$

39) $\sqrt{94}$ 40) $\sqrt{120}$

41) $\sqrt{140}$ 42) $\sqrt{163}$

43) $\sqrt{195}$ 44) $\sqrt{211}$

45) $\sqrt{250}$ 46) $\sqrt{283}$

47) $\sqrt{300}$ 48) $\sqrt{315}$

49) $\sqrt{327}$ 50) $\sqrt{342}$

EXPONENTS—CHANGE TO SCIENTIFIC NOTATION

1) 42,500   2) 1,300   3) 800,000

4) .0042   5) .00009   6) .032

7) 600   8) 71,000   9) 1,001,000

10) .005   11) .000102   12) .02

13) 650,000   14) 7,000,010   15) 23,000,000

16) 18.45   17) 924.003   18) 7000.007

19) 606,000   20) 99,900   21) 500,000,000

22) .00075   23) .0000006   24) 59.005

25) 92,000

CHANGE TO STANDARD NUMERALS

26) 1.43×10^5 27) 6×10^8 28) 7.2×10^3

29) 5.2×10^{-4} 30) 8.75×10^{-6} 31) 5×10^{-3}

32) 6.754×10^7 33) 3.17×10^5 34) 8.1×10^4

35) 3×10^{-1} 36) 4.72×10^{-2} 37) 7.51×10^{-6}

38) 8.4×10^5 39) 5.555×10^2 40) 1.2345×10^6

41) 2.73×10^{-4} 42) 8.15×10^{-7} 43) 6×10^{-4}

44) 9.2×10^2 45) 6.52×10^1 46) 4.85×10^0

47) 2.145×10^{-3} 48) 3.2×10^{-6} 49) 1.72×10^{-1}

50) 4.832×10^8

EXPONENTS—
MULTIPLY—GIVE YOUR ANSWER IN SCIENTIFIC NOTATION

1) $\quad 2.5 \times 10^3$
$\times \quad 1.4 \times 10^4$

2) $\quad 6.3 \times 10^5$
$\times \quad 4 \times 10^3$

3) $\quad 8.32 \times 10^5$
$\times \quad 2.1 \times 10^2$

4) $\quad 8.5 \times 10^{\ 6}$
$\times \quad 1.4 \times 10^{-2}$

5) $\quad 9 \times 10^6$
$\times \quad 5 \times 10^7$

6) $\quad 2.3 \times 10^{-3}$
$\times \quad 1.5 \times 10^{-2}$

7) $\quad 6.8 \times 10^5$
$\times \quad 6 \times 10^4$

8) $\quad 3.64 \times 10^{-2}$
$\times \quad 5.8 \times 10^4$

9) $\quad 8.4 \times 10^5$
$\times \quad 2.2 \times 10^5$

10) $\quad 48,000$
$\times \quad 2,500$

11) $\quad 4,000,000$
$\times \quad 600,000$

12) $\quad 93,000,000$
$\times \quad 47,000$

13) $\quad 725,000$
$\times \quad 8,000$

14) $\quad 21,000,000$
$\times \quad 6,000,000$

15) $\quad 75,000$
$\times \quad 6,100$

DIVIDE—GIVE YOUR ANSWER IN SCIENTIFIC NOTATION

16) $\dfrac{4.8 \times 10^4}{2.4 \times 10^2}$

17) $\dfrac{8.6 \times 10^6}{2 \times 10^3}$

18) $\dfrac{4 \times 10^9}{8 \times 10^6}$

19) $\dfrac{6.36 \times 10^5}{6 \times 10^{-2}}$

20) $\dfrac{1.25 \times 10^{-3}}{2.5 \times 10^{-5}}$

21) $\dfrac{6 \times 10^5}{1.5 \times 10^5}$

22) $\dfrac{7.24 \times 10^3}{4 \times 10^0}$

23) $\dfrac{3.2 \times 10^0}{8 \times 10^3}$

24) $\dfrac{8.04 \times 10^6}{5 \times 10^4}$

25) $\dfrac{900,000}{45,000}$

26) $\dfrac{72,000,000}{3,000,000}$

27) $\dfrac{.000054}{.00009}$

28) $\dfrac{81,000,000}{.00018}$

29) $\dfrac{.00045}{500,000}$

30) $\dfrac{75,000,000}{.0000075}$

EXPONENTS—
WRITE THE STANDARD NUMERAL FOR EACH

1) 2^5 2) $(-3)^4$ 3) 5^3

4) 8^3 5) $(-7)^3$ 6) 2^{-8}

7) 6^4 8) $(-3)^6$ 9) 11^3

10) $(-12)^2$ 11) 9^{-4} 12) $(-10)^5$

13) $\dfrac{1}{4^3}$ 14) 10^7 15) $\dfrac{1}{7^{-2}}$

WRITE THE SIMPLEST EXPONENTIAL NOTATION FOR EACH

16) $5^3 \cdot 5^4$ 17) $6^0 \cdot 6^1 \cdot 6^5$ 18) $8^{-3} \cdot 8^4 \cdot 8^{-5}$

19) $\dfrac{9^5}{9^3}$ 20) $\dfrac{19^3}{19^6}$ 21) $\dfrac{25^6}{25^5}$

22) $(6^3)^4$ 23) $(8^2)^5$ 24) $(4^{-3})^8$

25) $\dfrac{6^4 \cdot 6^5}{6^3 \cdot 6^2 \cdot 6^1}$ 26) $\dfrac{(7^2 \cdot 7^3)^3}{7^3 \cdot 7^2 \cdot 7^5}$ 27) $\dfrac{8^{-3} \cdot 8^{-2}}{(8^2)^6}$

28) $(-3)^3 \cdot (-3)^{-8}$ 29) $\dfrac{(-8)^2 \cdot (-8)^{-5}}{(-8)^3}$ 30) $\dfrac{(-4)^2 \cdot (4)^{-8}}{4^{-3} \cdot ((-4)^2)^3}$

FIND THE SQUARE ROOT FOR EACH.
ROUND OFF TO THE NEAREST HUNDREDTH IF NECESSARY

31) $\sqrt{9}$ 32) $\sqrt{2}$ 33) $\sqrt{81}$

34) $\sqrt{10}$ 35) $\sqrt{1296}$ 36) $\sqrt{150}$

37) $\sqrt{121}$ 38) $\sqrt{6561}$ 39) $\sqrt{85}$

40) $\sqrt{275}$

WRITE EACH OF THE FOLLOWING IN SCIENTIFIC NOTATION

41) 395,000,000   42) 76,543,000

43) .000008   44) .0000000865

45) 70,000,000,000,000   46) 2000×8000

47) $.0008 \times .000027$ 48) $70,000 \times 8,000 \times 16,000$

49) $8,100,000,000 \div 27,000$ 50) $.0000064 \div .000000016$

GEOMETRY—COMPLETE THE FOLLOWING

1) 4 gal. = _____ qts.
2) 10 pts. = _____ qts.
3) 28 qts. = _____ gals.
4) 9 gal. = _____ pts.
5) 44 pts. = _____ qts.
6) 64 pts. = _____ gals.
7) 24 qts. = _____ gals.
8) 12 gals. = _____ qts.
9) 17 pts. = _____ qts.
10) 3 lbs. = _____ oz.
11) 4 tons = _____ lbs.
12) 144 oz. = _____ lbs.
13) 14,000 lbs. = _____ tons
14) 3 tons = _____ oz.
15) 3 miles = _____ ft.
16) 72 ft. = _____ yds.
17) 96 in. = _____ ft.
18) 64 ft. = _____ in.
19) 7 yds. = _____ in.
20) 8 miles = _____ yds.
21) 31,680 ft. = _____ miles
22) 504 in. = _____ yds.
23) 7 hrs. = _____ min.
24) 5 days = _____ min.
25) 3600 min. = _____ hrs.

26) 7 wks. = _____ hrs.
27) 312 hrs. = _____ days
28) 48 hrs. = _____ sec.
29) 1 wk. = _____ min.
30) 27,000 sec. = _____ min.

31)   3 gals. 2 qts. 1 pt.
    +   2 gals. 1 qt. 1 pt.

32)   2 lbs. 12 oz.
    +   4 lbs. 5 oz.

33)   3 days 19 hrs. 37 min.
    +   2 days 6 hrs. 13 min.

34)   8 ft. 7 in.
    −   4 ft. 9 in.

35)   5 days 6 hrs. 12 min.
    −   3 days 12 hrs. 17 min.

GEOMETRY—COMPLETE THE FOLLOWING

1) 14 ft. = _____ in.
2) 105 yds. = _____ ft.
3) 380,160 ft. = _____ miles
4) 7,596 in. = _____ yds.
5) 74 miles = _____ ft.
6) 3648 in. = _____ ft.
7) 13 miles = _____ yds.
8) 724 yds. = _____ in.
9) 12 gal. = _____ qts.
10) 62 pts. = _____ qts.
11) 15 gals. = _____ pts.
12) 64 pts. = _____ gal.
13) 48 qts. = _____ gal.
14) 21 qts. = _____ pts.
15) 33 gals. = _____ qts.
16) 56 pts. = _____ qts.
17) 12 lbs. = _____ oz.
18) 384 oz. = _____ lbs.
19) 6 tons = _____ lbs.
20) 44,000 lbs. = _____ tons
21) 2 tons = _____ oz.
22) 12,660 sec. = _____ min.
23) 408 hrs. = _____ days
24) 19 weeks = _____ days
25) 3 weeks = _____ hrs.

26) 46,800 sec. = _____ hrs.
27) 8 hrs. = _____ sec.
28) 6 days = _____ min.
29) 2,184 days = _____ weeks
30) 12 weeks = _____ hrs.

31)
$$+ \quad \frac{\begin{array}{r} 17 \text{ lbs. } 4 \text{ oz.} \\ 8 \text{ lbs. } 13 \text{ oz.} \end{array}}{}$$

32)
$$+ \quad \frac{\begin{array}{r} 5 \text{ yds. } 2 \text{ ft. } 7 \text{ in.} \\ 3 \text{ yds. } 2 \text{ ft. } 6 \text{ in.} \end{array}}{}$$

33)
$$- \quad \frac{\begin{array}{r} 9 \text{ days } 12 \text{ hrs. } 14 \text{ min.} \\ 3 \text{ days } 18 \text{ hrs. } 20 \text{ min.} \end{array}}{}$$

34)
$$+ \quad \frac{\begin{array}{r} 5 \text{ gal. } 3 \text{ qts. } 1 \text{ pt.} \\ 3 \text{ gal. } 2 \text{ qts. } 1 \text{ pt.} \end{array}}{}$$

35)
$$- \quad \frac{\begin{array}{r} 7 \text{ yds. } 1 \text{ ft. } 5 \text{ in.} \\ 2 \text{ yds. } 2 \text{ ft. } 8 \text{ in.} \end{array}}{}$$

GEOMETRY—COMPLETE THE FOLLOWING

1) 6.3 mm = _____ m

2) 87 dm = _____ mm

3) .93 km = _____ cm

4) 800 hm = _____ km

5) 9.472 m = _____ mm

6) 3 dm = _____ dam

7) 91.3 km = _____ mm

8) .004 cm = _____ m

9) 79.14 dam = _____ cm

10) .214 hm = _____ mm

11) 77.7 mg = _____ g

12) .0082 kg = _____ dg

13) 9.42 dag = _____ g

14) 1,000 mg = _____ kg

15) 1 kg = _____ mg

16) 3.04 hg = _____ cg

17) .63 cg = _____ mg

18) 88.1 dag = _____ dg

19) 3.4 cg = _____ kg

20) .08 g = _____ dg

21) 17 L = _____ dL

22) 9.35 cL = _____ mL

23) 111 kL = _____ L

24) 85.1 mL = _____ daL

25) 8.7 cL = _____ kL

26) .147 hL = _____ kL

27) 9.536 L = _____ daL

28) 17 cL = _____ mL

29) 7,250 dL = _____ kL

30) 47.1 kL = _____ cL

31) _____ mm = 4.7 m

32) _____ cL = 4.85 hL

33) _____ g = 84.2 mg

34) _____ kL = 18 L

35) _____ m = .47 dm

36) _____ mg = 8 Kg

37) _____ daL = 93 dL

38) _____ hm = 41 km

39) _____ dg = 32.4 g

40) _____ cm = 8 hm

41) _____ L = 93 kL

42) _____ mL = .81 cL

43) _____ hg = 94.14 cg

44) _____ m = 64.352 mm

45) _____ dag = 9 mg

46) _____ hL = 13.7 cL

47) _____ cm = .043 hm

48) _____ mg = 145 g

49) _____ dL = 14.3 daL

50) _____ km = 8,875 m

GEOMETRY—COMPLETE THE FOLLOWING

1) 49 g = _____ kg

2) 7.3 cg = _____ dag

3) 825 mg = _____ dg

4) .095 hg = _____ cg

5) 87.25 dag = _____ kg

6) 4 cg = _____ mg

7) .142 kg = _____ cg

8) 9.2 dg = _____ g

9) 3.76 mg = _____ dg

10) 997.3 cg = _____ hg

11) 9.4 L = _____ dL

12) .042 mL = _____ cL

13) 87.64 daL = _____ kL

14) 25 cL = _____ L

15) .485 hL = _____ mL

16) 2.74 mL = _____ cL

17) 88.1 dL = _____ daL

18) 3,675 cL = _____ hL

19) 7 kL = _____ mL

20) .004 hL = _____ L

21) 47 mm = _____ hm

22) 9.7 m = _____ km

23) 890 cm = _____ mm

24) 9.37 dam = _____ dm

25) 4.75 hm = _____ cm

26) 9.84 mm = _____ dm

27) 276 km = _____ cm

28) .0046 hm = _____ mm

29) 4.852 dm = _____ cm

30) 95.8 m = _____ mm

31) _____ mg = 8.7 g

32) _____ L = 45 mL

33) _____ cm = 8 km

34) _____ dL = 95 hL

35) _____ hm = 4.76 cm

36) _____ g = 8.5 mg

37) _____ cL = 415 L

38) _____ mm = 93 hm

39) _____ dag = .85 dg

40) _____ mm = 7.8 m

41) _____ kL = .54 mL

42) _____ m = 93 cm

43) _____ hL = 8.41 cL

44) _____ dg = 47.4 g

45) _____ km = 4,500 m

46) _____ cL = 8.4 kL

47) _____ daL = 73 cL

48) _____ hm = .4 cm

49) _____ g = 45 kg

50) _____ hL = .15 L

GEOMETRY—
FIND THE PERIMETER AND AREA OF THE FOLLOWING

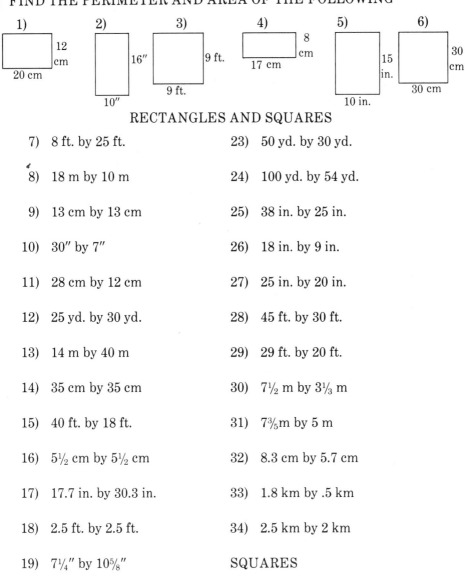

RECTANGLES AND SQUARES

7) 8 ft. by 25 ft.

8) 18 m by 10 m

9) 13 cm by 13 cm

10) 30" by 7"

11) 28 cm by 12 cm

12) 25 yd. by 30 yd.

13) 14 m by 40 m

14) 35 cm by 35 cm

15) 40 ft. by 18 ft.

16) 5½ cm by 5½ cm

17) 17.7 in. by 30.3 in.

18) 2.5 ft. by 2.5 ft.

19) 7¼" by 10⅝"

20) 20.6 ft. by 12½ ft.

21) 15 cm by 20 cm

22) 35 cm by 15 cm

23) 50 yd. by 30 yd.

24) 100 yd. by 54 yd.

25) 38 in. by 25 in.

26) 18 in. by 9 in.

27) 25 in. by 20 in.

28) 45 ft. by 30 ft.

29) 29 ft. by 20 ft.

30) 7½ m by 3⅓ m

31) 7⅗ m by 5 m

32) 8.3 cm by 5.7 cm

33) 1.8 km by .5 km

34) 2.5 km by 2 km

SQUARES

35) 25 cm   38) 15 m

36) 40 cm   39) 250 ft.

37) 14 m   40) 125 ft.

GEOMETRY—FIND THE PERIMETER
AND AREA OF THE FOLLOWING TRIANGLES

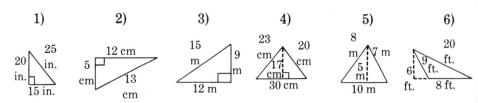

1) 2) 3) 4) 5) 6)

RIGHT TRIANGLES
LEGS   HYPOTENUSE
7) 3 ft. — 4 ft. — 5 ft.

8) 8 in. — 15 in. — 17 in.

9) 12 m — 16 m — 20 m

10) 10 in. — 24 in. — 26 in.

11) 30 ft. — 16 ft. — 34 ft.

12) 45 m — 60 m — 75 m

13) 24 in. — 7 in. — 25 in.

14) 8 cm — 6 cm — 10 cm

15) 36 m — 48 m — 60 m

16) 30 ft. — 40 ft. — 50 ft.

17) 45 in. — 24 in. — 51 in.

18) 14 cm — 48 cm — 50 cm

19) 4½ ft. — 6 ft. — 7½ ft.

20) 1.5 cm — 3.6 cm — 3.9 cm

NON-RIGHT TRIANGLES
BASE — ALTITUDE — OTHER SIDES
21) 20 in. — 16 in. — 22 in. — 22 in.

22) 35 cm — 25 cm — 30 cm — 40 cm

23) 10 cm — 13 cm — 15 cm — 18 cm

24) 20 m — 20 m — 22 m — 25 m

25) 30 ft. — 15 ft. — 18 ft. — 28 ft.

26) 12 in. — 20 in. — 25 in. — 25 in.

27) 50 cm — 20 cm — 25 cm — 40 cm

28) 60 cm — 65 cm — 100 cm — 75 cm

29) 30 m — 18 m — 25 m — 50 m

30) 28 ft. — 30 ft. — 37 ft. — 65 ft.

31) 18 in. — 10 in. — 13 in. — 14 in.

32) 80 cm — 65 cm — 80 cm — 80 cm

33) 50 ft. — 30 ft. — 35 ft. — 35 ft.

34) 100 m — 10 m — 15 m — 20 m

35) 45 in. — 25 in. — 30 in. — 30 in.

36) 8 ft. — 20 ft. — 25 ft. — 25 ft.

37) 18 cm — 14 cm — 18 cm — 18 cm

38) 20 m — 15 m — 20 cm — 20 cm

39) 12½ cm — 10 cm — 14⅕ cm — 13⅓ cm

40) 17.3 ft. — 8.5 ft. — 14.3 ft. — 15.7 ft.

GEOMETRY—
FIND THE PERIMETER AND AREA OF THE FOLLOWING

PARALLELOGRAMS—1-20   TRAPEZOIDS—21-40

1)
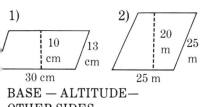

2)

21)
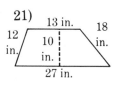

22)
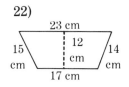

BASE — ALTITUDE—
OTHER SIDES

3) 15 cm — 10 cm — 14 cm

4) 30 m — 15 m — 20 m

5) 25 in. — 15 in. — 18 in.

6) 8 in. — 5 in. — 8 in.

7) 18 ft. — 30 ft. — 40 ft.

8) 18 ft. — 14 ft. — 18 ft.

9) 50 cm — 32 cm — 40 cm

10) 20 cm — 33 cm — 40 cm

11) 25 cm — 10 cm — 14 cm

12) 32 cm — 30 cm — 40 cm

13) 9 km — 6 km — 8 km

14) 22 in. — 14 in. — 22 in.

15) 24 in. — 20 in. — 25 in.

16) 15 ft. — 20 ft. — 25 ft.

17) 50 in. — 40 in. — 50 in.

18) 34 cm — 20 cm — 28 cm

19) 40 m — 32 m — 44 m

20) 14½ ft. — 8 ft. — 12 ft.

BASES—ALTITUDE—OTHER SIDES

23) 17 in. — 8 in. — 10 in. — 13 in. — 12 in.

24) 34 in. — 16 in. — 25 in. — 27 in. — 29 in

25) 28 cm — 19 cm — 20 cm — 22 cm — 26 cm

26) 31 cm — 9 cm — 30 cm — 34 cm — 36 cm

27) 18 ft. — 14 ft. — 24 ft. — 30 ft. — 30 ft.

28) 31 ft. — 19 ft. — 22 ft. — 27 ft. — 28 ft.

29) 38 ft. — 27 ft. — 30 ft. — 39 ft. — 41 ft.

30) 15 ft. — 25 ft. — 20 ft. — 29 ft. — 26 ft.

31) 18 cm — 12 cm — 15 cm — 20 cm — 22 cm

32) 37 in. — 33 in. — 20 in. — 26 in. — 24 in.

33) 50 m — 40 m — 30 m — 35 m — 35 m

34) 65 m — 35 m — 40 m — 48 m — 52 m

35) 23 in. — 17 in. — 30 in. — 36 in. — 34 in.

36) 41 m — 39 m — 35 m — 38 m — 42 m

37) 100 in. — 50 in. — 60 in. — 75 in. — 75 in.

38) 65 ft. — 35 ft. — 25 ft. — 32 ft. — 28 ft.

39) 20 cm — 30 cm — 18 cm — 22 cm — 24 cm

40) 50 in. — 46 in. — 30 in. — 34 in. — 36 in.

GEOMETRY—FIND THE CIRCUMFERENCE
AND AREA OF THE FOLLOWING CIRCLES

1)   2) 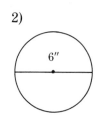   3) 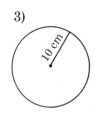   4) 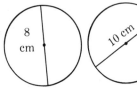   5)

1-20 USE 3.14 FOR π

6) R = 7″   11) R = 9 cm   16) D = 1000 miles

7) D = 100 m   12) R = 12 cm   17) D = 400 ft.

8) R = 30 m   13) R = 1000 miles   18) D = .6 cm

9) D = 30 m   14) R = 150 ft.   19) D = .25 in.

10) R = 40 cm   15) R = 2500 m   20) D = .9 m

FOR 21-40 USE 22/7 FOR π

21) D = 14 in.   31) R = 140 in.

22) R = 14 in.   32) R = 56 ft.

23) R = 21 cm   33) R = .14 m

24) D = 70 m   34) R = 91 cm

25) D = 140 m   35) R = 5¼ ft.

26) R = 3.5 ft.   36) D = 28 ft.

27) R = 42 ft.   37) D = .14 m

28) D = .7 m   38) D = 5¼ ft.

29) D = 35 m   39) D = 91 in.

30) R = 700 cm   40) D = .07 m

GEOMETRY—NAME EACH FIGURE
FIND THE PERIMETER AND AREA FOR EACH

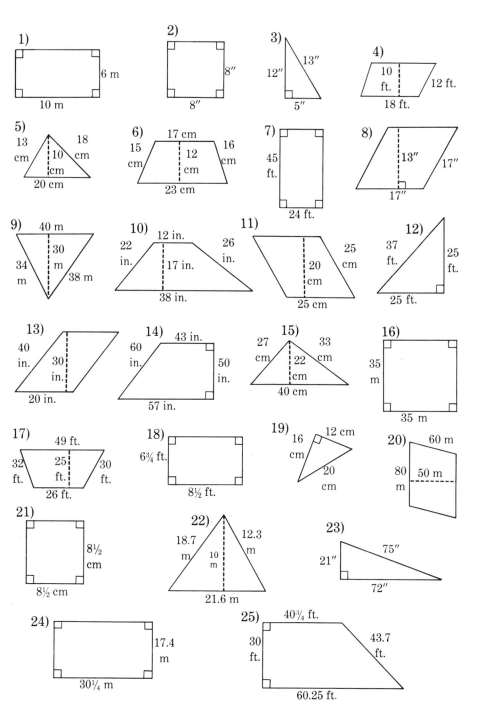

1) 6 m, 10 m

2) 8″, 8″

3) 13″, 12″, 5″

4) 10 ft., 12 ft., 18 ft.

5) 13 cm, 18 cm, 10 cm, 20 cm

6) 17 cm, 15 cm, 16 cm, 12 cm, 23 cm

7) 45 ft., 24 ft.

8) 13″, 17″, 17″

9) 40 m, 30 m, 34 m, 38 m

10) 12 in., 22 in., 26 in., 17 in., 38 in.

11) 25 cm, 20 cm, 25 cm

12) 37 ft., 25 ft., 25 ft.

13) 40 in., 30 in., 20 in.

14) 43 in., 60 in., 50 in., 57 in.

15) 27 cm, 33 cm, 22 cm, 40 cm

16) 35 m, 35 m

17) 49 ft., 32 ft., 25 ft., 30 ft., 26 ft.

18) 6¾ ft., 8½ ft.

19) 16 cm, 12 cm, 20 cm

20) 60 m, 80 m, 50 m

21) 8½ cm, 8½ cm

22) 18.7 m, 12.3 m, 10 m, 21.6 m

23) 75″, 21″, 72″

24) 17.4 m, 30¼ m

25) 40¾ ft., 43.7 ft., 30 ft., 60.25 ft.

- 111 -

GEOMETRY—NAME EACH FIGURE
FIND THE PERIMETER (CIRCUMFERENCE)
AND AREA OF EACH

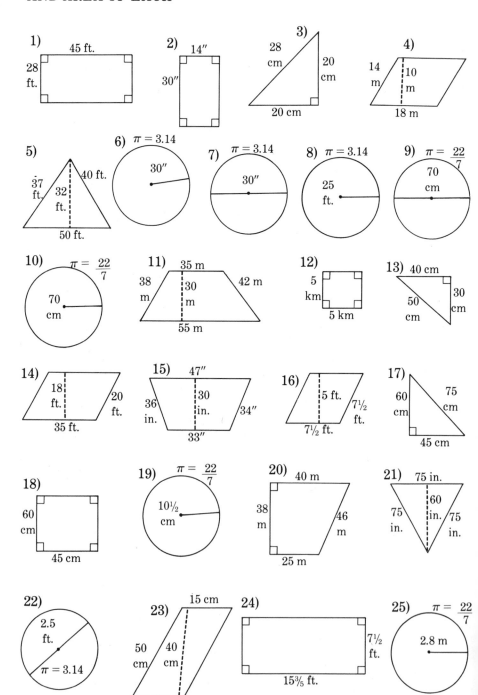

1) 45 ft. 28 ft.

2) 14″ 30″

3) 28 cm 20 cm 20 cm

4) 14 m 10 m 18 m

5) 37 ft. 40 ft. 32 ft. 50 ft.

6) π = 3.14 30″

7) π = 3.14 30″

8) π = 3.14 25 ft.

9) π = 22/7 70 cm

10) π = 22/7 70 cm

11) 35 m 38 m 30 m 42 m 55 m

12) 5 km 5 km

13) 40 cm 50 cm 30 cm

14) 18 ft. 20 ft. 35 ft.

15) 47″ 36 in. 30 in. 34″ 33″

16) 5 ft. 7½ ft. 7½ ft.

17) 60 cm 75 cm 45 cm

18) 60 cm 45 cm

19) π = 22/7 10½ cm

20) 40 m 38 m 46 m 25 m

21) 75 in. 60 in. 75 in. 75 in.

22) 2.5 ft. π = 3.14

23) 15 cm 50 cm 40 cm

24) 7½ ft. 15³⁄₅ ft.

25) π = 22/7 2.8 m

- 112 -

GEOMETRY—NAME EACH FIGURE
FIND THE PERIMETER (CIRCUMFERENCE)
AND AREA OF EACH

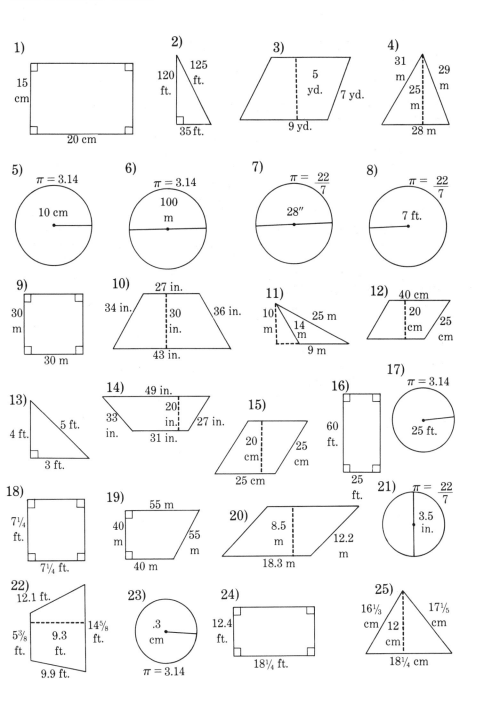

1)
15 cm
20 cm

2)
120 ft.
125 ft.
35 ft.

3)
5 yd.
7 yd.
9 yd.

4)
31 m
29 m
25 m
28 m

5)
π = 3.14
10 cm

6)
π = 3.14
100 m

7)
π = 22/7
28″

8)
π = 22/7
7 ft.

9)
30 m
30 m

10)
27 in.
34 in.
30 in.
36 in.
43 in.

11)
10 m
25 m
14 m
9 m

12)
40 cm
20 cm
25 cm

13)
5 ft.
4 ft.
3 ft.

14)
49 in.
20 in.
33 in.
27 in.
31 in.

15)
20 cm
25 cm
25 cm

16)
60 ft.
25 ft.

17)
π = 3.14
25 ft.

18)
7¼ ft.
7¼ ft.

19)
55 m
40 m
55 m
40 m

20)
8.5 m
12.2 m
18.3 m

21)
π = 22/7
3.5 in.

22)
12.1 ft.
5⅜ ft.
9.3 ft.
14⅝ ft.
9.9 ft.

23)
.3 cm
π = 3.14

24)
12.4 ft.
18¼ ft.

25)
16⅓ cm
17⅕ cm
12 cm
18¼ cm

- 113 -

GEOMETRY

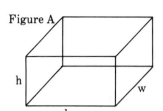 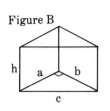 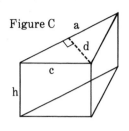

Figure A   Figure B   Figure C

FIND THE SURFACE AREA AND VOLUME OF THE FOLLOWING
RECTANGULAR PRISMS. (Figure A)

1) l = 4 cm	2) l = 10 m	3) l = 10 mm	4) l = 25 cm	5) l = 50 mm
w = 30 cm	w = 8 m	w = 12 mm	w = 30 cm	w = 45 mm
h = 4 cm	h = 5 m	h = 15 mm	h = 15 cm	h = 65 mm

6) l = .6 m	7) l = 1.8 cm	8) l = .08 cm	9) l = .8 mm	10) l = .06 m
w = .6 m	w = 2 cm	w = .16 cm	w = 1.7 mm	w = 16 mm
h = .6 m	h = 2.4 cm	h = .09 cm	h = 2.1 mm	h = 5.2 cm

11) l = ¾ ft.	12) l = ⅚ in.	13) l = 1½ yd.	14) l = 6⅔ in.	15) l = ½ yd.
w = ¾ ft.	w = ³⁄₁₀ in.	w = 2¾ yd.	w = 5⅕ in.	w = 1¾ ft.
h = ¾ ft.	h = ½ in.	h = 1⅚ yd.	h = 4¾ in.	h = 16 in.

FIND THE SURFACE AREA AND VOLUME OF THE FOLLOWING
TRIANGULAR PRISMS. (Figure B)

16) a = 3 cm	17) a = 5 mm	18) a = .6 m	19) a = 1.5 cm	20) a = ½ in.
b = 4 cm	b = 12 mm	b = .8 m	b = 3.6 cm	b = ⅔ in.
c = 5 cm	c = 13 mm	c = 1 m	c = 3.9 cm	c = ⅚ in.
h = 5 cm	h = 7 mm	h = 1.2 m	h = 5 cm	h = ¾ in.

FIND THE SURFACE AREA AND VOLUME OF THE FOLLOWING
TRIANGULAR PRISMS. (Figure C)

21) a = 8 cm	22) a = 12 m	23) a = 20 cm
b = 6 cm	b = 10 m	b = 30 cm
c = 9 cm	c = 20 m	c = 25 cm
d = 7 cm	d = 24 m	d = 27 cm
h = 10 cm	h = 15 m	h = 25 cm

24) a = .5 mm	25) a = .25 m	26) a = .016 m
b = .3 mm	b = .15 m	b = .8 cm
c = .6 mm	c = .15 m	c = 12 mm
d = .4 mm	d = .12 m	d = .6 cm
h = 1.2 mm	h = .35 m	h = 20 mm

27) a = ⅚ in.	28) a = 2½ ft.	29) a = 5¼ yd.
b = ¼ in.	b = 3⅓ ft.	b = 4½ yd.
c = ⅔ in.	c = 4 ft.	c = 4⅔ yd.
d = ⅙ in.	d = 2⅔ ft.	d = 3⅐ yd.
h = ¾ in.	h = 5½ ft.	h = 6¼ yd.

30) a = ½ yd.
b = 2¼ ft.
c = 24 in.
d = 1⅔ ft.
h = 1¼ yd.

GEOMETRY

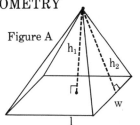

Figure A

Figure B

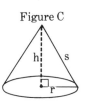

Figure C

FIND THE SURFACE AREA AND VOLUME OF THE FOLLOWING
RECTANGULAR PYRAMIDS. (Figure A)

1) $l = 8$ cm
   $w = 8$ cm
   $h_1 = 6$ cm
   $h_2 = 7$ cm

2) $l = 3$ ft.
   $w = 4$ ft.
   $h_1 = 6$ ft.
   $h_2 = 8$ ft.

3) $l = 15$ m
   $w = 20$ m
   $h_1 = 12$ m
   $h_2 = 14$ m

4) $l = 50$ mm
   $w = 75$ mm
   $h_1 = 40$ mm
   $h_2 = 45$ mm

5) $l = 6.3$ m
   $w = 8.1$ m
   $h_1 = 7$ m
   $h_2 = 8.3$ m

6) $l = .09$ cm
   $w = .12$ cm
   $h_1 = .15$ cm
   $h_2 = .2$ cm

7) $l = 2\frac{1}{2}$ in.
   $w = 3$ in.
   $h_1 = 4\frac{1}{4}$ in.
   $h_2 = 5\frac{1}{2}$ in.

8) $l = 3\frac{1}{3}$ yd.
   $w = 1\frac{1}{2}$ yd.
   $h_1 = 4\frac{1}{5}$ yd.
   $h_2 = 5\frac{1}{4}$ yd.

9) $l = 1.5$ m
   $w = 200$ cm
   $h_1 = 1700$ mm
   $h_2 = 2$ m

10) $l = 1\frac{1}{4}$ yd.
    $w = 2\frac{1}{2}$ ft.
    $h_1 = 24$ in.
    $h_2 = 27$ in.

FIND THE SURFACE AREA AND VOLUME OF THE FOLLOWING
TRIANGULAR PYRAMIDS. (Figure B)

11) $a = 6$ cm
    $b = 6$ cm
    $c = 6$ cm
    $h_1 = 5$ cm
    $h_2 = 10$ cm
    $h_3 = 8$ cm

12) $a = 10$ cm
    $b = 8$ cm
    $c = 9$ cm
    $h_1 = 11$ cm
    $h_2 = 15$ cm
    $h_3 = 12$ cm

13) $a = 20$ ft.
    $b = 30$ ft.
    $c = 25$ ft.
    $h_1 = 13$ ft.
    $h_2 = 40$ ft.
    $h_3 = 35$ ft.

14) $a = 7$ m
    $b = 10$ m
    $c = 9$ m
    $h_1 = 6$ m
    $h_2 = 150$ m
    $h_3 = 125$ m

15) $a = .5$ m
    $b = .7$ m
    $c = .9$ m
    $h_1 = .4$ m
    $h_2 = 1.2$ m
    $h_3 = .9$ m

16) $a = 2.4$ cm
    $b = 1.8$ cm
    $c = 1.6$ cm
    $h_1 = 1.2$ cm
    $h_2 = 3.6$ cm
    $h_3 = 2.8$ cm

17) $a = 3\frac{1}{2}$ in.
    $b = 4$ in.
    $c = 5\frac{3}{4}$ in.
    $h_1 = 3\frac{1}{8}$ in.
    $h_2 = 2\frac{3}{4}$ in.
    $h_3 = 2\frac{1}{4}$ in.

18) $a = 7\frac{1}{2}$ ft.
    $b = 6\frac{1}{4}$ ft.
    $c = 2\frac{1}{2}$ ft.
    $h_1 = 5$ ft.
    $h_2 = 8\frac{1}{5}$ ft.
    $h_3 = 5\frac{1}{4}$ ft.

19) $a = 2$ m
    $b = 240$ cm
    $c = 3600$ mm
    $h_1 = 1.6$ m
    $h_2 = 750$ cm
    $h_3 = 6000$ mm

20) $a = 3\frac{1}{2}$ ft.
    $b = 1$ yd.
    $c = 30$ in.
    $h_1 = 24$ in.
    $h_2 = 2\frac{1}{2}$ yd.
    $h_3 = 5\frac{1}{4}$ ft.

FIND THE SURFACE AREA AND VOLUME OF THE FOLLOWING
CONES. (Figure C). Use $\pi \approx 3.14$ Unless Specified.

21) $r = 6$ cm
    $h = 8$ cm
    $s = 10$ cm

22) $r = 15$ in.
    $h = 30$ in.
    $s = 35$ in.

23) $r = 6$ m
    $h = 1.2$ m
    $s = 6.8$ m

24) $r = 3\frac{1}{2}$ in.
    $h = 3$ in.
    $s = 4\frac{3}{4}$ in.
    $\pi = \frac{22}{7}$

25) $r = 3$ cm
    $h = .02$ m
    $s = 40$ mm

26) $d = 14$ m
    $h = 21$ m
    $s = 25$ m
    $\pi = \frac{22}{7}$

27) $d = 20$ ft.
    $h = 12$ ft.
    $s = 16$ ft.

28) $d = 3.4$ cm
    $h = 9$ cm
    $s = 13$ cm

29) $d = 3$ ft.
    $h = 5\frac{1}{3}$ ft.
    $s = 8\frac{3}{4}$ ft.
    $\pi = \frac{22}{7}$

30) $d = 3$ yd.
    $h = 6\frac{1}{2}$ ft.
    $s = 120$ in.

GEOMETRY

Figure A

Figure B

FIND THE SURFACE AREA AND VOLUME OF THE FOLLOWING CYLINDERS. (Figure A)

USE $\pi \approx 3.14$

1) r = 5 cm   2) r = 6 cm   3) r = 10 m   4) r = 20 mm   5) r = .8 m
   h = 10 cm   h = 11 cm   h = .5 m   h = 30 mm   h = .7 m

6) d = 8 mm   7) d = 4 cm   8) d = .2 m   9) d = 25 mm   10) d = 6 m
   h = 12 mm   h = 4.8 cm   h = .6 m   h = 16 mm   h = 750 cm

USE $\pi \approx {}^{22}\!/_7$

11) r = 1 in.   12) r = 7 ft.   13) r = 8 in.   14) r = 3½ yd.   15) r = ³/₁₁ in.
   h = 10 in.   h = 20 ft.   h = 14 in.   h = 4 yd.   h = 2½ in.

16) d = 20 in.   17) d = ⁷/₁₁ ft.   18) d = 3½ yd.   19) d = 35 in.   20) d = 2⅓ ft.
   h = 21 in.   h = 1⁴/₇ ft.   h = 4⅕ yd.   h = 1 yd.   h = 2 yd.

FIND THE SURFACE AREA AND VOLUME OF THE FOLLOWING SPHERES (Figure B)

USE $\pi \approx 3.14$

21) r = 5 cm   22) r = 10 cm   23) r = 9 cm   24) r = .3 cm   25) r = 1.2 cm

26) d = 12 m   27) d = 1.8 m   28) d = 1.2 mm   29) d = 150 cm   30) d = 30 m

USE $\pi \approx {}^{22}\!/_7$

31) r = 7 in.   32) r = ½ yd.   33) r = 3 ft.   34) r = 3½ ft.   35) r = 21 in.

36) d = 21 yd.   37) d = 1³/₁₁ in.   38) d = 3½ ft.   39) d = ³/₁₁ in.   40) d = 10½ ft.

GEOMETRY
FIND THE SURFACE AREA AND VOLUME OF THE FOLLOWING
USE $\pi \approx 3.14$ if not specified.

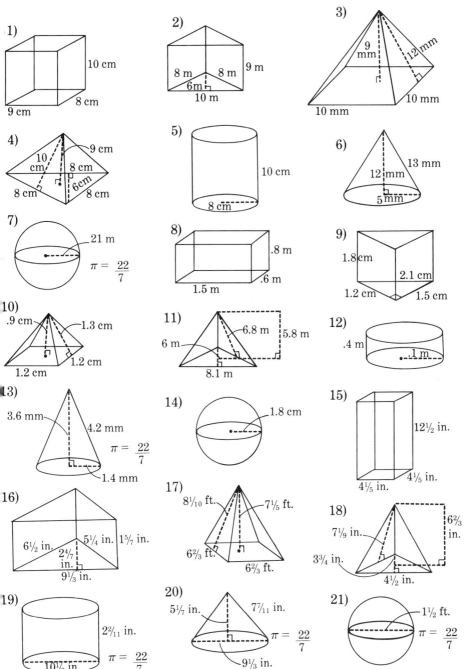

1) 10 cm, 8 cm, 9 cm

2) 8 m, 8 m, 9 m, 6 m, 10 m

3) 9 mm, 12 mm, 10 mm, 10 mm

4) 10 cm, 9 cm, 8 cm, 8 cm, 6 cm, 8 cm

5) 10 cm, 8 cm

6) 13 mm, 12 mm, 5 mm

7) 21 m, $\pi = \frac{22}{7}$

8) .8 m, .6 m, 1.5 m

9) 1.8 cm, 2.1 cm, 1.2 cm, 1.5 cm

10) .9 cm, 1.3 cm, 1.2 cm, 1.2 cm

11) 6.8 m, 5.8 m, 6 m, 8.1 m

12) .4 m, .1 m

13) 3.6 mm, 4.2 mm, 1.4 mm, $\pi = \frac{22}{7}$

14) 1.8 cm

15) $12\frac{1}{2}$ in., $4\frac{1}{5}$ in., $4\frac{1}{5}$ in.

16) $6\frac{1}{2}$ in., $5\frac{1}{4}$ in., $1\frac{5}{7}$ in., $2\frac{4}{7}$ in., $9\frac{1}{3}$ in.

17) $8\frac{1}{10}$ ft., $7\frac{1}{5}$ ft., $6\frac{2}{3}$ ft., $6\frac{2}{3}$ ft.

18) $7\frac{1}{9}$ in., $6\frac{2}{3}$ in., $3\frac{3}{4}$ in., $4\frac{1}{2}$ in.

19) $2\frac{2}{11}$ in., $10\frac{1}{2}$ in., $\pi = \frac{22}{7}$

20) $5\frac{1}{7}$ in., $7\frac{7}{11}$ in., $9\frac{1}{3}$ in., $\pi = \frac{22}{7}$

21) $1\frac{1}{2}$ ft., $\pi = \frac{22}{7}$

- 117 -

GEOMETRY

ANGLES—Acute, obtuse, right, vertical,
complementary, supplementary, alternate
interior, alternate exterior, degrees.

TRIANGLES—Right, acute, obtuse.

Use Figure I for 1-7.

  Given—Angle NEK is a right angle.

1) Name 4 acute angles.

2) Name 3 obtuse angles.

3) Name another right angle besides
   angle NEK.

4) What angle is complementary to angle:
   a. LEN   b. KER   c. SER

5) What angle is supplementary to angle:
   a. LEN   b. SER   c. LES   d. NEK

6) If angle LEN = 20 degrees and angle KER =
   30 degrees, find the measurement of angle:
   a. LEK   b. RES   c. KES   d. LER   e. LES   f. REN

7) If angle LER equals 85 degrees and angle KER
   equals 25 degrees, find the measure of angle:
   a. LEK   b. LEN   c. LES   d. RES   e. REN   f. KES

FIG. I

Use Figure II for 8-15

  Given—Line segment TB is perpendicular
         to line segment WE.

8) Name 4 acute angles.

9) Name 4 right angles.

10) Name 4 obtuse angles.

11) What angle is complementary to angle:
    a. RYW   b. MYB   c. TYR

12) What angle is supplementary to angle:
    a. RYE   b. RYB   c. TYM   d. WYM
    e. TYW   f. BYW

13) What angle is a vertical angle
    of angle:
    a. RYW   b. TYR   c. TYE

14) If angle RYW equals 55
    degrees, find the measure
    of angle:
    a. TYR   b. EYM   c. MYB
    d. BYE   e. WYB   f. RYE
    g. MYT   h. WYM   i. RYB

15) If angle RYW equals 50
    degrees, find the measure-
    ment of angle:
    a. TYR   b. EYM   c. MYB
    d. BYE   e. WYB   f. RYE
    g. MYT   h. WYM   i. RYB

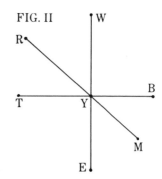

FIG. II

Use Figure III for 16-29
   Given—Segment BP perpendicular to segments TZ and CX and parallel to ZX and △ ARI is equilateral.
WITH A FOR A VERTEX
16) Name four right angles.
17) Name four acute angles.
18) Name four obtuse angles.
WITH I FOR A VERTEX
19) Name four right angles.
20) Name four acute angles.
21) Name four obtuse angles.
WITH R FOR A VERTEX
22) Name two acute angles.
23) Name two obtuse angles.
24) Name one rectangle.
25) Name four right triangles.
26) Name two acute triangles.
27) Name two obtuse triangles.
28) Name an alternate interior angle to angle:
      a. IAR   b. RZA   c. TAI   d. ZAI
29) Name a corresponding angle to angle:
      a. RXI   b. AZR   c. MAB   d. PIN
30) If angle RAZ equals 30 degrees, find the measurement of angle:
      a. RAI   b. MAT   c. MAB   d. AIX   e. AIR
      f. RIX   g. CIN   h. PIN   i. RIA   j. ARI   k. ZRX
      l. IRX   m. ARZ   n. RXI   o. RZX   p. PIX   q. ZXI

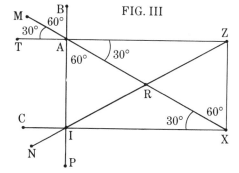

FIG. III

- 119-

GEOMETRY

ANGLES—Acute, obtuse, right, vertical,
complementary, supplementary, alternate
interior, alternate exterior, degrees.

TRIANGLES—Right, acute, obtuse.
Use Figure I for 1-7.
  Given—Angle BAM is a right angle.

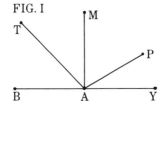

FIG. I

1) Name 4 acute angles.
2) Name 3 obtuse angles.
3) Name another right angle besides
   angle BAM.
4) What angle is complementary to angle:
   a. BAT   b. YAP   c. MAT
5) What angle is supplementary to angle:
   a. BAT   b. MAB   c. PAY   d. TAY
6) If angle BAT = 60 degrees and angle YAP =
   20 degrees, find the measurement of angle:
   a. MAT   b. MAP   c. TAP   d. MAY   e. TAY   f. BAP
7) If angle TAP equals 95 degrees and angle MAP
   equals 60 degrees, find the measurement of angle:
   a. MAT   b. BAT   c. PAY   d. MAY   e. BAP   f. YAT

Use Figure II for 8-15
  Given—Line segment KC is perpendicular
          to segment RN.

8) Name 4 acute angles.
9) Name 4 right angles.
10) Name 4 obtuse angles.
11) What angle is complementary to angle:
    a. DUC   b. KUL   c. RUD
12) What angle is supplementary to angle:
    a. CUD   b. KUL   c. RUL   d. NUD
    e. RUK   f. NUK
13) What angle is a vertical angle
    of angle:
    a. RUD   b. CUD   c. CUN
14) If angle LUN equals 60
    degrees, find the measure-
    ment of angle:
    a. LUK   b. NUK   c. RUD
    d. DUC   e. NUC   f. DUK
    g. DUN   h. RUL   i. LUC
    j. RUC

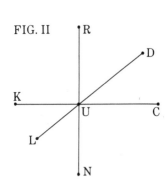

FIG. II

15) If angle LUN equals 57
    degrees, find the measure-
    ment of angle:
    a. LUK   b. NUK   c. RUD
    d. DUC   e. NUC   f. DUK
    g. DUN   h. RUL   i. LUC
    j. RUC

Use Figure III for 16-33
　Given—Segment ZB perpendicular to AM and ZP and parallel to TM and △
ZYN is isosceles.

16) Name one rectangle.
17) Name four right triangles.
18) Name two acute triangles.
19) Name two obtuse triangles.

WITH X VERTEX

20) Name 4 right angles.
21) Name 4 acute angles.
22) Name 4 obtuse angles.

WITH I FOR A VERTEX

23) Name 4 right angles.
24) Name 4 acute angles.
25) Name 4 obtuse angles.

WITH N FOR A VERTEX

26) Name two acute angles.
27) Name two obtuse angles.

NAME THE FOLLOWING TYPES OF ANGLES:

28) Vertical of: a. ZNX　　b. BXR　　c. CIP
29) Corresponding of: a. ZXA　　b. MIP　　c. ZXN　　d. ZIN
30) Alternate interior of: a. ZXN　　b. NMX　　c. NMI　　d. NXM
31) Alternate exterior of: a. AXR　　b. BXR　　c. AXB
32) If angle NZX = 65 degrees, find angle:
　　a. NZI　　　b. XZI　　　c. NXM　　　d. NXZ　　　e. AXB
　　f. AXR　　　g. BXR　　h. ZNX　　i. XNM　　j. ZNI　　k. MNI
　　l. TIP　　　m. TIC　　n. CIP　　o. MIN　　p. ZIN　　q. MXB

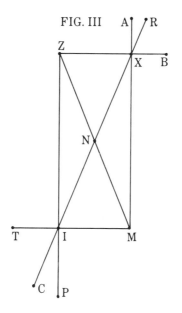

FIG. III

- 121-

GEOMETRY—FIND THE MISSING ANGLE IN EACH TRIANGLE

1) 45° — 55° — ?

2) 37° — 91° — ?

3) 64° — 56° — ?

4) 35° — 35° — ?

5) 26° — 120° — ?

6) 93° — 47° — ?

7) 57° — 33° — ?

8) 65° — 25° — ?

9) 31° — 59° — ?

10) 44° — 46° — ?

11) 91° — 75° — ?

12) 65° — 65° — ?

13) 77° — 43° — ?

14) 51° — 66° — ?

15) 78° — 32° — ?

16) 55° — 49° — ?

17) 21° — 21° — ?

18) 7° — 24° — ?

19) 6° — 35° — ?

20) 94° — 26° — ?

21) 53° — 96° — ?

22) 44° — 35° — ?

23) 73° — 63° — ?

24) 51° — 59° — ?

25) 25° — 25° — ?

26) 38° — 104° — ?

27) 45° — 90° — ?

28) 63° — 54° — ?

29) 95° — 15° — ?

30) 100° — 40° — ?

IN THE FOLLOWING
RIGHT TRIANGLES

31) 27° — ?

32) 45° — ?

33) 30° — ?

34) 55° — ?

35) 61° — ?

36) 42° — ?

37) 15° — ?

38) 37° — ?

39) 71° — ?

40) 25° — ?

41) 54° — ?

42) 33° — ?

43) 29° — ?

44) 75° — ?

45) 21° — ?

46) In an Equilateral Triangle

IN THE FOLLOWING
ISOSCELES TRIANGLES
WITH TWO OF THE
ANGLES MEASURING:

47) 35°

48) 45°

49) 54½°

50) 75°

GEOMETRY—COMPLEMENTARY ANGLES, SUPPLEMENTARY ANGLES, AND ANGLES IN A TRIANGLE

Name the complementary angle of the following angles:

1) 25° 2) 40° 3) 45° 4) 56° 5) 60° 6) 85°

7) 15° 8) 30° 9) 32° 10) 51° 11) 28° 12) 54°

13) 75° 14) 7° 15) 66°

Name the supplementary angle of the following angles:

16) 30° 17) 60° 18) 90° 19) 45° 20) 100° 21) 110°

22) 150° 23) 75° 24) 105° 25) 15° 26) 85° 27) 120°

28) 144° 29) 87° 30) 27°

The following represent two angles in a triangle.
A. Give the degrees in the remaining angle.
B. Tell whether the triangle is acute, right, or obtuse.
C. Tell whether the triangle is scalene, isosceles, or equilateral.

31) 30° — 60°   32) 54° — 36°   33) 28° — 110° 34) 45° — 45°

35) 65° — 65°   36) 46° — 44°   37) 85° — 35°   38) 15° — 15°

39) 110° — 47° 40) 103° — 38° 41) 60° — 60°   42) 75° — 75°

43) 29° — 39°   44) 50° — 80°   45) 48° — 42°   46) 75° — 15°

47) 45° — 90°   48) 36° — 92°   49) 25° — 130° 50) 43° — 94°

GEOMETRY—FIND THE LENGTH OF THE MISSING SIDE OF EACH RIGHT TRIANGLE

Leg	Leg	Hypotenuse		Leg	Leg	Hypotenuse
1) 6	8	?	26) 27	?	45	
2) 15	8	?	27) 63	?	65	
3) 35	12	?	28) ?	6	10	
4) 7	24	?	29) ?	11	61	
5) 9	40	?	30) ?	80	89	
6) 11	60	?	31) 21	?	221	
7) 27	36	?	32) ?	20	29	
8) 35	12	?	33) 4	?	5	
9) 3	4	?	34) ?	84	85	
10) 21	20	?	35) 14	?	50	
11) 9	12	?	36) 18	?	30	
12) 24	10	?	37) ?	28	35	
13) 14	48	?	38) ?	36	39	
14) 30	16	?	39) 20	?	52	
15) 70	24	?	40) 27	?	123	
16) 63	16	?	41) 75	100	?	
17) 18	80	?	42) 65	?	97	
18) 22	120	?	43) 39	80	?	
19) 15	20	?	44) 45	108	?	
20) 15	36	?	45) ?	140	149	
21) ?	8	17	46) 75	308	?	
22) 12	?	37	47) 17	144	?	
23) ?	40	41	48) 33	56	?	
24) ?	24	25	49) 55	48	?	
25) 5	?	13	50) 65	?	97	

PROBABILITY AND STATISTICS—

FIND THE MEAN, MEDIAN, AND MODE FOR EACH
OF THE FOLLOWING GROUPS. ROUND THE MEAN
TO THE NEAREST TENTH IF NECESSARY.

1) 6, 5, 7, 5, 8, 4

2) 105, 98, 102, 106, 105

3) 17, 18, 16, 17, 18, 21, 18

4) 950, 900, 850, 875, 805, 900

5) 58, 55, 60, 52, 41, 39, 69, 73

6) 1152, 1213, 1346, 1058, 1213, 1163, 1284

7) 35, 40, 36, 42, 37, 36, 36, 42, 36

8) 15, 13, 15, 14, 13, 16, 13, 17, 16, 13

9) 87, 95, 63, 78, 65, 73, 84, 80, 65, 91, 78

10) 25, 50, 25, 75, 100, 125, 200, 75, 50, 25

11) 95, 95, 93, 96, 94, 93, 99, 90, 91, 93, 95, 94

12) 215864, 418348, 348653, 418158, 152343

13) 40, 60, 50, 60, 70, 30, 40, 60, 60, 70

14) 8, 12, 15, 9, 11, 10, 7, 9, 12, 11, 10, 15, 10, 8, 10

15) 2153, 4158, 6214, 2483, 3280, 4184, 5808, 9505

16) 25, 27, 31, 39, 35, 28, 27, 32, 38, 36, 27, 35, 26

17) 375, 385, 363, 374, 382, 363, 385, 391, 383, 376

18) 650, 750, 700, 650, 850, 700, 650, 800, 950, 600, 750, 650

19) 21586, 72438, 52348, 49165, 39414, 62852, 49165

20) 52, 65, 8, 95, 108, 75, 42, 17, 86, 42, 9, 96, 87, 13, 15, 71

21) 156, 180, 173, 175, 165, 175, 172, 159, 160, 190, 121, 168

22) 87, 91, 65, 43, 86, 75, 58, 94, 86, 42, 43, 52, 56, 40, 69

23) 7, 8, 6, 5, 4, 8, 7, 3, 9, 7, 5, 4, 5, 6, 7, 9, 8, 4, 3

24) 2143, 2463, 2222, 2343, 2514, 2234, 2343, 2565, 2453, 2143, 2583, 2431

25) 58, 44, 59, 52, 69, 44, 45, 60, 48, 63, 51, 60, 50, 49, 66, 60, 48, 62, 47, 65

PROBABILITY AND STATISTICS—

FIND THE MEAN, MEDIAN, AND MODE FOR EACH
OF THE FOLLOWING GROUPS. ROUND OFF WHOLE NUMBERS
MEANS TO NEAREST TENTH. ROUND OFF DECIMAL MEANS
TO ONE MORE PLACE VALUE THAN THE MOST PRECISE
OF THE DATA.

1) 10, 12, 8, 10, 9, 11, 10

2) 25, 45, 30, 35, 30

3) 72, 75, 81, 70, 64, 72, 68, 70

4) 125, 235, 178, 201, 156, 185

5) 8, 6, 9, 5, 4, 6, 9, 7, 8, 9, 2, 5

6) 42, 48, 36, 43, 49, 43, 45, 38, 44, 47

7) 1001, 1100, 1050, 1076, 1027, 1100, 1065

8) 4.6, 7.8, 6.7, 5.3, 8.1

9) .8, 1.0, .9, 1.2, .9, 1.5, 1.1

10) 10.5, 11.5, 14.5, 14, 13, 15.5, 15, 14.5, 12, 9.5, 10

11) .0005, .00008, .00045, .000075

12) .29, .356, .333, .4, .33, .356, .37, .3

13) .0158, .02, .0225, .0175, .02, .0225

14) 2.2, 3.1, 4.8, 1.9, 3.6, 4.8, 5, 2.4, 3.4, 4.4

15) $\frac{2}{3}$, $\frac{1}{2}$, $\frac{1}{4}$, $\frac{7}{12}$, $\frac{5}{12}$, $\frac{1}{3}$, $\frac{3}{4}$

16) $\frac{2}{5}$, $\frac{3}{10}$, $\frac{1}{2}$, $\frac{4}{10}$, $\frac{1}{5}$, $\frac{4}{5}$, $\frac{7}{10}$, $\frac{1}{10}$

17) $22\frac{1}{2}$, $4\frac{1}{2}$, 3, $5\frac{1}{2}$, 4, $5\frac{1}{2}$, $4\frac{1}{2}$, 6, $3\frac{1}{2}$

18) $2\frac{1}{12}$, $3\frac{1}{3}$, $4\frac{1}{9}$, $3\frac{3}{4}$, $2\frac{5}{6}$, $3\frac{2}{6}$

19) $3\frac{2}{7}$, $6\frac{1}{2}$, $4\frac{2}{3}$, $5\frac{5}{21}$, $4\frac{2}{3}$, $6\frac{1}{2}$, $3\frac{5}{6}$

20) $2\frac{2}{3}$, $4\frac{1}{3}$, $8\frac{1}{6}$, $5\frac{5}{6}$, 7

21) $2\frac{3}{4}$, $1\frac{1}{2}$, $2\frac{1}{4}$, 3, $4\frac{1}{4}$, $3\frac{3}{4}$, $3\frac{1}{2}$, $4\frac{3}{4}$, $3\frac{1}{2}$, $3\frac{3}{4}$

22) $5\frac{1}{2}$, 4.3, $6\frac{1}{4}$, 4.2, $5\frac{1}{5}$, $4\frac{1}{5}$

23) $3\frac{1}{8}$, 2.25, 3, $2\frac{1}{2}$, 2.75, 3.5, $3\frac{1}{4}$

24) .05, $\frac{1}{8}$, .15, $\frac{1}{4}$, .125, .1, $\frac{5}{40}$, .15, .25, $\frac{1}{20}$

25) $\frac{3}{16}$, .0156, $\frac{5}{16}$, .0172, $\frac{23}{250}$

PROBABILITY AND STATISTICS—

FIND THE PROBABILITY OF DRAWING OUT THE DESIGNATED MARBLES FROM A SACK OF MARBLES THAT CONTAINS:

5 red marbles, 6 white marbles, 4 blue marbles, and 3 green marbles.

For 1 - 20   you are to draw out one marble, then *put it back in the sack* before drawing the second (or third) marble.

1)	A red, then blue.	11)	A blue, then white.
2)	A blue, then green.	12)	A blue, then red.
3)	A white, then red.	13)	Two blue in a row.
4)	A red, then green.	14)	Two red in a row.
5)	A red, then white.	15)	Two white in a row.
6)	A white, then blue.	16)	Two green in a row.
7)	A white, then green.	17)	Two blue, then a red.
8)	A green, then white.	18)	Two red, then white.
9)	A green, then red.	19)	Two green, then blue.
10)	A green, then blue.	20)	Three blue in a row.

For 21 - 40   you are to draw out one marble, *keep it out*, then draw another marble.

21)	A red, then blue.	31)	Two blue in a row.
22)	A green, then blue.	32)	Two red in a row.
23)	A white, then blue.	33)	Two white in a row.
24)	A blue, then white.	34)	Two green in a row.
25)	A green, then white.	35)	Two blue, then a green.
26)	A red, then white.	36)	Two white, then a red.
27)	A green, then red.	37)	Two green, then a white.
28)	A blue, then green.	38)	Three blue in a row.
29)	A red, then green.	39)	A blue, then green, then white.
30)	A white, then green.	40)	A red, then white, then blue.

For 41 - 50   you are to draw out *two marbles at once, leave them out* and draw two more marbles at once.

41)   Two blue, then a red and white.

42)   A blue and white, then a red and white.

43)   Two green, then a green and white.

44)   Two red, then a red and blue.

45)   A green and white, then a blue and white.

46)   Two white, then two more white.

47)   Two blue, then two more blue.

48)   A blue and green, then another blue and green.

49)   A red and white, then two blue.

50)   A green and red, then two white.

PROBABILITY AND STATISTICS—

FIND THE PROBABILITY OF DRAWING OUT THE DESIGNATED MARBLES FROM A SACK OF MARBLES THAT CONTAINS:

8 pink, 6 purple, 4 white, 3 black, 2 yellow, and one orange.

For 1 - 20 you are to draw out one marble, then *put it back in the sack* before drawing the second (or third) marble.

1) A pink, then white.
2) A purple, then pink.
3) A black, then yellow.
4) A white, then orange.
5) A white, then purple.
6) A yellow, then orange.
7) A pink, then yellow.
8) A black, then white.
9) A pink, then black.
10) A purple, then white.
11) Two pink in a row.
12) Two purple in a row.
13) Two white in a row.
14) Two black in a row.
15) Two yellow in a row.
16) Two orange in a row.
17) Two pink, then a purple.
18) Two black, then an orange.
19) Three purple in a row.
20) Three white in a row.

For 21 - 40 you are to draw out one marble, *keep it out*, then draw another marble.

21) A pink, then purple.
22) A purple, then white.
23) A black, then orange.
24) A white, then orange.
25) A purple, then pink.
26) A pink, then black.
27) A purple, then yellow.
28) An orange, then purple.
29) A pink, then white.
30) A black, then white.
31) Two pink in a row.
32) Two purple in a row.
33) Two white in a row.
34) Two black in a row.
35) Two yellow in a row.
36) Two orange in a row.
37) Two purple, then a white.
38) Two white, then a black.
39) Two purple in a row, then two pink.
40) Three pink in a row.

For 41 - 50 you are to draw out *two marbles at once, leave them out, then draw two more marbles at once.*

41) Two pink, then a purple and a white.
42) Two purple, then a yellow and an orange.
43) Two white, then two black.
44) A black and white, then another black and white.
45) A white and a purple, then a pink and black.
46) A pink and purple, then two black.
47) A white and yellow, then two orange.
48) A yellow and an orange, then a pink and a black.
49) Two pink, then two more pink.
50) Two white, then two more white.

PROBABILITY AND STATISTICS—

WHAT IS THE PROBABILITY OF ROLLING EACH
OF THE FOLLOWING NUMBERS WITH 2 DICE?

1) 2   2) 5   3) 7   4) 8   5) 10

WITH 3 DICE?

6) 3   7) 5   8) 6   9) 9   10) 11

11) 13   12) 14   13) 17

WITH 4 DICE?

14) 4   15) 8

WHAT IS THE PROBABILITY OF DRAWING THE FOLLOWING
CARDS FROM A 52 CARD DECK WITHOUT REPLACEMENT?

16) A heart

17) A ten

18) A ten of hearts

19) Two spades

20) Two jacks

21) Two jacks of spades

22) Three clubs

23) Three fives

24) Four diamonds

25) Four sixes

26) Three consecutive cards drawn from least to greatest

27) Three consecutive clubs drawn in any order

28) Five cards of any one suit

29) Five consecutive cards drawn from least to greatest

30) Any three of a kind and two of a kind

PROBABILITY AND STATISTICS—

WHAT IS THE PROBABILITY OF ROLLING EACH
OF THE FOLLOWING NUMBERS WITH 2 DICE?

1) 3   2) 4   3) 6   4) 9   5) 12

WITH 3 DICE?

6) 4   7) 7   8) 8   9) 10   10) 12

11) 15   12) 16   13) 18

WITH 4 DICE?

14) 24   15) 10

WHAT IS THE PROBABILITY OF DRAWING THE FOLLOWING
CARDS FROM A 52 CARD DECK WITHOUT REPLACEMENT?

16)   A spade

17)   An ace

18)   A five of hearts

19)   A card below a five. (Aces are high)

20)   A spade and then a heart

21)   A five and then a six

22)   Two consecutive cards of any suit (Aces are high or low)

23)   Two consecutive hearts

24)   Two consecutive cards of any one suit

25)   A heart, then a spade, and then a club

26)   Two hearts and then two spades

27)   The five of diamonds and then the six of hearts

28)   Five consecutive cards of any one suit drawn from least to greatest

29)   An Ace, King, queen, jack, and ten of any one suit

30)   Four of a kind with any other card

ORDER OF OPERATIONS—SOLVE THE FOLLOWING

1) $6 \times 5 + 3$ 2) $6 + 5 \times 3$ 3) $8 - 3 \times 2$

4) $15 \div 5 - 3$ 5) $20 \div 5 + 5$ 6) $2 \times 3 + 8 \times 6$

7) $2 + 3 \times 8 + 6$ 8) $16 \div 8 + 4 \times 3$ 9) $18 \div 2 \div 3 \div 3$

10) $6 - 2 + 3 \times 4$ 11) $15 - 7 \times 2 - 1$ 12) $6 \times 2 \times 3 \times 5$

13) $6 + 8 \times 8 - 60$ 14) $3 \times 8 - 5 + 6$ 15) $20 \div 5 \div 4 \times 18$

16) $2 + 3 \times 5 + 3 + 24$ 17) $10 + 12 \times 12 \div 2 + 6$ 18) $6 \times 3 + 2 \times 8 + 3$

19) $18 - 3 \times 4 \div 2 + 8$ 20) $7 + 8 \times 2 \times 8 + 6$

21) $6 \times (3 + 2)$ 22) $(14 - 3 + 4) \div 5$

23) $(4 - 2) \times 5 + 3$ 24) $(23 + 13) \div 6 + 18$

25) $(6 + 8) \times 8 - 60$ 26) $(3 + 8) \div 11 + 23$

27) $49 \div 7 \times 8 + 4 \times (3 + 2)$ 28) $3 \times (8 - 5) + 6 + 3 \times 8$

29) $5 \times (6 + 8 + 18) \times 0 + 8$ 30) $4 \times 9 + 6 \times (3 + 4)$

31) $(4 + 3) \times (8 + 3)$ 32) $(10 + 12) \times 12 \div (2 + 6)$

33) $(6 - 2) \times (8 - 3) \div 4$ 34) $15 + 7 \times (2 + 5) \times 4 \times (2 - 2)$

35) $(6 + 10) + 3 \times 3 \times (8 \times 2)$

36) $4 \times (8 + 2) - 1 + (9 - 6) + 4 \times 2$

37) $(4 + 3) + (6 + 2) \div (10 - 8)$

38) $(6 + 4) \times 10 \div (5 \times 5 - 5)$

39) $(7 + 8) \times 2 \times (8 - 6)$

40) $(4 + 3) \times (6 + 2) \div (10 - 8)$

41) $[6 \times (3 + 2)] \times (8 + 3)$

42) $[(24 + 6 + 6) \div 9] \times 3$

43) $[(2 + 3) \times (5 + 3)] + 24$

44) $[(18 - 6) \times 12] \div (24 \times 2)$

45) $(20 + 8) \div 7 \times [(3 + 6) \div 9]$

46) $[16 \div (4 \times 2) + 5] + [(6 - 3) \times 8]$

47) $[288 \div (2 \times 3) \div (6 \times 2)] \times 2$

48) $[(288 \div 2) \times 3] \div (6 \times 2 \times 2)$

49) $[2 + (8 - 3) \times 4] + 16 \div 4 + 2 \times 3$

50) $[2 \times (3 + 4) + 6] \times [3 \times (2 + 5)]$

ORDER OF OPERATIONS—SOLVE THE FOLLOWING

1) $8 \times 3 + 4$

2) $7 + 6 \times 5$

3) $8 + 3 \times 4$

4) $7 \times 6 + 5$

5) $5 + 7 \times 6 + 7$

6) $18 - 5 \times 3$

7) $16 \div 8 + 9 - 7$

8) $18 \times 5 - 3$

9) $12 + 8 \div 2 + 7$

10) $6 + 4 \times 3 \times 5$

11) $3 \times 6 \times 5 + 8$

12) $2 \times 7 - 3 \times 4$

13) $12 + 7 + 3 \times 10$

14) $8 \times 9 + 7 \times 6$

15) $20 - 15 \div 3 + 6$

16) $8 - 3 - 2 + 5 \times 4$

17) $35 - 4 \times 5 - 15$

18) $3 \times 8 - 2 + 5 - 6 \div 1$

19) $4 \times 5 + 3 \times 6 + 1$

20) $7 + 8 \times 9 - 3 \times 4$

21) $4 + 3 \, (2 + 6 \times 5)$

22) $8 + 9(3 + 7 \times 2)$

23) $2(3 \times 4 + 8) + 6 \times 2$

24) $4(5 \times 2 + 3) - 4 \times 3$

25) $7 + 5(2 \times 3 + 6) \times 2 + 7$

26) $6(7 - 2 \times 3) \times 4 - 2 \times 5$

27) $(4 \times 9) - (6 \times 3)2 + 4$

28) $15 + 7 \times 2 + 5(4 \times 2 + 8)$

29) $8 + 7(6 + 18 \div 3) + 28 \div 2$

30) $5(6 + 9 \times 2) - (3 \times 4 + 7)2 - 4$

31) $20 - (14 - 2 \times 6) + 3 \times 9$

32) $6 + 7(8 + 2 \times 5) \times 5 - 7 \div 1$

33) $6(4 \times 7 - 3 \div 1) \times 5 + 7$

34) $9 \times 8 - 5(6 + 3 \times 2) + 8$

35) $5(8 \times 8 - 7) - 2(6 + 4 \div 2) \times 3 - 6$

36) $5 + 7(3 + 2 \times 5) \times 2 + 9$

37) $6 + 10(9 - 2 \times 3) \times 5 + 7$

38) $4(25 - 4 \times 5) - 6 + 5 \times 9$

39) $15(10 + 7 \times 6) - 4 - 15 \div 3 + 7$

40) $4(2 \times 6 + 15 \div 5) \times 5 - 3(17 - 8 \times 2) \times 3$

41) $13 + 7[5 + 3(4 + 7 \times 3)]$

42) $20 + 5[6 + 5(4 \times 2 - 5)] \times 2 + 4$

43) $6[8 + 2(7 - 2 \times 2)] + 6$

44) $100 - 3[24 - (8 + 2 \times 6)] + 3 \times 4$

45) $18 + 2[2 + 9(3 + 5 \times 1)] \times 4$

46) $25 + [15 + 3(14 - 2 \times 6)]4 + 24 \div 6$

47) $4(14 - 3 \times 3) + 5[25 + 4(3 + 5 \times 3)] \times 2 + 6$

48) $7 + 5[6 + 3(2 \times 3 - 4)] \times 8 + 3(3 \times 8 + 12 \div 4) + 5 \div 1$

49) $20[28 - 3(18 - 3 \times 5)] - [25 - (4 + 5 \times 4)] + 7 \times 6 \div 3$

50) $10(20 - 3 \times 6) + 7[15 + 5(6 + 2 \times 4)] \times 5 + 14 \div 7 + 2$

ORDER OF OPERATIONS—SOLVE THE FOLLOWING

1) $\frac{1}{2} + \frac{2}{3} - \frac{1}{4}$

2) $\frac{3}{8} \div \frac{1}{2} \times \frac{1}{3}$

3) $\frac{1}{5} + \frac{3}{4} \times \frac{2}{3}$

4) $\frac{5}{6} - \frac{7}{9} \div \frac{14}{15}$

5) $\frac{9}{10} + \frac{3}{5} \times \frac{5}{8}$

6) $2\frac{1}{4} \times 8 \div \frac{1}{3}$

7) $3\frac{1}{3} - 4\frac{1}{2} \div 9$

8) $2\frac{1}{2} + \frac{3}{4} \times \frac{5}{6} - 1\frac{1}{3}$

9) $5\frac{2}{5} + 4\frac{1}{8} \div 11 \times \frac{4}{5}$

10) $6\frac{2}{7} \div 22 + 4\frac{2}{9} \times \frac{3}{19}$

11) $4.8 + 2.4 \times 2.7$

12) $6.13 \times 2.1 - 3.08$

13) $6.9 \div 2.3 \times 4.5$

14) $7.04 - 3.6 \div 0.9$

15) $8.4 \div 4.2 + .63 \times 4$

16) $7.58 - 5.3 \times .13 + 2.8$

17) $88.4 + 6.5 - 3.8 \times 4.5$

18) $63.9 \div 21.3 - .45 + 3.72$

19) $7.9 + 3.9 \times 0 - 4.75$

20) $6.56 \times 0 + 4.9 \div 2$

21) $(6\frac{1}{4} + 3\frac{1}{2}) \div \frac{1}{8}$

22) $\frac{4}{9} \times (\frac{3}{5} + \frac{1}{4})$

23) $\frac{5}{16} \div (\frac{9}{10} \times 1\frac{1}{4})$

24) $9\frac{1}{3} - (2\frac{2}{5} + 3\frac{7}{10})$

25) $(6\frac{1}{8} - 3\frac{5}{6}) \times 4\frac{1}{2}$

26) $(\frac{5}{9} + \frac{2}{3}) \times (\frac{1}{4} + \frac{3}{8})$

27) $(\frac{7}{12} - \frac{2}{9}) \times (\frac{6}{7} + \frac{1}{4})$

28) $2\frac{1}{3} \div (4\frac{1}{2} + \frac{5}{9}) + 15$

29) $4\frac{1}{5} \times 2\frac{1}{2} \div (8 - 4\frac{1}{3})$

30) $(\frac{5}{8} + \frac{2}{5} + \frac{3}{4}) \div \frac{5}{16}$

31) $(4.5 + 3.8) \times 2.6$

32) $88.4 \div (40.24 \div 10.06)$

33) $79.5 - (6.4 \times 9)$

34) $6.04 + (8.4 \div .07)$

35) $(5.9 \times 8.5) - 8.13$

36) $(4.7 + 2.8) \div (1.36 + 1.14)$

37) $87.5 - (3.6 \times 6) - 1.14$

38) $(28.8 \div 0.3) - (9.5 \times 0.8)$

39) $(6.34 + .16) \times (4.3 - 4.3)$

40) $8.9 + (8.8 \div 2.2) \times 1.4$

41) $[(4.3 - 2.1) \times 8] - 1\frac{3}{5}$

42) $6\frac{1}{4} + [8 + (4.5 \times 4)]$

43) $5.6 - [(4\frac{1}{4} + 2\frac{1}{2}) \times \frac{1}{2}]$

44) $[(6.3 \div 0.7) - 4\frac{3}{5})] \div 3\frac{1}{7}$

45) $8 - [(4.4 \div 2) + 1\frac{1}{4}]$

46) $4\frac{1}{5} + [(6.7 + 4.9) \times 0]$

47) $9 \times [6.5 - (2\frac{1}{4} + 4\frac{1}{4})]$

48) $[(9.7 - 2.3) \div \frac{1}{5}] + 3$

49) $6\frac{3}{5} - [4.2 + (1.1 \times 2)]$

50) $[(8\frac{3}{5} - 2\frac{1}{4}) \times 40] + 4.9$

ORDER OF OPERATIONS—SOLVE THE FOLLOWING

1) $-6 + -5 \times -6$

2) $-8 \times 3 + 4$

3) $-11 + 15 \times 3 \times -2$

4) $-7 \times -2 + 7 \times 2$

5) $-8 - -3 \times 5$

6) $-8 - 3 \times 5 + -8$

7) $-15 \times 3 + -5 \times -15$

8) $-3 - -8 + -4 - -9$

9) $-9 \times -3 + -9 + -2 - -5$

10) $-6 \div 2 - -8 \times 3$

11) $-16 \div 4 + -32 \div -8$

12) $-8 + -32 \div 8 + -4$

13) $18 \div -3 + 5 - -18 \div -3$

14) $-6 \times -5 \times -3 \times -4$

15) $-8 - -16 \div -8 + 12$

16) $-16 \times -4 \div -8 \times -2$

17) $-8 \times -8 \div -16 + -28$

18) $-16 - -16 + -42 \div -6$

19) $7 + 8 \times 2 \times -8 + -6$

20) $-16 + -8 \div -2 \times -3 + -5$

21) $8 + -9(-3 + 7 \times 2)$

22) $-4 \times (-3 - -2)$

23) $-4 \times (-2 + -4) - 8$

24) $(-6 + -8)8 \div 4 + -8$

25) $4 \times 9 + (6 \times -3 \times -4)$

26) $(-5 + -8) \times (-7 - 3)$

27) $(-8 + -6) \times 2 + -6$

28) $-16 \div -4 + 2 \times (-8 + -3)$

29) $-16 \div -4 \times (-8 + -2)$

30) $-4 \times 9 + 6(3 + 4)$

31) $-7 \times (-8 + -4) \div -14$

32) $(16 + -16) \times 5 \times -23$

33) $-43 + 8 \times -4 + 3(-6 - 2)$

34) $(-6 + 4) \times 10 \div (-5 \times -5 - 20)$

35) $-(4 \times 3) + -(6 \times 8)$

36) $-(-6 - -8) \times -4$

37) $-6(-4 - 3) + -6 \times -8$

38) $48 \div -6 + (-36 + -12) \div -8$

39) $-8 + 4 - 9 + (-16 - -6) \times 3$

40) $-7 \times (3 + -4 + -8) + -23$

41) $[2(-4 + -5) + -8]-3$

42) $[(-4 \times -3) \times (-2 + -3)] + -3 \times -8$

43) $25 + [-15 + 3(-8 + -5)] \times 4 - 3$

44) $[-2 + (8 - 3) \times 4] + -16 \div 4$

45) $[(-4 + -8 - -3) \times -4] + (-4 - -8)$

46) $[(-3 \times -2 + -4) - 2] + -2 \times (-3 + 2)$

47) $[2(6 + 8) - -3] \times [3(-4 - -8)]$

48) $[-16 \div (-8 + -8) \times -4] + -3(-5 - 1)$

49) $-3(-5 + -9) - [4 \times -5(-3 + -2)]$

50) $[-2(-8 + 5) + 6][3(-2 - 5)]$

ORDER OF OPERATIONS—SOLVE THE FOLLOWING

1) $9 + -6 \times 7$

2) $\frac{1}{2} + 40 \times \frac{3}{8}$

3) $-9 + -6 \times 7$

4) $\frac{1}{2} \times 40 + \frac{3}{8}$

5) $-9 \div -6 + 7$

6) $.8 + -24 \times .5$

7) $-9 + -6 \times -7$

8) $.8 \times -24 + .5$

9) $\frac{2}{5} \times 15 + 6$

10) $-.8 \times -24 + .5$

11) $\frac{2}{5} - 15 \times -6$

12) $-25 + -20 \times -2.5$

13) $7 \div 3\frac{1}{2} + -14$

14) $-20 \times -25 + -2.5$

15) $7 + 3\frac{1}{2} \div -14$

16) $\frac{3}{4} + \frac{3}{8} \times \frac{4}{9}$

17) $4.8 \times .5 + -3.7$

18) $-\frac{3}{4} + \frac{3}{8} \div \frac{4}{9}$

19) $24.12 + 48.6 \div -1.2$

20) $-\frac{3}{4} + \frac{3}{8} \times 24 + -18 \div \frac{2}{3}$

21) $-8 + -3(4 + -3 \times 2)$

22) $14 + -6(7 + -5.2)$

23) $14\frac{1}{2} + -6(5\frac{1}{2} + -3 \times 3)$

24) $-24 + -5(8 + -3 \times -2) \times 2 + 4$

25) $-24.31 + -.8(4.2 + -5 \times 2)$

26) $-19.17 + -.8(4 + -3 \times 5)$

27) $5(24.6 \div -12 + 4) \times 2 + -7.1$

28) $50\frac{1}{3} + -\frac{3}{4}(19 + -8.2)$

29) $(8 + -5 \times 4) \div (12 - 6 \div 2) + 9$

30) $-25.7 + 12(2.4 \div -6 + 1) + 9$

31) $14\frac{3}{8} - -6(8\frac{1}{4} - 3 \times 3) \times 2$

32) $9\frac{5}{8} + -\frac{3}{4}(\frac{1}{2} + -\frac{3}{4} \times 6)$

33) $18.1 + -.6(15 - -3 \times 3)$

34) $.5(8 + -6 \times .2) \div 17 + 3.9$

35) $-5(4 + -6 \times -5) + -2(3 \times 5 + -9)$

36) $100 - 1\frac{1}{2}(-5 + 3 \times -4 + 3) + -8\frac{1}{3}$

37) $\frac{2}{3}(-6 \times 6 + 9) + \frac{3}{4} \times -14 + 3$

38) $28.7 \div 14 + -.3(8 + -6 \times .8) + 1$

39) $\frac{1}{2}(12 \div -4 + 3) + -.9(6 + -3 \times 3)$

40) $\frac{1}{4}(16 - -5 \times 4) + -.7(-4 + -3 \times 2)$

41) $24 + -8[-6 + (-5 \times -3 + -11.4)] + -7.6$

42) $-17\frac{1}{3} + -\frac{1}{2}[-8 + 5(-3 + \frac{1}{2} \times 2)] + -\frac{3}{4} \times 8$

43) $-29.7 + \frac{3}{4}[-5 + 4(-3 + 12 \div 2) + 1] + -5\frac{1}{4}$

44) $-.12 \div 8 + .5[2.3 + -5(6 + 3 \times -2)] \times .2 + \frac{3}{4} \times -6$

45) $-.8 + 3(-5\frac{1}{2} + 2 \times 3) + -5[-8\frac{1}{4} + -4(-3 \times 3 + 4) \times 3] \times 2 + -8\frac{1}{5}$

46) $-5(-.8 + .3 \times .4) + -9[-6 + -3(-.5 \times 2 + 1.5)] \times .5 + 3 \times -4\frac{1}{3}$

47) $-2[-9 + -7(3 + -3 \times -3)] + -5(-2 \times 3 + -3 \times -4)$

48) $.4[4\frac{3}{5} + -5(-.3 + .4 \times .5) + 4\frac{3}{4}] + .5 \times .2$

49) $-\frac{5}{8}(\frac{1}{2} + \frac{3}{4} \times -6) + -.4[-.8 + .5(3 + -6 \times .5)] + 1\frac{1}{2}$

50) $-\frac{3}{4}(\frac{2}{5} + 8 \times 1.2) + -\frac{5}{8}[2\frac{1}{3} + \frac{8}{9}(-\frac{3}{4} + \frac{3}{8} \times 4)] \times \frac{8}{15}$

ORDER OF OPERATIONS—SOLVE THE FOLLOWING

1) $-3 + 2^3$

2) $4^2 + -3 \times 5$

3) $-7 + (-3)^2 + 2 \times -4$

4) $5^3 + (-3)^2 \times 2$

5) $-5 \times 3 + -2^3$

6) $-2^3 + 3^2 \times 5^2$

7) $-5^2 \times 6^2 + -4 \times 7$

8) $8^2 + -9^3 + 3 \times -5$

9) $11^2 + -2^3 \times 5 \times 2^3$

10) $9 + -4 \times 5$

11) $-6 \times 3 + 7$

12) $-8^2 \times 5 + -4^3$

13) $-6 + -3^3 \times 4^2$

14) $10^3 + -2^3 \times -5^3$

15) $13^2 + -5^3 \times 2$

16) $-14^2 + -14^3 \times 2$

17) $-7^3 + 5 \times 2 \times -3^5$

18) $(-4)^2 \times 5^2 + 7 \times 3^2$

19) $5 \times 7^2 - 3 \times 4^2$

20) $-8 \times 2^5 + -3^4$

21) $9^2 + -7^3 + -6^2 \times 5$

22) $20^2 + -10^3 \times 3^2$

23) $-5^3 \times 5^2 \times 3 + -4^3$

24) $3^3 + 30^2 \times 7^2 + -5 \times -4$

25) $8^2 + 9^2 \times 10$

26) $-4^3 \times 5^2 + 6^2 \times -5$

27) $-5 \times -4 + 3 + -6 \times 5$

28) $8 \times -3 + 5 \times 6^2 \times -2 + -7$

29) $-11^2 + -3^2 \times 5$

30) $-4 + -7 \times -6 + (-5)^2$

31) $.7^2 + -.2 \times 30$

32) $-.5 \times 1.4 + -.2^3$

33) $(-.4)^2 \times 5^2 + -7 \times .3^2$

34) $-.8^3 + -.5 \times -.4^3$

35) $-10^3 + -20^2 \times -.04^2$

36) $144 \times (-\tfrac{3}{4})^2 + (\tfrac{5}{8})^2 \times \tfrac{48}{75}$

37) $(\tfrac{2}{3})^3 + \tfrac{3}{4} \times (\tfrac{1}{2})^3$

38) $(\tfrac{3}{5})^2 + (-\tfrac{1}{4})^2 \times (-\tfrac{2}{5})^2$

39) $(\tfrac{4}{5})^3 \times 1000 + (-\tfrac{1}{5})^3 \times 1000$

40) $(8)^3 \times (-\tfrac{1}{2})^3 + (\tfrac{1}{6})^2 \times -18$

41) $\tfrac{3}{4}(3^2 + -4 \times 2) + (-5)^2$

42) $.3^2(2 + -3 \times 5 + -4^3) \times \tfrac{1}{2} + -7^2$

43) $20(3^3 + -2^2 \times 5) + -8^3$

44) $6^2 + 3(4 + -2 \times 5)^2 + 2^2 \times 3^2$

45) $-8^3 + -2^3(15 + -4 \times 2^2) + -5^3$

46) $.9^2 + -5^2(24 + (-3)^2 \times -2) + -5$

47) $-8[-5(-2^3 \times 5 + 6^2)] + 3^2$

48) $-\tfrac{1}{2}[-3^2(-5^3 + 15 \times 2^3)] \times 4 + 3$

49) $(6^2)[-6 + 3(2^2 + 3 \times -1) \times 4] \times (\tfrac{1}{2})^2 + -7$

50) $5^2 + 3^2[-4^2(5^2 + 3 \times -9) + -2^3] + 5^2$

EVALUATING EXPRESSIONS—
EVALUATE THE FOLLOWING EXPRESSIONS:

FOR 1-20 USE: A = 5, B = 2, C = 10, D = 4, E = 15, F = 20

1) 2A + B

2) 2C + 3E

3) 4F − 5C

4) D + 3B

5) 8E − F

6) 2C + AB

7) 4F ÷ C

8) AB − C

9) 2B ÷ D

10) ABC − DF

11) 4C + 3EF

12) 9D ÷ 3B

13) 4CD − ABE

14) 9F ÷ 2E

15) BAD + DEC

16) 25D − 5F

17) AE + CD − BF

18) 24F ÷ 3BD

19) DE − 3F

20) 2ACE ÷ 4E

FOR 21-40 USE: U = 5, C = 24, L = 3, A = 4, T = 2, M = 18

21) UC + LA

22) 8T − 3L

23) 2MUT + CA

24) 5U − 3U + U

25) MC − AT + UL

26) 5TC ÷ LAU

27) CM ÷ TAL + 4U

28) 9ML ÷ 27T − 2A

29) CU + 4A − TC

30) 15A + 15U − 15L

31) 2L + 2M

32) 7C − 7M

33) TU − 3L + 20M

34) $\dfrac{8M}{C} + \dfrac{C}{TA}$

35) 6C − LM + 5U

36) 8M + 6C + 36A + 48A

37) 3C − 4M + 20U − 25A

38) 180T + 72U − 40M

39) 20L ÷ 3U + 7T

40) 6M ÷ 3 ÷ 3 + 5UCLA

EVALUATING EXPRESSIONS—
EVALUATE THE FOLLOWING EXPRESSIONS

USE $c = 2\pi R$ FOR 1-8

1) $\pi = 3.14$, $R = 10$

2) $\pi = 3.14$, $R = 20$

3) $\pi = 3.14$, $R = 15$

4) $\pi = 3.14$, $R = 80$

5) $\pi = 22/7$, $R = 14$

6) $\pi = 22/7$, $R = 35$

7) $\pi = 22/7$, $R = 70$

8) $\pi = 22/7$, $R = .21$

USE $P = 2L + 2W$ FOR 9-16

9) $L = 12$, $W = 8$

10) $L = 15$, $W = 10$

11) $L = 25$, $W = 15$

12) $L = 100$, $W = 100$

13) $L = 7\frac{1}{2}$, $W = 10$

14) $L = 9.5$, $W = 8.5$

15) $L = 10.25$, $W = 8.6$

16) $L = 12\frac{1}{4}$, $W = 9\frac{1}{3}$

USE $A = \dfrac{L \times W}{2}$

FOR 17-20

17) $L = 12$, $W = 8$

18) $L = 15$, $W = 10$

19) $L = 25$, $W = 12.5$

20) $L = 8\frac{1}{3}$, $W = 4\frac{1}{5}$

USE $V = LWH$ FOR 21-24

21) $L = 15$, $W = 15$, $H = 15$

22) $L = 10\frac{1}{2}$, $W = 3\frac{1}{3}$, $H = 8$

23) $L = 12$, $W = 7.5$, $H = 8.5$

24) $L = 30$, $W = 20$, $H = 3.25$

USE $I = PRT$ FOR 25-28

25) $P = \$750.00$, $R = .08$, $T = 2.5$

26) $P = \$9500.00$, $R = .125$, $T = 3$

27) $P = \$5000.00$, $R = .085$, $T = 2.6$

28) $P = \$80{,}000.00$, $R = .11$, $T = 30$

USE $F = \frac{8}{5}c + 32$ FOR 29-32

29) $c = 20$

30) $c = 0$

31) $c = 35$

32) $c = 45$

USE $V = \dfrac{\pi R R H}{3}$ FOR 33-36

FOR 33-36

33) $\pi = 3.14$, $R = 5$, $H = 30$

34) $\pi = 3.14$, $R = 15$, $H = 10$

35) $\pi = 22/7$, $R = 14$, $H = 6$

36) $\pi = 22/7$, $R = .35$, $H = 9$

USE $V = \frac{1}{2}BHA + \frac{1}{2}THA$ FOR 37-40

37) $B = 15$, $H = 20$, $A = 25$, $T = 12$

38) $B = 40$, $H = 25$, $A = 30$, $T = 32$

39) $B = 4\frac{1}{2}$, $H = 8$, $A = 3\frac{1}{3}$, $T = 1\frac{1}{5}$

40) $B = 10.5$, $H = 20$, $A = 5.25$, $T = 12$

EVALUATING EXPRESSIONS—
EVALUATE THE FOLLOWING EXPRESSIONS:

USE V = $\frac{1}{6}$ LWH FOR 1-5

1) L = 15, W = 15, H = 15

2) L = 18, W = 10, H = 20

3) L = 25, W = 15, H = 12

4) L = 14, W = 18, H = 10

5) L = 16, W = 10, H = 9

USE A = π R^2 FOR 6-10

6) π = 3.14, R = 10

7) π = 3.14, R = 3

8) π = $^{22}/_7$, R = 7

9) π = $^{22}/_7$, R = 70

10) π = $^{22}/_7$, R = .35

USE A = (T + B) $\dfrac{W}{2}$ FOR 11-15

11) T = 23, B = 17, W = 10

12) T = 54, B = 46, W = 28

13) T = 11.2, B = 7.8, W = 2.5

14) T = 9$\frac{3}{4}$, B = 6$\frac{1}{2}$, W = 12

15) T = 14$\frac{3}{4}$, B = 5.2, W = 40

USE V = $\frac{1}{3}$ π R^2 H FOR 16-20

16) π = 3.14, R = 6, H = 15

17) π = 3.14, R = 50, H = 30

18) π = 3.14, R = 20, H = 18

19) π = $^{22}/_7$, R = 14, H = 9

20) π = $^{22}/_7$, R = .28, H = .6

USE V = $\frac{1}{3}$ (T + B) WH FOR 21-25

21) T = 41, B = 29, W = 30, H = 25

22) T = 13, B = 7, W = 15, H = 20

23) T = 7.5, B = 13.5, W = 9$\frac{3}{4}$, H = 7.25

24) T = 7$\frac{1}{2}$, B = 4$\frac{3}{4}$, W = 4$\frac{4}{5}$, H = 2$\frac{1}{7}$

25) T = 15$\frac{3}{5}$, B = 14.4, W = 9.5, H = 20

USE U = C^2 + $\frac{1}{2}$ (4L + A) + 2C

26) C = 5, L = 5, A = 6

27) C = -6, L = .07, A = -7

28) C = $\frac{4}{5}$, L = $\frac{1}{2}$, A = 3

29) C = .4, L = -3, A = 6

30) C = 1$\frac{1}{2}$, L = 23, A = 5

USE U = $\frac{4}{3}$ π R^3 FOR 31-35

31) π = 3.14, R = 10

32) π = 3.14, R = 50

33) π = 3.14, R = .3

34) π = $^{22}/_7$, R = 7

35) π = $^{22}/_7$, R = .21

USE Z = $\frac{3}{4}$ (M^2 − N) − $\frac{1}{2}$ (M − N^2)

36) M = 2, N = 4

37) M = 20, N = 8

38) M = 1, N = 1

39) M = $\frac{1}{2}$, N = $\frac{1}{4}$

40) M = .6, N = .4

EQUATIONS—SOLVE THE FOLLOWING

1) $X + 7 = 35$

2) $X - 7 = 35$

3) $N - 5 = 21$

4) $N + 5 = 21$

5) $N + 38 = 75$

6) $N - 38 = 75$

7) $B + 19 = 51$

8) $B - 19 = 51$

9) $A + 6 = 13$

10) $A - 6 = 13$

11) $U + 8 = 39$

12) $C + 21 = 117$

13) $L - 34 = 3$

14) $A + 1 = 95$

15) $B - 7 = 27$

16) $R - 14 = 31$

17) $U - 95 = 6$

18) $I - 8 = 81$

19) $N + 24 = 27$

20) $S + 412 = 500$

21) $X + 8 = 9$

22) $X - 8 = 9$

23) $M + 24 = 31$

24) $M - 31 = 24$

25) $Z + 3 = 42$

26) $Z - 7 = 38$

27) $X - 35 = 7$

28) $X - 25 = 0$

29) $M + 32 = 41$

30) $Q + 25 = 68$

31) $R - 29 = 58$

32) $E - 39 = 4$

33) $G + 77 = 111$

34) $Q + 55 = 66$

35) $N - 55 = 55$

36) $S - 36 = 41$

37) $T - 85 = 71$

38) $A - 43 = 43$

39) $T + 43 = 43$

40) $E - 714 = 398$

41) $B + 71 = 530$

42) $E + 97 = 113$

43) $A - 46 = 4$

44) $V - 33 = 117$

45) $E - 401 = 399$

46) $R + 59 = 71$

47) $S + 96 = 107$

48) $M + 5 = 71$

49) $M - 8 = 46$

50) $M - 85 = 84$

EQUATIONS—SOLVE THE FOLLOWING

1) $N + 9 = 47$

2) $N - 9 = 47$

3) $X + 5 = 66$

4) $X + 74 = 417$

5) $N - 5 = 66$

6) $N - 74 = 417$

7) $T + 47 = 71$

8) $I - 63 = 3$

9) $M - 51 = 17$

10) $T + 33 = 88$

11) $Z - 33 = 88$

12) $X + 6 = 19$

13) $Z + 7 = 331$

14) $Y + 3\frac{1}{2} = 8$

15) $Z - 3\frac{1}{2} = 8$

16) $W + 41 = 7$

17) $A - 35 = -8$

18) $S - 44 = 6$

19) $H + 64 = 41$

20) $I + 17 = 3$

21) $N - 7\frac{1}{2} = 8$

22) $G - 6\frac{1}{4} = 3\frac{3}{4}$

23) $T + 8.3 = 5$

24) $Q - .63 = 3$

25) $N - .63 = -.3$

26) $S - .63 = .3$

27) $T - .63 = -3$

28) $A + 5\frac{1}{3} = 2\frac{3}{5}$

29) $T + 6\frac{1}{4} = 4\frac{1}{8}$

30) $E + 3 = 9\frac{1}{8}$

31) $C + 3 = 2\frac{1}{8}$

32) $Q + .8 = 12.3$

33) $U + 8 = 12.3$

34) $G - 8 = 12.3$

35) $A - .8 = 12.3$

36) $R - .08 = 12.3$

37) $S + 9\frac{1}{4} = 3\frac{2}{3}$

38) $M + 4\frac{3}{8} = 1\frac{5}{6}$

39) $N + 7 = 3\frac{2}{7}$

40) $R - 5 = -7\frac{1}{4}$

41) $X - 7\frac{1}{8} = -9\frac{3}{5}$

42) $Z + 6 = 4\frac{3}{8}$

43) $Z + .6 = -4.375$

44) $R - 2\frac{3}{5} = -9.6$

45) $T + 5\frac{1}{4} = 5.25$

46) $C - .75 = -6\frac{1}{4}$

47) $C - 5.01 = 5\frac{2}{5}$

48) $B + 8\frac{1}{8} = 3.375$

49) $A + .6 = 7\frac{4}{5}$

50) $G + 5\frac{1}{6} = 3\frac{3}{8}$

EQUATIONS—SOLVE THE FOLLOWING

1) $5N = 35$

2) $\dfrac{N}{5} = 35$

3) $8A = 96$

4) $7B = 91$

5) $\dfrac{N}{3} = 13$

6) $\dfrac{R}{6} = 5$

7) $9M = 108$

8) $6N = 54$

9) $\dfrac{R}{8} = 10$

10) $\dfrac{T}{7} = 20$

11) $5M = 95$

12) $6Z = 84$

13) $\dfrac{Q}{2} = 15$

14) $\dfrac{R}{7} = 30$

15) $5E = 85$

16) $12G = 84$

17) $\dfrac{Q}{10} = 22$

18) $\dfrac{N}{4} = 80$

19) $4D = 80$

20) $8U = 120$

21) $\dfrac{C}{8} = 120$

22) $\dfrac{K}{9} = 72$

23) $9S = 72$

24) $\dfrac{X}{2} = 54$

25) $\dfrac{X}{3} = 54$

26) $2X = 54$

27) $3X = 54$

28) $14Z = 42$

29) $18Y = 144$

30) $16Y = 144$

31) $\dfrac{M}{18} = 20$

32) $\dfrac{N}{25} = 16$

33) $\dfrac{M}{20} = 7$

34) $\dfrac{R}{60} = 20$

35) $\dfrac{T}{50} = 24$

36) $24Z = 144$

37) $36Z = 144$

38) $48Y = 144$

39) $72M = 144$

40) $9W = 144$

41) $40Z = 6000$

42) $\dfrac{R}{40} = 6000$

43) $\dfrac{T}{200} = 7$

44) $\dfrac{M}{15} = 3$

45) $\dfrac{N}{50} = 75$

46) $9M = 117$

47) $8A = 13{,}600$

48) $\dfrac{W}{45} = 28$

49) $\dfrac{Y}{60} = 8$

50) $\dfrac{Z}{125} = 40$

EQUATIONS—SOLVE THE FOLLOWING

1) $8N = 120$

2) $\frac{1}{8} N = 120$

3) $.8N = 120$

4) $-8N = 120$

5) $-8N = -120$

6) $\frac{2}{5}M = 18$

7) $-\frac{3}{4}M = 18$

8) $-\frac{5}{6}M = -20$

9) $12M = 18$

10) $24M = .6$

11) $6C = 72$

12) $\frac{A}{6} = 72$

13) $-4L = 56$

14) $-.04I = 56$

15) $4F = .56$

16) $\frac{7}{8}Q = 56$

17) $-25R = 500$

18) $.25N = 500$

19) $\frac{5}{8}I = -30$

20) $\frac{A}{7} = .98$

21) $7B = .98$

22) $-8E = 48$

23) $-13A = -65$

24) $9R = -.018$

25) $3S = -9$

26) $\frac{A}{18} = -5$

27) $\frac{B}{-18} = -5$

28) $9C = .27$

29) $.009B = 27$

30) $-18B = 27$

31) $14M = .7$

32) $\frac{M}{14} = .7$

33) $-13N = 182$

34) $-.13U = 182$

35) $7N = .182$

36) $7N = \frac{14}{15}$

37) $\frac{3}{4}Z = \frac{5}{6}$

38) $-\frac{2}{3}X = \frac{8}{9}$

39) $-\frac{7}{8}Z = -1\frac{2}{5}$

40) $.45A = 180$

41) $45A = -180$

42) $-45A = -.018$

43) $9B = \frac{3}{4}$

44) $-6B = 22$

45) $-.08C = 1$

46) $\frac{M}{25} = 4.5$

47) $\frac{2}{5}Z = .4$

48) $1\frac{3}{4}Z = .14$

49) $8A = -3\frac{1}{5}$

50) $-8A = -3.2$

EQUATIONS—SOLVE THE FOLLOWING

1) $R + 7 = 63$

2) $7R = 63$

3) $R - 7 = 63$

4) $\dfrac{R}{7} = 63$

5) $5T = 75$

6) $\dfrac{T}{5} = 75$

7) $T + 5 = 75$

8) $T - 5 = 75$

9) $12Z = 60$

10) $Z - 12 = 60$

11) $Z + 12 = 60$

12) $\dfrac{Z}{12} = 60$

13) $M + 7 = 41$

14) $\dfrac{N}{20} = 15$

15) $8Z = 120$

16) $X - 7 = 3$

17) $Z + 4 = 71$

18) $5N = 65$

19) $\dfrac{N}{9} = 130$

20) $Z - 45 = 3$

21) $T + 94 = 944$

22) $14A = 42$

23) $\dfrac{B}{25} = 400$

24) $C - 75 = 4$

25) $E + 64 = 311$

26) $6K = 366$

27) $\dfrac{K}{40} = 250$

28) $M + 35 = 63$

29) $A - 9 = 44$

30) $15R = 135$

31) $I + 48 = 48$

32) $36Z = 720$

33) $Q + 5 = 91$

34) $\dfrac{N}{13} = 91$

35) $13A = 91$

36) $W - 13 = 91$

37) $I + 39 = 47$

38) $25L = 2000$

39) $\dfrac{D}{7} = 30$

40) $C + 4 = 411$

41) $A - 7 = 28$

42) $9T = 108$

43) $\dfrac{S}{3} = 54$

44) $18Z = 54$

45) $\dfrac{T}{30} = 15$

46) $A + 461 = 1000$

47) $B - 350 = 1000$

48) $25C = 1000$

49) $\dfrac{D}{75} = 1000$

50) $49E = 14798$

EQUATIONS—SOLVE THE FOLLOWING

1) $M + 9 = 36$

2) $N - 9 = 36$

3) $9R = 36$

4) $\frac{1}{9}S = 36$

5) $.9T = 36$

6) $U + .9 = 36$

7) $U - .9 = 36$

8) $-9V = 36$

9) $W + \frac{3}{4} = 3$

10) $\frac{3}{4}X = 3$

11) $\frac{Y}{7} = -5$

12) $-\frac{2}{3}Z = -14$

13) $A + \frac{2}{3} = 14$

14) $R - 1.7 = 51$

15) $-1.7I = -51$

16) $\frac{Z}{-4} = 9$

17) $Q + 8 = 5$

18) $\frac{4}{5}N = -12$

19) $A + \frac{4}{5} = 12$

20) $.8S = 12$

21) $T - 8 = .12$

22) $-8A = .12$

23) $1\frac{2}{5}T = \frac{14}{15}$

24) $E + 1\frac{2}{5} = \frac{14}{15}$

25) $S + 8 = 56$

26) $\frac{1}{8}U = 56$

27) $N - 8 = 56$

28) $8D = 56$

29) $-.08E = 56$

30) $-8V = .056$

31) $I - 8 = -56$

32) $L + \frac{1}{8} = 56$

33) $S - \frac{1}{8} = .56$

34) $N + 3.1 = 5$

35) $N + .31 = 5$

36) $2.4N = 96$

37) $\frac{N}{.15} = -40$

38) $9N = -57$

39) $M + 75 = 75$

40) $-.75M = 15$

41) $M + 8 = 1$

42) $8M = -1$

43) $R + \frac{3}{8} = -1\frac{2}{5}$

44) $\frac{4}{5}T = -1\frac{1}{4}$

45) $\frac{V}{48} = -700$

46) $Z + 4.8 = 3.91$

47) $1.5Z = 900$

48) $A + 1.34 = 2.1$

49) $1.8B = -9$

50) $C - 345 = -7.9$

EQUATIONS—SOLVE THE FOLLOWING

1) $12A = 48$

2) $A - 12 = 48$

3) $A + 12 = 48$

4) $\dfrac{A}{12} = 48$

5) $.12A = -48$

6) $A + .12 = 48$

7) $A - 1.2 = 48$

8) $12A = -.048$

9) $-\tfrac{3}{4}A = 48$

10) $A + \tfrac{3}{4} = 48$

11) $S + 17 = 51$

12) $17T = -5.1$

13) $A - 17 = -5.1$

14) $.17N = -51$

15) $\dfrac{F}{-17} = 51$

16) $Q - \tfrac{2}{3} = 3\tfrac{1}{4}$

17) $15R = -50$

18) $\dfrac{D}{.25} = -.6$

19) $C + 3\tfrac{3}{4} = 1\tfrac{2}{3}$

20) $\tfrac{15}{16}A = -\tfrac{8}{25}$

21) $R + \tfrac{15}{16} = \tfrac{8}{24}$

22) $D - 1\tfrac{4}{5} = -3\tfrac{1}{5}$

23) $.15I = 60$

24) $N + 15 = 60$

25) $A + .15 = 60$

26) $\dfrac{L}{.15} = 60$

27) $Z + 7 = 3.3$

28) $Z - 5 = 51.3$

29) $5Z = 51.3$

30) $-5Z = 51.3$

31) $A + 9 = 7$

32) $8B = 24$

33) $6C = -.24$

34) $E + .24 = 6$

35) $M + 44 = 7$

36) $35N = 70,000$

37) $9Z = 126$

38) $Z + 9 = 126$

39) $\tfrac{1}{9}N = 126$

40) $5R = .3$

41) $R + 5 = .3$

42) $T + .88 = -7$

43) $.005Z = 4$

44) $12M = .096$

45) $\tfrac{2}{3}N = -54$

46) $N + \tfrac{2}{3} = 54$

47) $3\tfrac{3}{4}N = .75$

48) $M + 5.2 = 14$

49) $Z + 25 = .125$

50) $25Z = .125$

EQUATIONS—SOLVE THE FOLLOWING

1) $4M + 3 = 11$

2) $5N - 2 = 13$

3) $9Z - 6 = 39$

4) $8X + 4 = 60$

5) $2Y + 7 = 35$

6) $6B + 8 = 50$

7) $7C + 1 = 50$

8) $9A - 4 = 68$

9) $5B - 4 = 61$

10) $3M - 14 = 13$

11) $4I + 31 = 31$

12) $6C + 3 = 39$

13) $10H - 13 = 77$

14) $2I - 1 = 51$

15) $7G + 12 = 103$

16) $8A + 15 = 111$

17) $9N + 7 = 124$

18) $2W - 19 = 103$

19) $4Q - 17 = 55$

20) $12L - 40 = 44$

21) $13V - 38 = 14$

22) $15E - 95 = 10$

23) $11R + 21 = 98$

24) $8I + 14 = 118$

25) $3N + 98 = 155$

26) $8E - 1 = 87$

27) $4S - 3 = 53$

28) $14B - 17 = 25$

29) $20C + 41 = 201$

30) $17A - 24 = 27$

31) $15E - 9 = 66$

32) $25I - 40 = 185$

33) $19Z + 47 = 85$

34) $11H + 8 = 140$

35) $9M + 28 = 172$

36) $3Z - 13 = 41$

37) $5M - 24 = 76$

38) $7H - 35 = 91$

39) $8X + 94 = 238$

40) $24M + 7 = 79$

41) $32N - 136 = 56$

42) $24Z + 13 = 157$

43) $15H + 75 = 330$

44) $72A - 100 = 188$

45) $6M + 127 = 271$

46) $21B - 13 = 71$

47) $36Y + 36 = 180$

48) $75L - 225 = 900$

49) $9Z - 342 = 774$

50) $3H + 401 = 545$

EQUATIONS—SOLVE THE FOLLOWING

1) $4N + 9 = 61$

2) $5M - 7 = 68$

3) $3Z + 14 = 65$

4) $8N + 34 = 162$

5) $9N - 4 = 185$

6) $7T - 17 = 11$

7) $6Z - 120 = 24$

8) $2Y + 13 = 311$

9) $4R + 43 = 139$

10) $12Z + 57 = 153$

11) $5W + 47 = 2$

12) $6A - 24 = -84$

13) $7S - 15 = -71$

14) $10H - 33 = 67$

15) $9I - 55 = -163$

16) $15N - 85 = 5$

17) $8G + 300 = -100$

18) $25T + 275 = 50$

19) $18Q + 54 = -360$

20) $17N - 68 = 51$

21) $\frac{3}{5}H + 24 = 60$

22) $1\frac{1}{4}U + 30 = 20$

23) $.4S + 12 = 36.8$

24) $15K + 8 = 8.3$

25) $.07I + 49 = 42$

26) $-\frac{1}{2}E + 40 = -56$

27) $.8S - 35 = -3$

28) $.004M + 1.2 = 4.8$

29) $-\frac{2}{3}N - \frac{1}{4} = \frac{7}{12}$

30) $\frac{3}{4}N - 1\frac{1}{5} = \frac{2}{3}$

31) $12T + 60 = 68$

32) $18T + 54 = 0$

33) $15T + 39 = 39.06$

34) $8T + 75 = 54$

35) $-12Z + 14 = 80$

36) $-.12Z + 14 = 80$

37) $35N + 28 = 0$

38) $-\frac{1}{5}X + 7 = 47$

39) $30T - 15 = 135$

40) $.005B - 47 = 91$

41) $16E - 4 = 16$

42) $25 + 3T = 100$

43) $15 - 6M = 78$

44) $44 = 9N - 1$

45) $75 = 10R + 45$

46) $19 - A = 31$

47) $-\frac{4}{5}B + 6 = 6.32$

48) $-400C + 7 = -13$

49) $50X - 3.75 = -3$

50) $1\frac{1}{5}M - 24 = 72.06$

EQUATIONS—SOLVE THE FOLLOWING

1) $N + 14 = 84$

2) $14N = 84$

3) $N - 14 = 84$

4) $\dfrac{N}{14} = 84$

5) $\dfrac{N}{3} = 18$

6) $3N = 18$

7) $N - 3 = 18$

8) $N + 3 = 18$

9) $N + 13 = 78$

10) $13N = 78$

11) $\dfrac{N}{13} = 78$

12) $N - 13 = 78$

13) $4W - 1 = 35$

14) $6I - 24 = 72$

15) $8S + 7 = 95$

16) $2C + 17 = 121$

17) $4Q + 14 = 78$

18) $3N + 45 = 51$

19) $7S - 35 = 105$

20) $5I - 98 = 107$

21) $12N - 45 = 135$

22) $25B - 75 = 500$

23) $17A + 51 = 731$

24) $9D + 7 = 124$

25) $15G + 101 = 176$

26) $14E + 28 = 140$

27) $R + 17 = 54$

28) $S - 31 = 5$

29) $6M + 3 = 45$

30) $13M = 52$

31) $5M - 7 = 108$

32) $\dfrac{M}{6} = 31$

33) $M - 6 = 31$

34) $9M + 1 = 82$

35) $7R - 17 = 165$

36) $6T = 168$

37) $U - 6 = 168$

38) $8Z + 39 = 167$

39) $9Y - 43 = 146$

40) $8A + 360 = 1000$

41) $3B = 318$

42) $\dfrac{B}{3} = 318$

43) $B + 3 = 318$

44) $18F - 31 = 113$

45) $35F + 350 = 420$

46) $19L - 57 = 380$

47) $24L + 48 = 192$

48) $25M = 975$

49) $Z - 713 = 1051$

50) $4T + 152 = 976$

EQUATIONS—SOLVE THE FOLLOWING

1) $M + 8 = 96$

2) $8N = 96$

3) $\frac{1}{8}N = 96$

4) $R + .8 = 96$

5) $-8R = 96$

6) $-.08R = 96$

7) $M - 8 = 96$

8) $M + .08 = 96$

9) $N + 8 = .96$

10) $8N = -.96$

11) $6M + 7 = 61$

12) $8I + 5 = 77$

13) $9N - 14 = 85$

14) $12N - 1 = 131$

15) $8E + 40 = 40$

16) $\frac{1}{2}S + 24 = -48$

17) $.05Q + 15 = 3$

18) $9T + 45 = 45.54$

19) $15A - 60 = 0$

20) $.007G + 3 = -4.56$

21) $Q + 9 = 24.23$

22) $5P + 3 = 98$

23) $7H - 45 = 53$

24) $-6E = 20$

25) $\frac{3}{4}R = -36$

26) $7S - .35 = .098$

27) $20M + 3 = 1$

28) $-25M - 30 = 75$

29) $12N = 60$

30) $N + 12 = 60$

31) $12N + 12 = 60$

32) $-.12N = 60$

33) $N + .12 = 60$

34) $\frac{3}{5}N - 6 = 60$

35) $.003N + 240 = 6$

36) $8 + M = 32$

37) $\frac{1}{7}M = -45$

38) $14N + 24 = 66$

39) $4R + 6 = 98.64$

40) $4R + .6 = 98.64$

41) $\frac{2}{3}T + \frac{1}{4} = 1\frac{1}{2}$

42) $\frac{5}{8}T = \frac{4}{5}$

43) $T - \frac{5}{8} = \frac{4}{5}$

44) $48 = 5T - 17$

45) $12 = 24A + 36$

46) $-.1B + 3.6 = 3$

47) $B - 9 = 30$

48) $9 - B = 30$

49) $.007B + 14 = -.098$

50) $1\frac{1}{5}M + 36 = -.054$

EQUATIONS—SOLVE THE FOLLOWING

1) $4M + 3M = 21$

2) $5M - 2M = 21$

3) $8M + 4M = 36$

4) $3M + 7M = 80$

5) $6M + 2M = 48$

6) $5M - 2M = 51$

7) $8M - 6M = 64$

8) $7M - M = 42$

9) $13M + 7M = 160$

10) $9M + 7M = 144$

11) $7I + 2I = 63$

12) $5Q + Q = 24$

13) $5W - W = 24$

14) $15A - 7A = 120$

15) $20H - 8H = 84$

16) $4A - A = 15$

17) $5W + 4W = 72$

18) $2K + 13K = 60$

19) $9E + 2E = 132$

20) $7Y + 3Y = 1400$

21) $15E - E = 42$

22) $4S - 2S = 38$

23) $24M - 6M = 54$

24) $15M - 12M = 57$

25) $14M + 3M = 102$

26) $8P + 7P = 90$

27) $9U + 5U = 84$

28) $12R - 8R = 56$

29) $20D + 7D = 54$

30) $15U + 4U = 76$

31) $13E - E = 156$

32) $18B + 7B = 325$

33) $7Q - Q = 102$

34) $12I + 6I = 216$

35) $7L + 11L = 360$

36) $15E + 6E = 84$

37) $30R + 5R = 910$

38) $8M - M = 91$

39) $12A - 7A = 95$

40) $16K - 2K = 168$

41) $36E - 17E = 114$

42) $31R + 11R = 210$

43) $9S + 4S = 156$

44) $17M + 10M = 108$

45) $4M + M = 60$

46) $4M - M = 60$

47) $13M + 12M = 575$

48) $8M + 9M = 102$

49) $19M - 5M = 56$

50) $45M - 13M = 96$

EQUATIONS—SOLVE THE FOLLOWING

1) $9M + 4M = 26$

2) $9M - 4M = 35$

3) $7M - M = 54$

4) $7M + M = 48$

5) $6M - 9M = 27$

6) $5M - 9M = 48$

7) $4M + 6M = 15$

8) $12M + 18M = 75$

9) $13M + 5M = .72$

10) $12M - 5M = .56$

11) $7I + \frac{1}{2}I = 30$

12) $\frac{3}{4}L + \frac{1}{2}L = -20$

13) $\frac{2}{3}L + \frac{3}{4}L = -51$

14) $.8I - .6I = 38$

15) $8N - .5N = .225$

16) $5Q - \frac{1}{2}Q = 135$

17) $5I + \frac{1}{2}I = -165$

18) $9S + S = -35$

19) $12F + 24F = .072$

20) $15I - 18I = .2418$

21) $-\frac{1}{2}G + -\frac{5}{8}G = 18$

22) $9H + .8H = 49$

23) $-8T + -9T = 68$

24) $-3I + 5I = -37$

25) $-3N - 5N = 40$

26) $-3G - -5G = -37$

27) $3I - -5I = 40$

28) $8L - 5L = -.24$

29) $8L - .5L = -.15$

30) $8I - -5I = -.52$

31) $8N - -.5N = -.51$

32) $-8I - .5I = -.68$

33) $6M + -2.4M = 144$

34) $-6M - -2.4M = 288$

35) $7T - 2T = -39$

36) $8K + 5K = 78$

37) $8K - 5K = 78$

38) $8K - -5K = 78$

39) $8K + -5K = 78$

40) $\frac{1}{2}Z + \frac{3}{4}Z = .35$

41) $3\frac{1}{2}Z - \frac{3}{4}Z = .22$

42) $5A + 3A + 6A = -168$

43) $9A + -5A + -6A = 42$

44) $8B - 5B - B = -78$

45) $6B + 9B - 4B = .154$

46) $\frac{3}{4}H + \frac{1}{2}H + \frac{7}{8}H = 51$

47) $9K - .8K - .6K = -152$

48) $3\frac{1}{2}L - 5L - 4L = 16.5$

49) $18M - 1.8M - .18M = -48.06$

50) $4\frac{3}{4}N + 1.8N + .35N = 345$

EQUATIONS—SOLVE THE FOLLOWING

1) $9M = 3M + 24$

2) $8M = 5M + 48$

3) $8M = 6M + 48$

4) $5M = M + 28$

5) $7M = 3M + 52$

6) $10M = 7M + 27$

7) $9M = M + 56$

8) $3M = M + 98$

9) $6M = 4M + 66$

10) $12M = 3M + 63$

11) $9N = 2N + 56$

12) $11N = 6N + 105$

13) $15M = M + 42$

14) $19I = I + 36$

15) $17C = 3C + 56$

16) $20H = 13H + 91$

17) $20I = 7I + 91$

18) $25G = 12G + 65$

19) $15A = 11A + 92$

20) $9N = 4N + 135$

21) $8S = 5S + 57$

22) $7T = T + 84$

23) $6A = A + 315$

24) $21T = 11T + 70$

25) $5E = 2E + 51$

26) $24S = 8S + 144$

27) $30P = 12P + 144$

28) $27A = 3A + 144$

29) $25R = 16R + 144$

30) $40T = 4T + 144$

31) $40A = 10A + 270$

32) $15N = N + 98$

33) $7S = S + 96$

34) $45M = 23M + 88$

35) $14M = 11M + 87$

36) $21M = 7M + 28$

37) $10M = M + 216$

38) $13M = M + 156$

39) $20M = 5M + 90$

40) $50M = 12M + 760$

41) $20M = 3M + 102$

42) $15M = 3M + 240$

43) $9M = M + 120$

44) $6M = M + 120$

45) $14M = M + 182$

46) $39T = 15T + 120$

47) $15T = 3T + 96$

48) $40K = 28K + 720$

49) $21K = 13K + 720$

50) $19K = 3K + 720$

EQUATIONS—SOLVE THE FOLLOWING

1) $8N = 5N + 39$

2) $8N = -5N + 39$

3) $6N = 2N + 60$

4) $9N = N + 96$

5) $6N = -2N + 60$

6) $9N = -N + 60$

7) $-7N = 5N + -48$

8) $-7N = -5N + -48$

9) $7N = 5N + -48$

10) $7N = -5N + -48$

11) $5I = I + 72$

12) $5N = -N + 72$

13) $4D = 7D + 57$

14) $4I = -7I + 55$

15) $12A = 5A + 84$

16) $12N = -5N + 85$

17) $A = 9A + -20$

18) $H = -9H + -20$

19) $7Q = 3Q + -92$

20) $-8Q = 5Q + -104$

21) $6S = 1\frac{1}{2}S + 18$

22) $15I = 17I + .18$

23) $4E = 1.6E + 96$

24) $6R = 7.2R + 96$

25) $7S = S + .003$

26) $3M = 3.6M + 42$

27) $\frac{3}{4}M = \frac{1}{2}M + -15$

28) $\frac{5}{6}M = 1\frac{1}{3}M + -\frac{4}{5}$

29) $\frac{4}{5}M = \frac{2}{3}M + \frac{4}{25}$

30) $\frac{5}{8}M = \frac{5}{6}M + \frac{25}{32}$

31) $7M = 2\frac{1}{2}M - 45$

32) $7\frac{1}{2}M = 2M - 33$

33) $4\frac{1}{3}M = 5\frac{3}{4}M + \frac{24}{34}$

34) $6.4N = 3N + .102$

35) $6.4N = .3N + .183$

36) $.9N = .5N + 120$

37) $.9N = .05N + 1700$

38) $.9N = N + 37$

39) $15N = 15.04N + 75$

40) $7.5N = 20N + 750$

41) $1\frac{4}{5}T = .7T + 143$

42) $3.5T = \frac{3}{4}T - 110$

43) $3.4T = 5\frac{4}{5}T - 120$

44) $6\frac{3}{5}T = 5.4T + 96$

45) $5K = 3\frac{3}{5}K + 42$

46) $8K = 7\frac{2}{5}K + -42$

47) $.2K = .8K + 48$

48) $3.54M = 3.545M + 3$

49) $2T = 26T + .12$

50) $4M + 3M = M + .03$

EQUATIONS—SOLVE THE FOLLOWING

1) $M + 6 = 84$

2) $M - 6 = 84$

3) $6M = 84$

4) $\dfrac{M}{6} = 84$

5) $4M + 12 = 84$

6) $4M - 12 = 84$

7) $5M + 7M = 84$

8) $9M - 5M = 84$

9) $8M = 5M + 84$

10) $8M = M + 84$

11) $Q + 9 = 57$

12) $7H - 45 = 46$

13) $9I - I = 72$

14) $\dfrac{Q}{3} = 31$

15) $17S = 459$

16) $9T + 12T = 105$

17) $18A = 4A + 98$

18) $T + 34 = 51$

19) $15E + 29 = 194$

20) $9B = 126$

21) $16U = U + 135$

22) $8C + 4C = 36$

23) $8K + 4 = 36$

24) $8E - 4E = 36$

25) $8Y - 4 = 36$

26) $8E = 4E + 36$

27) $S - 47 = 6$

28) $9M + 31M = 720$

29) $17T - 19 = 134$

30) $\dfrac{M}{15} = 30$

31) $14K - K = 130$

32) $N + 45 = 317$

33) $18M + 31 = 31$

34) $14Z - 5Z = 108$

35) $R - 35 = 35$

36) $14T = T + 39$

37) $25T - 900 = 0$

38) $N - 19 = 61$

39) $25Z + Z = 78$

40) $25T + 1 = 126$

41) $8M + 5M - 7M = 216$

42) $\dfrac{T}{8} = 103$

43) $K + K = 48$

44) $K + 1 = 48$

45) $12K + 14K = 208$

46) $35K = 15K + 2000$

47) $18M - M = M + 48$

48) $19Z = 456$

49) $\dfrac{T}{6} + 24 = 29$

50) $28B = B + 729$

EQUATIONS—SOLVE THE FOLLOWING

1) $N + 7 = 98$

2) $N - 7 = 98$

3) $7N = 98$

4) $\dfrac{N}{7} = 98$

5) $4N + 2 = 98$

6) $4N - 2 = 98$

7) $4N + 2N = 98$

8) $4N - 2N = 98$

9) $4N = 2N + 98$

10) $-\tfrac{2}{3}N = 98$

11) $T + \tfrac{2}{3} = 98$

12) $8E = 11E + 51$

13) $9X - 15X = -48$

14) $9A - 15 = 48$

15) $\tfrac{1}{2}S + 8 = -46$

16) $-5L + -8L = 52$

17) $Q + 3\tfrac{1}{3} = 2\tfrac{7}{8}$

18) $3\tfrac{1}{3}N = -40$

19) $\dfrac{G}{-9} = .33$

20) $8H = -7H + .75$

21) $Q - 4\tfrac{1}{8} = 5\tfrac{3}{4}$

22) $5R - R = -.03$

23) $.005N = -45$

24) $S + .05 = 1.7$

25) $9N + N = .03$

26) $9N + 87 = 6$

27) $A + 5\tfrac{1}{2} = 22$

28) $6R + 3 = 3.03$

29) $8K - 14K = 66$

30) $5A + 45 = 0$

31) $N - 5\tfrac{1}{2} = 22$

32) $-.03S = 375$

33) $1.8A - A = 36$

34) $S + \tfrac{3}{4} = .4$

35) $3.4R = .7R + 162$

36) $\tfrac{3}{4}A = -\tfrac{5}{8}$

37) $5Z + 4Z = .02763$

38) $Q + 75 = 7.5$

39) $\dfrac{R}{-.8} = 3.1$

40) $9B + .8B = 490$

41) $12A - 4.8A = -360$

42) $15C = 3C + 144$

43) $40K = 42K - 38$

44) $S + .25 = 3.1$

45) $9T - T + 3T = -.143$

46) $4\tfrac{1}{2}Z = 5.25Z + 2.25$

47) $3.4M - 102 = 0$

48) $2N + 5N + 9 = -5$

49) $5N - 2 = 2.35$

50) $8N + 5N - 24N = .253$

EQUATIONS—SOLVE THE FOLLOWING

1) $5N + 2 = 3N + 44$

2) $7N - 3 = 2N + 42$

3) $6N - 24 = N + 71$

4) $4N + 33 = N + 96$

5) $12N + 1 = 5N + 92$

6) $35N - 17 = 10N + 383$

7) $16M - 3 = 4M + 9$

8) $40M + 19 = 17M + 111$

9) $35M + 60 = 20M + 750$

10) $24M + 37 = 10M + 79$

11) $13M - 3 = 9M + 73$

12) $16M - 9 = M + 6$

13) $12M - 37 = 2M + 333$

14) $75N - 1 = 30N + 89$

15) $14N + 24 = 5N + 87$

16) $17B + 200 = 5B + 344$

17) $6R - 1 = R + 244$

18) $15A - 17 = 11A + 51$

19) $34S + 4 = 22S + 100$

20) $29K + 34 = 15K + 146$

21) $8A + 23 = A + 107$

22) $6C + 71 = C + 126$

23) $7Q + 9 = 3Q + 25$

24) $13R - 7 = 5R + 89$

25) $15N - 33 = 6N + 3$

26) $14H - 99 = 12H + 311$

27) $7U + 51 = 4U + 342$

28) $8S + 32 = 2S + 176$

29) $17K + 13 = 4K + 208$

30) $18E - 18 = 8E + 2$

31) $19R - 37 = 5R + 5$

32) $3S - 97 = S + 333$

33) $14Q - 15 = 6Q + 57$

34) $12K - 6 = K + 82$

35) $34L + 3 = 15L + 60$

36) $28A + 5 = 4A + 77$

37) $9H + 7 = H + 159$

38) $25Q - 4 = 18Q + 94$

39) $50M - 3 = 5M + 132$

40) $32A - 9 = 29A + 126$

41) $21S + 1 = 20S + 8$

42) $12Q + 7 = 9Q + 28$

43) $19Q + 1 = Q + 109$

44) $31N + 18 = 18N + 135$

45) $13E - 7 = 12E + 31$

46) $15R - 7 = 8R + 91$

47) $8S - 7 = 2S + 455$

48) $12M + 7 = 5M + 917$

49) $22M + 6 = 6M + 310$

50) $8M - 1 = 3M + 314$

EQUATIONS—SOLVE THE FOLLOWING

1) $8M + -4 = -3M + 18$

2) $6M + 7 = 3M + 16$

3) $12M - 13 = M + 9$

4) $12M - 13 = -M + 13$

5) $-12M - 13 = M + 26$

6) $-12M - 13 = -M + 20$

7) $25M + 94 = -8M + 28$

8) $35M + 31 = 20M - 74$

9) $20M - 84 = 27M - 14$

10) $19M + 47 = 23M + 1$

11) $-6K + 20 = -2.4K + 92$

12) $1.5A + 24 = .6A + 204$

13) $1.5N + 24 = 6N + 204$

14) $1.5S + -.15 = -.6S + .0075$

15) $1.5A + -.15 = -6A + .0075$

16) $10S + 4 = -14S + -4$

17) $25J - .20 = J + .28$

18) $3.4A + 17 = 1.7A + -34$

19) $8Y + 48 = 3Y + 99$

20) $12H + 31 = 3H - 77$

21) $1\frac{1}{4}A + 8 = \frac{1}{2}A - 7$

22) $2\frac{2}{3}W + 9 = 1\frac{4}{5}W - 17$

23) $5\frac{3}{8}K - 17 = 6K + 113$

24) $\frac{1}{2}S - \frac{4}{5} = \frac{2}{3}S + \frac{3}{8}$

25) $\frac{4}{9}M + 4 = \frac{1}{3}M + 4$

26) $15M + 2 = 10M + 4$

27) $2M + 31 = 5M + 20$

28) $8M + 9 = M + 9.91$

29) $15M - 24 = -7M + 9$

30) $30M + 17 = 18M + 107$

31) $.05Z - 34 = .2Z + 11$

32) $4.7Z + 65 = 2.3Z + 185$

33) $\frac{5}{8}X - 30 = \frac{3}{4}X + 14$

34) $1\frac{3}{5}X - 17 = .4X + 31$

35) $\frac{3}{8}X - 49 = .125X + 91$

36) $\frac{5}{12}X - \frac{3}{4} = \frac{1}{3}X + \frac{1}{4}$

37) $.6Z + 44 = .48Z + 8$

38) $1.8Z + 240 = Z + 16$

39) $45Z + .8 = 5Z + .88$

40) $18Z + .9 = 3Z + .3$

41) $75N + 46 = 78N + 44$

42) $34N + 95 = 40N + 90$

43) $52N + .26 = 13N - .13$

44) $4\frac{1}{4}X + 1\frac{1}{3} = 3\frac{3}{4}X + \frac{2}{3}$

45) $5\frac{1}{5}X + .09 = 5X + .085$

46) $200M + 3.5 = 20M + 3.32$

47) $54M - 4 = 50M - 8$

48) $35M + 50 = 3.5M - 13$

49) $.04N - 4 = .2N + .8$

50) $5B - .007 = -2B + 3.5$

EQUATIONS—SOLVE THE FOLLOWING

1) $M + 12 = 108$

2) $12M = 108$

3) $M - 12 = 108$

4) $\dfrac{M}{12} = 108$

5) $12M + 36 = 108$

6) $12M - 36 = 108$

7) $12M + 6M = 108$

8) $12M - 6M = 108$

9) $12M = 3M + 108$

10) $12M + 18 = 6M + 108$

11) $D + 40 = 71$

12) $3U + 2U = 65$

13) $\dfrac{K}{8} = 26$

14) $7E = E + 66$

15) $8B + 4 = 100$

16) $7L + 4 = 4L + 55$

17) $9U - 36 = 108$

18) $E - 715 = 4$

19) $24D = 120$

20) $8E + 7 = 3E + 112$

21) $\dfrac{V}{9} = 54$

22) $I + 29 = 141$

23) $4L + 9L = 182$

24) $S + 84 = 217$

25) $16N = 144$

26) $8T = T + 112$

27) $9B + 7B = 192$

28) $M + 43 = 91$

29) $9B - 7B = 192$

30) $9B - 7 = 191$

31) $8N = 128$

32) $4T = 2T + 268$

33) $6T + 1 = 2T + 93$

34) $M - 75 = 113$

35) $7R - 3 = 2R + 72$

36) $5B = 2B + 216$

37) $\dfrac{N}{17} = 17$

38) $7R - R = 84$

39) $5Z - 16 = 104$

40) $M + 37 = 97$

41) $6K + K = 84$

42) $6K + 1 = 85$

43) $9N = 342$

44) $10B - 2B = 112$

45) $21M = 11M + 340$

46) $3Z + 71 = 221$

47) $25B + 10B = 5B + 270$

48) $M - 21 = 19$

49) $12B + 5B = 85$

50) $28R + 1 = R + 82$

EQUATIONS—SOLVE THE FOLLOWING

1) $M + 9 = 5$

2) $9M = 126$

3) $M + \frac{3}{4} = 17$

4) $-\frac{3}{4}M = 18$

5) $7M + 3 = -53$

6) $-\frac{1}{2}M - 9 = 27$

7) $8M + 4M = 20$

8) $7M - 15M = .72$

9) $6M - .42 = 3M + 18$

10) $10M + 14 = 12M + 93$

11) $\dfrac{L}{15} = -20$

12) $S + 3.5 = 8$

13) $9U + 4U = -65$

14) $9B + 4 = 67$

15) $9E - 4E = -65$

16) $9N + 4 = 13N + 48.2$

17) $G - 4.5 = .68$

18) $3.4A = 510$

19) $8L - .6 = 5L + .012$

20) $5T = T + .052$

21) $8I + I = -.216$

22) $8G - 8 = G + .4$

23) $E + 8.31 = 4$

24) $-.06R + 5 = 23$

25) $14S = .021$

26) $9M - 4 = 2M + 80$

27) $9M - 4 = -2M + 84$

28) $3T + -8T = 24$

29) $14T = 2T + -8$

30) $\frac{5}{8}B = -\frac{3}{4}$

31) $B + \frac{5}{8} = -\frac{3}{4}$

32) $6R = 9R + 414$

33) $9R + 9R = -12$

34) $9M + \frac{1}{4} = 8\frac{1}{2}M + \frac{2}{3}$

35) $6M = -9M + 3000$

36) $25Z + 1 = 16$

37) $24Z - 48Z = .72$

38) $.0005K = -34$

39) $K + .0005 = 4$

40) $8K - 26 = 9\frac{1}{2}K + 25$

41) $45E - .225 = 0$

42) $27E - .78 = E$

43) $4B + 3B - 9 = .142$

44) $4B + 3B - 9B = .142$

45) $6M + 3 = 4M + 1$

46) $6M + 3 = 4M + M$

47) $30K + 4 = 28 + 12K$

48) $3K = .03 + 7K$

49) $1\frac{3}{5}N + 9 = .8N + 9.3$

50) $4.7N + 34 = 5\frac{1}{4}N + 144$

EQUATIONS—SOLVE THE FOLLOWING

1) $5(2M - 5) = 35$

2) $3(M - 4) = 27$

3) $8(2M - 7) = 24$

4) $9(3M - 4) = 0$

5) $6(7M - 5) = 54$

6) $4(M + 7) = 8$

7) $7(2M + 9) = 7$

8) $2(5M + 7) = -126$

9) $8(M + 5) = 0$

10) $5(3M + 32) = 10$

11) $-4(M - 7) = 80$

12) $-4(-M - 7) = 80$

13) $4(M - 7) = 80$

14) $4(-M - 7) = 80$

15) $-7(3I + 8) = 28$

16) $8(5A + 15) = -200$

17) $-2(M + 9) = 47$

18) $-3(I + 4) = -57$

19) $6(2H - 13) = 0$

20) $4(5U + 1) = 84$

21) $-12(3R - 1) = 0$

22) $-15(5R - 1) = 0$

23) $7(2I + 9) = 42$

24) $9(4G + 15) = 32$

25) $-10(A + 9) = 125$

26) $\frac{1}{2}(6N + 8) = 55$

27) $\frac{3}{4}(8E + 12) = 0$

28) $-\frac{5}{8}(16S + 120) = 90$

29) $-\frac{5}{6}(12M + 42) = 90$

30) $\frac{2}{3}(3M - 21) = 124$

31) $.8(5M - 3) = 0$

32) $.08(5M - 3) = 0$

33) $.25(2M + 5) = -75$

34) $.5(3M + 8) = -124$

35) $-.75(8M - 1) = .3$

36) $7(2M + 3) = 5(4M - 3)$

37) $4(6M - 7) = 5(4M - 5)$

38) $8(7M + 1) = 9(6M - 1)$

39) $-5(2M + 5) = 3(4M - 1)$

40) $9(8M + 3) = 16(3M + 2)$

41) $3(3N - 4) = 4(2N - 15)$

42) $4(3N - 5) = .5(4N - 35)$

43) $8(-5N - 1) = 2(4N + 5)$

44) $-6(-3N + 4) = 5(3N + .15)$

45) $\frac{1}{2}(4N + 5) = .3(5N - 12)$

46) $6(3N - 5) + -4(4N + 7) = 0$

47) $8(5N + 4) + 2(5N + 59) = 0$

48) $7(2N - 3) + 3(4N - 5) = 42$

49) $9(2N + 5) + -6(3N + 7) + 4N = -.6$

50) $3N + -5(2N + 7) + 4(3N + 5) = 136$

EQUATIONS—SOLVE THE FOLLOWING

1) $3M - M = 50$

2) $9 + M = 4$

3) $15M = 3M + 2M + 70$

4) $4(3M - 1) = 80$

5) $48 = 3M - 8M$

6) $9M + 3 = 2 + M$

7) $6M + 5 = M$

8) $7(2M + 3) = 4(3M - 8)$

9) $48 - M = 4M + -7$

10) $9M + 3 + 2M - 4 + M = 83$

11) $6T - 4 = T + 31$

12) $6E + 4 = E - 31$

13) $6X - 4 = 31 - X$

14) $\frac{3}{4}A = \frac{1}{3}A - .65$

15) $\frac{4}{5}S = -.32$

16) $L + \frac{4}{5} = -.32$

17) $\frac{5}{8}Q = 3\frac{3}{4}$

18) $\frac{2}{3}N + 1\frac{3}{4}N = N + -51$

19) $-8(3G - 4) = -64$

20) $45 - H = 3H + 45.03$

21) $Q + \frac{7}{8} = .8$

22) $5R + 3 + 8R + 5 - 6R = 8.91$

23) $12N = 3(N - 15)$

24) $S + 4.7 = 3\frac{4}{5}$

25) $24 = M + .6 + 8M$

26) $.7M + .7 = .7$

27) $5(M + 8) = 335$

28) $6(N + 4) = 3(N - 2) + 51$

29) $\frac{1}{2}(12M + 7) = -.112$

30) $6(N - 3) = 54$

31) $20N + 7 = 12N$

32) $25 - 3T = 4(2T - 5) - 8T$

33) $T + 1.3 = 3\frac{1}{8}$

34) $1\frac{1}{3}T = -.112$

35) $6T - 5 - 5T = 7 - 3T$

36) $6W = W - .03$

37) $8Z = 8.005Z + 600$

38) $X + X + X + X + X + X = 1$

39) $25R - R = .06$

40) $25R - 1 = .06$

41) $30 + -8B = 0$

42) $0 = 45 - 3B$

43) $4(3F - 5) - 12F = 2(2F + 5)$

44) $4R - 5 = R$

45) $\frac{3}{4}R + 8 = \frac{2}{3}R - 37$

46) $.8R + 1 = .08R + 1.54$

47) $\frac{2}{3}(48 - B) = 0$

48) $6T - 9 = 4T - 2T$

49) $4(3B + \frac{1}{2}) = 2(5B + 4) + 46$

50) $5(2B + 3) + -4(3B + 1) = 19.01$

INEQUALITIES—SOLVE THE FOLLOWING

1) $M + 8 > 40$

2) $M - 8 < 40$

3) $8M > 40$

4) $\dfrac{M}{8} < 40$

5) $M + 8 \geq 40$

6) $M - 8 \leq 40$

7) $8M \geq 40$

8) $\dfrac{M}{8} \leq 40$

9) $M + 17 \geq 31$

10) $M + 17 > 31$

11) $9P \leq 72$

12) $I + 9 \leq 72$

13) $T - 42 \geq 20$

14) $\dfrac{T}{5} < 41$

15) $S + 21 > 21$

16) $B + 21 \geq 21$

17) $13U > 91$

18) $13R \leq 91$

19) $\dfrac{G}{13} > 91$

20) $H + 13 \leq 91$

21) $P - 13 \geq 91$

22) $A - 28 > 5$

23) $N + 28 \leq 31$

24) $T + 91 \geq 101$

25) $H - 9 < 47$

26) $8E \geq 56$

27) $8R > 56$

28) $S + 8 < 56$

29) $M + 7 > 11$

30) $7M \geq 28$

31) $M + 43 < 45$

32) $N - 43 \leq 45$

33) $N - 51 > 37$

34) $N + 29 \geq 41$

35) $8N \leq 144$

36) $9N \geq 144$

37) $16N \geq 144$

38) $24N < 144$

39) $36N \leq 144$

40) $48N < 144$

41) $M - 9 \geq 24$

42) $M - 35 > 4$

43) $4M \leq 92$

44) $7M \leq 35$

45) $9M < 45$

46) $M - 9 < 45$

47) $M + 9 < 45$

48) $35M > 105$

49) $8M \geq 2000$

50) $4M < 1,000,000$

INEQUALITIES—SOLVE THE FOLLOWING

1) $N + 8 > 5$

2) $N - 8 \geq 5$

3) $N + 8 \leq -5$

4) $N - 8 \leq -5$

5) $8N \geq 48$

6) $8N > -48$

7) $-8N > 48$

8) $-8N \geq -48$

9) $N + 3 < 3$

10) $N + 25 \leq 22$

11) $6M \geq 42$

12) $-6M \geq 42$

13) $9M < 54$

14) $9M < -54$

15) $-9M < 54$

16) $-9M < -54$

17) $N + 45 > 60$

18) $N + 34 \geq 25$

19) $N + 17 \leq -4$

20) $N - 17 \leq -4$

21) $\frac{3}{4}N \geq -6$

22) $-\frac{3}{4}N \geq -6$

23) $N + \frac{3}{4} \geq -6$

24) $N - \frac{3}{4} \geq -6$

25) $N + \frac{5}{8} < 1\frac{1}{3}$

26) $M + .7 < 3$

27) $I + 7 < 3$

28) $S + .07 < 3$

29) $S - 3.4 \geq 15.23$

30) $7I > 3.5$

31) $.7S \geq 35$

32) $-.7S \geq 35$

33) $-7I \geq .35$

34) $.003P < -57$

35) $P + .003 > 2.4$

36) $I + 28 \geq 3.71$

37) $R + \frac{2}{5} \geq 1\frac{1}{3}$

38) $E - 1\frac{1}{5} < 1\frac{1}{4}$

39) $B + 4 \leq 3\frac{3}{25}$

40) $\frac{4}{5}E \geq \frac{5}{9}$

41) $-\frac{7}{3}L \leq 1\frac{1}{6}$

42) $\frac{5}{6}S \geq -\frac{2}{3}$

43) $\frac{4}{5}X \leq 1.6$

44) $-\frac{3}{5}Z < 246$

45) $Y + 1\frac{7}{8} < 3.1$

46) $M - 2.53 > 4\frac{1}{5}$

47) $R + 24.3 \leq 24\frac{3}{5}$

48) $T - 1\frac{7}{10} > 3.3$

49) $-6B \leq 20$

50) $7B > -33$

INEQUALITIES—SOLVE THE FOLLOWING

1) $9M + 3 > 57$

2) $6M - 5 < 19$

3) $2M + 13 \geq 31$

4) $3M - 4 \leq 11$

5) $4M - 1 > 7$

6) $5M + 3 < 13$

7) $7M + 1 \geq 1$

8) $8M + 6 \geq 22$

9) $10M - 1 \leq 19$

10) $12M - 4 < 20$

11) $3S + 25 < 28$

12) $5M + 3 > 18$

13) $4U - 17 > 3$

14) $2M - 91 < 3$

15) $13U - 14 \leq 77$

16) $8S + 9 \geq 33$

17) $5T - 81 \geq 44$

18) $2A - 1 \leq 1$

19) $14N + 19 > 61$

20) $15G + 7 < 37$

21) $7S - 1 \geq 104$

22) $9N + 17 \geq 17$

23) $14N + 30 < 114$

24) $4N + 27 < 35$

25) $18N + 31 \geq 175$

26) $36N - 35 \leq 109$

27) $9N + 17 > 161$

28) $3N - 27 < 117$

29) $16N - 77 \leq 67$

30) $4N + 87 \geq 231$

31) $48N - 33 > 111$

32) $6N + 133 \geq 277$

33) $2N - 56 \leq 88$

34) $3N + 18 < 69$

35) $19N + 7 \leq 83$

36) $18M - 4 > 68$

37) $17M - 33 > 18$

38) $23T - 36 < 56$

39) $25R + 17 < 242$

40) $19B - 41 \geq 54$

41) $28B - 3 \geq 137$

42) $30C - 57 \leq 123$

43) $35C + 3 \leq 108$

44) $45R - 3 > 132$

45) $75R - 49 > 101$

46) $64A + 39 < 295$

47) $60A + 240 < 540$

48) $32B - 128 \geq 128$

49) $55B - 165 \geq 550$

50) $3T - 342 \leq 711$

INEQUALITIES—SOLVE THE FOLLOWING

1) $3N + 1 > -5$

2) $3N + 1 \geq -5$

3) $5N - 4 \leq 16$

4) $8N + 1 < -15$

5) $7N + 3 \geq 24$

6) $9N + 4 < -77$

7) $6N + 5 \leq -49$

8) $4N + 8 \geq -84$

9) $2N + 3 < 17$

10) $5N - 17 > 68$

11) $-4M + 1 \leq 73$

12) $-2M + 9 \geq -33$

13) $2M + 9 \geq -33$

14) $-\frac{1}{2}M + 1 < 4$

15) $-\frac{3}{5}M + 5 \leq 23$

16) $.7M + 14 < 35$

17) $-.03M + 1 < 1.6$

18) $-6M - 3 \geq 3$

19) $4M + 27 \leq -25$

20) $5M - 2 \leq 1.6$

21) $-7M + 1.4 > 7$

22) $-9R + 3 \leq 3.18$

23) $.003R + 1 > 7$

24) $\frac{4}{5}R + 7 \geq -9$

25) $8R + 5 \leq 5.12$

26) $6R - 4.5 \geq 4\frac{1}{2}$

27) $\frac{3}{4}R + 6 < 33$

28) $1.2R - 18 \geq .6$

29) $25R - \frac{3}{4} \leq -.5$

30) $-.8R + 12 < 108$

31) $.8R + 12 < 108$

32) $15 > 3T - 9$

33) $.24 < -6T + .36$

34) $.18 \geq -24T + -48$

35) $6 \leq -\frac{1}{5}T + 9$

36) $12 \geq \frac{4}{5}T - 36$

37) $12 > .8T - 36$

38) $3.6 < 2T + 3\frac{3}{5}$

39) $1\frac{7}{8} \leq 9T + 1.875$

40) $41 > .004T + 17$

41) $6B \geq -.15$

42) $B + 6 \geq -.15$

43) $\frac{1}{6}B \leq -.15$

44) $B + \frac{1}{5} < -.15$

45) $5A - 3 > 57$

46) $6A + 19 \geq 79$

47) $15A - 13\frac{1}{2} < 46.5$

48) $12A + 14.375 \leq 74\frac{3}{8}$

49) $8A - 17\frac{7}{8} < 42.125$

50) $-\frac{3}{5}A - 51.48 \geq 8\frac{13}{25}$

INEQUALITIES—SOLVE THE FOLLOWING

1) $N + 3 > 12$

2) $3N < 12$

3) $-3N \leq 12$

4) $N - 3 \geq 12$

5) $4N + 5 > 13$

6) $-4N + 5 > 13$

7) $5N - 7 \leq 17$

8) $-5N - 7 \leq 17$

9) $8N + 3 \geq 35$

10) $-8N + 5 < 25$

11) $6N + 4 > 19$

12) $L + 9 > 5$

13) $\frac{1}{2}S - 4 < -3$

14) $-4U \leq 52$

15) $T + 3 < 3$

16) $I - 4 > 4$

17) $\frac{3}{4}G \geq 12$

18) $4E - 3 < -4$

19) $-7R + 9 \geq 100$

20) $S + 14 \geq 14$

21) $9M > 57$

22) $-9M > 57$

23) $3N + .5 < 16.1$

24) $.4N \geq -2$

25) $N + .4 \geq -2$

26) $-.4N \geq -2$

27) $N - .4 \geq -2$

28) $12N + 43 < 40$

29) $-13N - 20 \geq 32$

30) $9N - 18 \geq .27$

31) $25N - 6 \leq -6.15$

32) $.005N \leq -3$

33) $N - .005 \leq -3$

34) $\frac{3}{5}R > 1\frac{1}{3}$

35) $\frac{3}{4}R \leq -39$

36) $T + \frac{3}{5} \geq 1\frac{1}{3}$

37) $T + \frac{3}{4} < 39$

38) $\frac{1}{5}B - .4 \leq 3.15$

39) $5B - .4 \leq 3.15$

40) $6A + 7 \geq 3$

41) $9A - 5 \leq 7$

42) $-.004Z + .2 \leq .12$

43) $-\frac{3}{5}Z > 1\frac{2}{3}$

44) $-4\frac{5}{6}T < 5\frac{4}{5}$

45) $400L + .4 < .28$

46) $-50L + .3 \geq .05$

47) $.003Y + 1 \leq .043$

48) $.004Y + 30 \geq -62$

49) $-34T + 20 \leq 20.51$

50) $16T + 7\frac{3}{8} < 7.375$

INEQUALITIES—SOLVE THE FOLLOWING

1) $5N + 3N > 24$

2) $5N - 3N > 24$

3) $6N + 7N < 39$

4) $9N - N < 16$

5) $9N + N \geq 30$

6) $20N - 8N \leq 72$

7) $15N + 6N < 84$

8) $30N - 9N > 105$

9) $24N + 6N \leq 150$

10) $7N + 4N \geq 33$

11) $7M > M + 42$

12) $9M \leq 3M + 42$

13) $20M \geq 6M + 42$

14) $17M < 14M + 42$

15) $9M < 2M + 42$

16) $3M \leq M + 86$

17) $9M > 2M + 182$

18) $7M \geq 4M + 213$

19) $9M < 4M + 75$

20) $12M \leq 5M + 112$

21) $4R - 3 > R + 18$

22) $9R + 7 < 2R + 84$

23) $12R + 9 \geq 5R + 100$

24) $13R - 8 \leq 10R + 43$

25) $19R - 14 > 7R + 70$

26) $12R - 15 < 9R + 123$

27) $17R + 25 \leq 8R + 169$

28) $40R + 17 \geq 35R + 112$

29) $17R - 19 > 9R + 93$

30) $30R + 1 < R + 59$

31) $9T - T \geq 96$

32) $15M + 6M \geq 84$

33) $14M - 8M < 84$

34) $10B < 2B + 56$

35) $14A \leq 3A + 143$

36) $9T > 4T + 135$

37) $6Z + 3 \leq Z + 38$

38) $14Z - 1 > 5Z + 35$

39) $4Z - 15 \geq 2Z + 133$

40) $12L + 13L > 325$

41) $9N - 5 \geq 4N + 95$

42) $6M < 3M + 57$

43) $5R + 14R > 95$

44) $24T \geq T + 92$

45) $14W - W < 2W + 33$

46) $9Y > 5Y + 104$

47) $15R < 13R + 96$

48) $30R + 25 \leq 13R + 127$

49) $25Z \geq 21Z + 148$

50) $14R + 6R \leq 14R + 102$

INEQUALITIES—SOLVE THE FOLLOWING

1) $3L + 4L > 91$

2) $5L - 2L \geq 51$

3) $6A - A \leq 45$

4) $8A + A \geq 117$

5) $4T - 9T < 30$

6) $6T - 13T > 105$

7) $9H \leq 2H - 56$

8) $6H < 3H + 57$

9) $7C > C - 72$

10) $5C \geq 9C + 56$

11) $A < 3A + 44$

12) $5A \leq 8A + 51$

13) $6R + 1 \geq 2R - 51$

14) $5R + 3 < R - 89$

15) $4T - 35 \leq 9T + 35$

16) $T + 1 > 3T - 71$

17) $9E + 17 \leq 119 - 8E$

18) $6E - 45 < 135 - 3E$

19) $5R - \frac{1}{2}R \geq 45$

20) $R - \frac{3}{5}R \leq -12$

21) $6W + 2 > 2W + 1$

22) $1.8W + 3 > -.6$

23) $.9E \leq 1\frac{1}{2}E + .54$

24) $12E - 3 > E + 52$

25) $5C + 4 \geq -6C + 26$

26) $2C \leq 5C + -.51$

27) $8A - 7.3A \geq 91$

28) $5A + 1 < 5.4A + 2$

29) $\frac{1}{2}N + .8N > -52$

30) $\frac{3}{4}N - .9N \leq 120$

31) $-4H - H > 1.4$

32) $9H - 7\frac{1}{2}H < -42$

33) $4A \leq 4.1A + 31$

34) $.9A < \frac{1}{2}A - 36$

35) $5N + N \geq -48$

36) $5N - N \leq -48$

37) $\frac{1}{2}D > 2D + 45$

38) $\frac{3}{4}D \geq D + -5$

39) $6L - 3 \leq 3L$

40) $14L + 30 < 8L$

41) $1\frac{1}{2}E + 1 \geq \frac{3}{4}E + 55$

42) $4E - 7 \leq 6E + 1$

43) $\frac{2}{3}I > \frac{1}{5}I + 91$

44) $.6I \leq \frac{1}{2}I - 24$

45) $9T - T + 3T > -143$

46) $6T - 4T - 7T \leq 1.5$

47) $8W + 3 > 2W - 4W$

48) $6W > 2W - 144 + -5W$

49) $2W + .7 \leq 5W + 8.8$

50) $\frac{3}{4}W + \frac{2}{5}W - \frac{1}{8}W < W + .46$

INEQUALITIES—SOLVE THE FOLLOWING

1) $10N - 3 \geq -37$

2) $8N \leq 1.6$

3) $N + 8 > 13$

4) $N - 8 \leq -2$

5) $7N + 3N < .4$

6) $6N + 2 \leq 3N + 7.1$

7) $6N > N + 3.5$

8) $-8N \leq 1.6$

9) $7N - 11N > 32$

10) $9N + 1 \geq 7.3$

11) $7N \leq 9N + 4.3$

12) $4N - 3 \geq 6N + 1$

13) $12N \geq 9N + 5.7$

14) $1.5N - N > .35$

15) $30N + 7 \geq 18N + 7.84$

16) $9N + 3 \geq 18$

17) $N + 7 < 5.3$

18) $14N > 15N + .8$

19) $12N + 7 > 5N$

20) $-8N \geq 5$

21) $9P \leq -3P + .72$

22) $\frac{3}{4}I - 6 > 9$

23) $-\frac{2}{5}T > -14$

24) $7T - T \geq 24.18$

25) $8S - 3 < 1.8$

26) $.03B + 9 \geq .9$

27) $6U + 17 < -9U + 14$

28) $4R + 3R - R < 24$

29) $\frac{3}{4}G + \frac{1}{2}G \geq .025$

30) $.03H > 15$

31) $P + .03 > 15$

32) $A < 4A + .087$

33) $5N + 4 \leq 8N + 10.9$

34) $4T - 3T > -.7$

35) $5H \geq H + .3$

36) $9E - 3 > 14E - 3.4$

37) $4R + 8 < 2R + 4.54$

38) $\frac{3}{5}S - 9 \geq 6$

39) $9M + 3 \leq 2$

40) $6M + 3 > M + 3.1$

41) $4(2M - 1) > 28$

42) $5(3N + 2) \leq -65$

43) $6(2R - 5) \geq 102$

44) $-8(R - 4) \leq 32.1$

45) $-9(2R + 3) < 7R + 23$

46) $7(R - 3) \leq 2R + 84$

47) $3(2M - 7) + 4M < 9$

48) $2(5M + 3) \geq 3(2M + 1) + 2$

49) $4(N - 1) \leq 0$

50) $5(3N - 7) > 10$

WORD PROBLEMS—
WRITE EACH EQUATION IN MATH SYMBOLS, THEN SOLVE IT.

1) Seven more than some number equals twenty-one.

2) Seven less than some number equals twenty-one.

3) Seven times some number equals 21.

4) Some number divided by seven equals twenty-one.

5) Twenty-four more than some number is forty-three.

6) Thirty-nine less than some number is twenty-one.

7) Five times some number is the same as fifty-five.

8) A certain number multiplied by eight equals ninety-six.

9) Five more than twice a number equals forty-three.

10) Seven less than three times some number is the same as twenty-nine.

11) Eight times a certain number increased by one equals 65.

12) Nine times some number decreased by 13 is ninety-five.

13) Seven times some number plus eight is the same as 99.

14) Six times some number plus three times the same number equals one hundred seventeen.

15) Five times some number decreased by two times the number is forty-two.

16) 7 times some number increased by 8 times the number equals 45.

17) Six times some number increased by the number itself equals 84.

18) Four times some number decreased by the number is eighty-seven.

19) Eight times some number equals 6 times the number plus 34.

20) Nine times some number is the same as 56 more than five times the number.

21) Four times some number equals twice the number increased by 104.

22) Three times some number equals seventy-eight more than the number itself.

23) 17 times some number is equal to 182 more than four times the number.

24) One more than six times some number equals two times the number plus 21.

25) Seven times some number increased by 17 equals three times the number increased by 109.

26) Eight less than fifteen times some number equals three times the number plus 76.

27) 34 less than a dozen times some number is equal to 36 more than five times the number.

28) Seventeen more than 21 times some number equals ten times the number plus 160.

29) 33 less than 14 times some number equals 5 times the number increased by 12.

30) Thirty-one more than five times a number is one hundred fifty-one.

31) Five times some number plus 3 times the number decreased by 2 times the number equals 54.

32) Fourteen times some number equals 57 more than 11 times the number.

33) Twenty-eight less than twelve times a number is the same as five times the number itself.

34) If you add one to eighteen times some number, you will get fifty-two more than the number itself.

35) 16 times some number equals 52 more than a dozen times the number decreased by 9 times the number.

WORD PROBLEMS—
CHANGE EACH TO MATH SENTENCES AND SOLVE.

1) Twenty-four more than some number is 31.

2) Eighteen added to some number equals 13.

3) Five less than some number is 27.

4) Some number decreased by 31 equals minus fifty-four.

5) 29 more than some number equals –18.

6) Fifteen less than a number equals –24.

7) Four times some number is the same as fifty-six.

8) Twice some number equals seventeen.

9) One third some number equals 14.

10) .5 times a number equals –75.

11) Three fourths of some number is equal to twelve.

12) ½ more than some number is 24.

13) Two thirds less than some number is the same as –17.

14) Eight more than some number equals zero.

15) Five less than three times some number equals –32.

16) Four times some number added to three is 31.

17) –7 times some number decreased by 6 equals 85.

18) One hundred forty more than twice a certain number equals 14.

19) Three fifths some number increased by twelve equals –15.

20) Five times some number added to four times the number is seventy-two.

21) Eight times a certain number increased by the number itself equals .513.

WORD PROBLEMS continued

22) Six times a certain number decreased by the number itself is the same as 85.

23) -5 times some number plus -7 times the number is equal to eighty-four.

24) 4 times some number decreased by seven times the same number is forty-eight.

25) Three fourths some number added to two thirds the number is fifty-one.

26) 8 times some number equals 147 more than the number itself.

27) Five times some number is the same as 42 more than twice the number.

28) Six times some number equals eight times the number increased by 66.

29) Four times some number equals seven times the number decreased by 42.

30) 7 more than 3 times a number equals 29 more than the number.

31) Five less than nine times a number equals four times the number added to 90.

32) 13 more than 8 times a number equals -92 increased by three times the number.

33) Thirteen less than eight times a number equals 97 decreased by three times the number.

34) A dozen times some number added to fifty-seven equals nine times the same number.

35) Four more than fourteen times some number decreased by five times the same number is the same as the number decreased by sixteen.

WORD PROBLEMS—
CHANGE EACH TO MATH SENTENCES AND SOLVE.

FIND THE NUMBER SUCH THAT:

1) Nine more than the number equals 54.

2) Nine less than the number equals 54.

3) Nine times the number equals 54.

4) A number divided by 9 equals 54.

5) -9 times the number equals 54.

6) Two thirds the number equals 54.

7) Two thirds more than the number equals 54.

8) Five less than four times some number equals 47.

9) 8 more than twice the number equals 82.

10) -5 times some number added to one equals 86.

11) One half some number decreased by 7 is the same as -18.

12) 44 more than .16 times the number equals twelve.

13) Four times some number plus three times the number equals 42.

14) Eight times some number decreased by three times the number equals -75.

15) Eight times a number increased by nine times the number is -51.

16) 20 times the number decreased by the number itself equals 95.

17) Three fifths the number added to five sixths the number equals -86.

18) Fourteen times a number is the same as 132 more than three times the number.

19) 5 times a number equals nine times the number plus 28.

20) Fifteen times a number equals the number decreased by 42.

21) Fifteen times a number equals 48 decreased by the number itself.

22) Three fifths a number is the same as twenty-five less than one half the number.

23) One less than eight times a number equals forty-one more than twice the number.

24) Three more than seven times a number equals 87 more than the number.

25) Twenty-one less than four times a number is the same as 54 plus 7 times the number.

26) 13 times a number added to 7 equals –5 times the number increased by 61.

27) Seven increased by eight times a number equals one half the number added to 52.

28) Four times a number increased by one is 85.

29) Four times a number increased by the number itself is 85.

30) Ten times a number equals –3 times the number added to 91.

31) Fourteen times the number is the same as five times the number plus twice the number added to 91.

32) Seven more than twenty-five times a number equals fifty-nine decreased by the number itself.

33) –17 times a number equals .14 more than 18 times the number.

34) Nine times a number added to ten times the number decreased by fourteen times the number is 3.1

35) Twice a number is the same as 153 more than 1.7 times the number.

WORD PROBLEMS—
CHANGE EACH TO MATH EQUATIONS AND SOLVE.

FIND THE NUMBER SUCH THAT:

1) Fifteen more than the number equals forty-five.

2) Fifteen less than the number equals 45.

3) 15 times the number equals 45.

4) One fifteenth the number equals 45.

5) Forty-five more than the number equals 15.

6) –8 times the number equals 32.

7) One half more than the number equals seven.

8) Twice the number is –24.

9) Three less than five times the number is forty-two.

10) One more than six times a number equals 43.

11) Five more than –3 times a number is fifty-six.

12) Seven times a number increased by 24 equals –67.

13) One half less than three times a number is 17.5.

14) Eight times a number decreased by four times the number equals 48.

15) Eight times a number increased by four times the number equals 48.

16) –8 times a number added to four times a number is 48.

17) .7 times a number plus 1.5 times the number is 176.

18) One half a number decreased by three fourths the number equals 13.

19) Four times a number is the same as 8 times the number added to 76.

20) Six times a number equals 41 more than seven times the number.

21) Five times a number equals twice the number decreased by 42.

22) Five times a number equals 42 decreased by twice the number.

23) 1.8 times a number is the same as three fifths the number added to 156.

24) Nine times a number added to three equals six less than eight times the number.

25) One more than a dozen times a number equals three less than four times the number.

26) Seven less than seven times a number is the same as negative five times the number plus 89.

27) Three fourths a number added to 15 equals one sixth the number decreased by 69.

28) Eight more than 3.5 times a number is the same as -28 added to three times the number.

29) Three times a number increased by eight times the number is equal to seven times the number decreased by .56.

30) Five times a number equals three times the number added to four times the number plus 8.

31) Six times the number plus one equals 49.

32) Six times the number plus the number itself equals 49.

33) If you add -7 times a number to -5 times the number, you will get .18 more than -15 times the number.

34) The number is the same as two sevenths times the number increased by 15.

35) 9.36 times a number equals 144 less than nine times the number.

REVIEW—ADD, SUBTRACT, MULTIPLY, OR DIVIDE THE FOLLOWING

1)   752
     916
  + 2043

2)   19
     37
  + 618

3)   2581
     307
  +   69

4)   5017
   − 4914

5)   39417
   − 8329

6)   7000
    − 858

7)   707
  ×   34

8)   509
  × 605

9)   218
  ×   83

10)   4⟌3256

11)   35⟌70105

12)   48⟌36096

13) 3.5 + 1.19 + .87

14) 4.2 + 918

15) 3 + 21.7 + .618

16) $7 + $3.71 + $45.19

17) 4.7 − .916

18) 21 − .79

19) 3 − .948

20) 48.71 − 19

21) $20 − $5.71

22)   24.9
   ×   5.8

23)   .63
   × .17

24) $9.19
   ×   .55

25) $47.91
   ×   .07

26)   32⟌.240

27)   .09⟌3114

28) .15⟌1.74

29) .008⟌7

30) 2.5⟌$753.44

31)   4²⁄₅
   + 1³⁄₄

32)   61¹⁄₃
   − 7¹⁄₅

33)   409⁵⁄₈
   +   71

34)   502
  − 497³⁄₅

35)   12⁵⁄₉
   − 7⁷⁄₁₂

36)   2¹¹⁄₁₂
   + 17⁷⁄₁₈

37)   8¹³⁄₁₆
  + 41¹¹⁄₁₂

38)   908¹⁷⁄₂₄
   − 149³⁵⁄₃₆

39) 4³⁄₈ × 1¹⁄₇ =

40) ⁹⁄₂₄ · ¹⁵⁄₃₀ =

41) 7½ ÷ 4½

42) ²⁴⁄₂₅ ÷ 8

43) 18 · ⅚ =

44) 10²⁄₃ ÷ 5⅓

45) ¹⁸⁄₂₇ ÷ 3³⁄₄ · 1¹⁄₁₅

46) 48 ÷ 1⅓ ÷ 6³⁄₄ =

47) ¹⁵⁄₄₅ × .8

48) 3¼ + .8 + ⅝

49) $360.54 · ⅔

50) ⅝ + 1.1 + .3 + 18.68

REVIEW—ADD, SUBTRACT, MULTIPLY, OR DIVIDE THE FOLLOWING

1)
$$
\begin{array}{r}
49 \\
386 \\
+\ 1075 \\
\hline
\end{array}
$$

2)
$$
\begin{array}{r}
823 \\
99 \\
+\ 654 \\
\hline
\end{array}
$$

3)
$$
\begin{array}{r}
7061 \\
258 \\
+\ 934 \\
\hline
\end{array}
$$

4)
$$
\begin{array}{r}
408 \\
-\ 39 \\
\hline
\end{array}
$$

5)
$$
\begin{array}{r}
1916 \\
-\ 907 \\
\hline
\end{array}
$$

6)
$$
\begin{array}{r}
3517 \\
-\ 1489 \\
\hline
\end{array}
$$

7)
$$
\begin{array}{r}
75 \\
\times\ 96 \\
\hline
\end{array}
$$

8)
$$
\begin{array}{r}
519 \\
\times\ 34 \\
\hline
\end{array}
$$

9)
$$
\begin{array}{r}
802 \\
\times\ 706 \\
\hline
\end{array}
$$

10) $8\overline{)12016}$

11) $19\overline{)38057}$

12) $14\overline{)7056}$

13) $8.5 + .67$

14) $98.1 - 7.34$

15) $452.18 + 8.9$

16) $94.7 - 8$

17) $94.7 - .8$

18) $6.1 + .94 + 33$

19) $431.618 + 9.7$

20) $\$20 - \$3.58$

21)
$$
\begin{array}{r}
34.6 \\
\times\ .8 \\
\hline
\end{array}
$$

22)
$$
\begin{array}{r}
59.7 \\
\times\ .052 \\
\hline
\end{array}
$$

23)
$$
\begin{array}{r}
.017 \\
\times\ .024 \\
\hline
\end{array}
$$

24)
$$
\begin{array}{r}
\$376.55 \\
\times\ .019 \\
\hline
\end{array}
$$

25) $12\overline{).10836}$

26) $.008\overline{)3}$

27) $.025\overline{).7}$

28) $32\overline{)\$64.22}$

29)
$$
\begin{array}{r}
2\frac{5}{8} \\
+\ 1\frac{2}{3} \\
\hline
\end{array}
$$

30)
$$
\begin{array}{r}
41\frac{3}{14} \\
+\ 9\frac{3}{4} \\
\hline
\end{array}
$$

31)
$$
\begin{array}{r}
\frac{5}{6} \\
\frac{3}{4} \\
+\ \frac{7}{12} \\
\hline
\end{array}
$$

32)
$$
\begin{array}{r}
35\frac{7}{18} \\
+\ 9\frac{7}{15} \\
\hline
\end{array}
$$

33)
$$
\begin{array}{r}
\frac{9}{10} \\
-\ \frac{3}{4} \\
\hline
\end{array}
$$

34)
$$
\begin{array}{r}
4\frac{5}{8} \\
-\ 1\frac{2}{5} \\
\hline
\end{array}
$$

35)
$$
\begin{array}{r}
30\frac{5}{6} \\
-\ 7\frac{8}{9} \\
\hline
\end{array}
$$

36)
$$
\begin{array}{r}
431 \\
-\ 28\frac{3}{5} \\
\hline
\end{array}
$$

37) $\frac{9}{10} \times \frac{5}{18}$

38) $3\frac{1}{3} \cdot 6$

39) $3\frac{5}{9} \cdot \frac{27}{48}$

40) $\frac{35}{49} \times 1\frac{2}{5} \times \frac{5}{8}$

41) $\frac{4}{7} \div \frac{4}{8}$

42) $5\frac{1}{3} \div 8$

43) $4\frac{1}{5} \div \frac{7}{8} \div 4\frac{4}{5}$

44) $\frac{4}{5} \times \frac{9}{10} \div 1\frac{11}{25}$

45) $\frac{3}{4} + \frac{5}{8} + .35$

46) $\frac{9}{10} \cdot \frac{3}{9} + \frac{2}{3}$

47) $15 - 3\frac{2}{5} - 5.17$

48) $\frac{3}{8} \times \$641.31$

49) $\$35.75 \div 1\frac{1}{4}$

50) $\frac{7}{10} + 1.7 + 62.38$

REVIEW—ADD, SUBTRACT, MULTIPLY, OR DIVIDE THE FOLLOWING

1)
```
   583
    74
+  926
```

2)
```
   408
   567
+  823
```

3)
```
   814
  5273
+   52
```

4)
```
  9218
-  649
```

5)
```
  6403
-  984
```

6)
```
  70,004
 -23,853
```

7)
```
    94
×   57
```

8)
```
   349
×   82
```

9)
```
   752
×  908
```

10) $6\overline{)8316}$

11) $47\overline{)1269}$

12) $18\overline{)71,136}$

13) $12.4 + .09 + 6.43$

14) $.65 + 1.8 + 4$

15) $.824 + .73 + 5.8$

16) $\$9.18 + \$.41 + \$9$

17) $77.14 - 8.6$

18) $43.6 - 7.58$

19) $76 - 14.71$

20) $\$24.14 - \$18.72$

21)
```
   7.94
×  8.6
```

22)
```
   4.07
× .085
```

23)
```
    .84
×   .96
```

24)
```
  $73.42
×    7.9
```

25) $9\overline{).4536}$

26) $1.6\overline{)32.08}$

27) $.007\overline{)149.1}$

28) $4.5\overline{)\$16.20}$

29)
```
   ³⁄₁₄
+  ⁷⁄₁₂
```

30)
```
   ¹¹⁄₁₅
+   ⁸⁄₉
```

31)
```
   7¹³⁄₁₈
+  4⁷⁄₁₀
```

32)
```
   15³⁄₅
   24⁵⁄₆
+   8⁷⁄₃₀
```

33)
```
   ¹⁹⁄₂₄
-   ⁷⁄₁₅
```

34)
```
   ³³⁄₄₀
-   ⁵⁄₁₆
```

35)
```
   15⁸⁄₂₁
-  6¹³⁄₁₄
```

36)
```
   18¹⁴⁄₂₇
-   9¹³⁄₁₈
```

37) $\frac{24}{35} \times \frac{50}{56}$

38) $\frac{21}{40} \times \frac{25}{30}$

39) $4\frac{1}{5} \times 5\frac{1}{3}$

40) $8\frac{2}{5} \times 3\frac{4}{5} \times 4\frac{1}{8}$

41) $\frac{21}{25} \div \frac{24}{35}$

42) $\frac{15}{26} \div \frac{40}{48}$

43) $7\frac{1}{5} \div 4\frac{2}{15}$

44) $8\frac{4}{7} \div 3\frac{3}{14} \div 6$

45) $16.8 \times 3\frac{1}{8}$

46) $7\frac{3}{5} \times .125$

47) $17.9 - 4\frac{1}{4}$

48) $8.8 \div \frac{1}{8}$

49) $5.28 + \frac{3}{5} + 6.7$

50) $8.4 \times \frac{3}{8} \times \frac{12}{15}$

REVIEW—ADD, SUBTRACT, MULTIPLY, OR DIVIDE THE FOLLOWING

1)
$$\begin{array}{r} 97 \\ 426 \\ + \ 508 \\ \hline \end{array}$$

2)
$$\begin{array}{r} 784 \\ 379 \\ + \ 521 \\ \hline \end{array}$$

3)
$$\begin{array}{r} 534 \\ 6781 \\ + \ 97 \\ \hline \end{array}$$

4)
$$\begin{array}{r} 8047 \\ - \ 568 \\ \hline \end{array}$$

5)
$$\begin{array}{r} 7943 \\ - \ 384 \\ \hline \end{array}$$

6)
$$\begin{array}{r} 90909 \\ - \ 2381 \\ \hline \end{array}$$

7)
$$\begin{array}{r} 68 \\ \times \ 59 \\ \hline \end{array}$$

8)
$$\begin{array}{r} 893 \\ \times \ 46 \\ \hline \end{array}$$

9)
$$\begin{array}{r} 608 \\ \times \ 473 \\ \hline \end{array}$$

10) $7 \overline{)6{,}549}$ 11) $24 \overline{)83{,}121}$ 12) $37 \overline{)46{,}107}$

13) $5.8 + .04 + 9.15$ 14) $.84 + 4.17$ 15) $.046 + 1.7 + .69$

16) $\$5.38 + \$13 + \$6.14$ 17) $90.83 - 5.9$ 18) $63.7 - 5.47$

19) $48 - 17.42$ 20) $\$18 - \$4.36$

21)
$$\begin{array}{r} 8.43 \\ \times \ 5.8 \\ \hline \end{array}$$

22)
$$\begin{array}{r} 6.08 \\ \times \ .072 \\ \hline \end{array}$$

23)
$$\begin{array}{r} .87 \\ \times \ .53 \\ \hline \end{array}$$

24)
$$\begin{array}{r} \$58.17 \\ \times \ 3.6 \\ \hline \end{array}$$

25) $5 \overline{).0435}$ 26) $2.5 \overline{)4.72}$ 27) $.004 \overline{)624}$

28) $4.8 \overline{)\$44.88}$

29)
$$\begin{array}{r} \tfrac{5}{8} \\ + \ \tfrac{5}{6} \\ \hline \end{array}$$

30)
$$\begin{array}{r} \tfrac{7}{12} \\ + \ \tfrac{9}{10} \\ \hline \end{array}$$

31)
$$\begin{array}{r} 9\tfrac{4}{15} \\ + \ 3\tfrac{11}{12} \\ \hline \end{array}$$

32)
$$\begin{array}{r} 18\tfrac{4}{9} \\ 12\tfrac{3}{8} \\ + \ 8\tfrac{1}{6} \\ \hline \end{array}$$

33)
$$\begin{array}{r} \tfrac{16}{25} \\ - \ \tfrac{7}{20} \\ \hline \end{array}$$

34)
$$\begin{array}{r} \tfrac{9}{16} \\ - \ \tfrac{3}{14} \\ \hline \end{array}$$

35)
$$\begin{array}{r} 8\tfrac{9}{40} \\ - \ 5\tfrac{11}{30} \\ \hline \end{array}$$

36)
$$\begin{array}{r} 12\tfrac{5}{27} \\ - \ \tfrac{5}{9} \\ \hline \end{array}$$

37) $\tfrac{18}{28} \times \tfrac{36}{45}$ 38) $\tfrac{30}{52} \times \tfrac{14}{35}$ 39) $8\tfrac{2}{5} \times 4\tfrac{2}{7}$

40) $3\tfrac{1}{8} \times 2\tfrac{2}{3} \times 5\tfrac{3}{5}$ 41) $\tfrac{13}{14} \div \tfrac{11}{35}$ 42) $\tfrac{24}{30} \div \tfrac{36}{45}$

43) $6\tfrac{2}{5} \div 4\tfrac{4}{15}$ 44) $5\tfrac{1}{4} \div \tfrac{15}{16} \div \tfrac{3}{8}$ 45) $14.4 \times 2\tfrac{1}{2}$

46 $5\tfrac{1}{8} \times .75$ 47) $46.8 - 2\tfrac{1}{5}$ 48) $6.4 \div \tfrac{4}{5}$

49) $3.6 + \tfrac{1}{4} + 5.37$ 50) $2.3 \times \tfrac{3}{4} \times 2\tfrac{2}{3}$

REVIEW—ADD, SUBTRACT, MULTIPLY, OR DIVIDE THE FOLLOWING

1)
```
   296
   483
+  295
```
2)
```
   6483
    298
+  2586
```
3)
```
   20514
    1864
+ 70839
```

4)
```
  285
-  46
```
5)
```
  7064
-  895
```
6)
```
  40638
- 15643
```

7)
```
    48
×   65
```
8)
```
    843
×    79
```
9)
```
    783
×   486
```

10) $7\overline{)986}$ 11) $75\overline{)9860}$ 12) $419\overline{)79648}$

13) $1.6 + 4.84 + .835$ 14) $.064 + 9.3 + 28$ 15) $16.45 + .986 + 6.2483$

16) $\$2.95 + \$24.00 + \$.48$ 17) $6.34 - .58$ 18) $9.3 - .4965$

19) $17 - 9.86$ 20) $\$17.48 - \$12.84$

21)
```
    .64
×   .09
```
22)
```
    8.6
×   .48
```
23)
```
    .148
×   .057
```
24)
```
   $2.86
×   9.3
```

25) $16\overline{)2.844}$ 26) $.5\overline{)9.84}$ 27) $.24\overline{)7.296}$

28) $18\overline{)\$9.72}$

29)
```
   2/3
+  4/5
```
30)
```
   5/8
+  5/6
```
31)
```
   4 7/12
+  8 9/15
```
32)
```
    4 8/9
    6 5/6
+  14 7/12
```

33)
```
   8/9
-  4/5
```
34)
```
   7/12
-  1/8
```
35)
```
   2 5/14
-  1 1/6
```
36)
```
   7 4/15
-  4 9/10
```

37) $8/10 \times 15/16$ 38) $15/28 \times 21/35$ 39) $4\,3/5 \times 1\,3/7$

40) $2\frac{1}{2} \times 4\frac{1}{5} \times 3\frac{2}{7}$ 41) $2/3 \div 5/6$ 42) $7/8 \div 9/10$

43) $6\frac{1}{5} \div 2\frac{2}{3}$ 44) $7\frac{1}{8} \div 1\frac{3}{16}$ 45) $6.8 \times 3/4$

46) $8\frac{2}{5} \times .25$ 47) $2\frac{1}{2} \times 6\frac{3}{4} \div 10$ 48) $\$87.64 \times 1.8$

49) $18/30 + 4.5 + .16$ 50) $14\,2/10 - 13.7 + 13/20$

- 183 -

REVIEW—ADD, SUBTRACT, MULTIPLY, OR DIVIDE THE FOLLOWING

1) $295 + 48 + 653$

2) $785 + 483 + 980$

3) $2943 + 853 + 29$

4) $7430 - 458$

5) $6148 - 2953$

6) $71053 - 8956$

7) 58×76

8) 943×82

9) 716×984

10) $856 \div 9$

11) $2864 \div 14$

12) $21864 \div 753$

13) $4.6 + 8.9 + 7.8$

14) $29 + 8.6 + 2.143$

15) $.056 + 9.8 + 15.215$

16) $\$7.15 + \$8.29 + \$19.64$

17) $4.21 - .46$

18) $7.8 - 2.856$

19) $15 - 9.64$

20) $\$18.25 - \$6.75$

21) 2.84×6.8

22) $46.3 \times .075$

23) $.068 \times 3.21$

24) $\$12.84 \times 58$

25) $1.446 \div 12$

26) $3.33 \div 4.5$

27) $645 \div .04$

28) $\$284.97 \div 7$

29) $\frac{3}{5} + \frac{5}{9}$

30) $\frac{2}{7} + \frac{5}{8}$

31) $5\frac{7}{12} + 3\frac{4}{9}$

32) $3\frac{1}{2} + 4\frac{2}{7} + 6\frac{3}{4}$

33) $\frac{9}{11} - \frac{3}{7}$

34) $\frac{5}{8} - \frac{1}{3}$

35) $3\frac{5}{6} - 1\frac{2}{13}$

36) $4\frac{6}{15} - 1\frac{9}{10}$

37) $\frac{8}{9} \times \frac{12}{18}$

38) $\frac{17}{50} \times \frac{35}{34}$

39) $2\frac{1}{2} \times 4\frac{3}{10}$

40) $6\frac{2}{3} \times 2\frac{3}{4} \times 5$

41) $\frac{3}{8} \div \frac{5}{6}$

42) $\frac{3}{14} \div 27$

43) $3\frac{1}{3} \div 1\frac{1}{9}$

44) $\frac{2}{3} \div 2\frac{5}{6} \div 1\frac{1}{2}$

45) $\frac{5}{7} \times .3$

46) $3.25 + 4\frac{1}{5}$

47) $2\frac{6}{7} \times 14 \div 5\frac{1}{2}$

48) $\$64.80 \times .18$

49) $\frac{23}{100} + 1.8 + 19.631$

50) $3\frac{8}{25} - 1.8 + 16.32$

REVIEW—SOLVE THE FOLLOWING

1) $14.6 - 9$

2) $14.6 - .9$

3) $14.6 + .09$

4) $15 - .34$

5) $417 + 1.26$

6)
$$\begin{array}{r} 2\frac{1}{3} \\ + 1\frac{3}{4} \\ \hline \end{array}$$

7)
$$\begin{array}{r} 6\frac{5}{8} \\ - 1\frac{1}{3} \\ \hline \end{array}$$

8) $2\frac{1}{2} \times \frac{4}{5}$

9) $\frac{8}{9} \div \frac{4}{6}$

10)
$$\begin{array}{r} 4 \\ - 1\frac{5}{8} \\ \hline \end{array}$$

11)
$$\begin{array}{r} \$14.35 \\ \times .5 \\ \hline \end{array}$$

12) $6\overline{)54.3}$

13) $.06\overline{)543}$

14) $8\overline{).1256}$

15) $\frac{4}{7} \times \frac{5}{6}$

16) $\frac{3}{5} \div 1\frac{2}{3}$

17)
$$\begin{array}{r} 2\frac{3}{5} \\ + 1\frac{7}{8} \\ \hline \end{array}$$

18)
$$\begin{array}{r} 3.7 \\ \times .9 \\ \hline \end{array}$$

19)
$$\begin{array}{r} .37 \\ \times .015 \\ \hline \end{array}$$

20) $2\frac{1}{4} \times \frac{4}{9}$

21) $\frac{15}{16} \div \frac{3}{4}$

22) $4\frac{1}{2} \div 6$

23) $\$20 + \$2.56 + \$.75$

24) $\$20 - \$3.71$

25) $6.4 + .89 + 13$

26)
$$\begin{array}{r} \frac{3}{7} \\ + \quad \frac{1}{4} \\ \hline \end{array}$$

27)
$$\begin{array}{r} 3\frac{1}{3} \\ - \quad 1\frac{3}{4} \\ \hline \end{array}$$

28)
$$\begin{array}{r} 5\frac{3}{8} \\ + \quad 2\frac{5}{6} \\ \hline \end{array}$$

29)
$$\begin{array}{r} \$271.75 \\ \times \quad .3 \\ \hline \end{array}$$

30)
$$\begin{array}{r} \$271.75 \\ \times \quad .0004 \\ \hline \end{array}$$

31) $.003\overline{).2163}$

32) $.0015\overline{)90}$

33) $8\overline{)\$647.31}$

34)
$$\begin{array}{r} 8\frac{3}{7} \\ - 3 \\ \hline \end{array}$$

35)
$$\begin{array}{r} 8 \\ - 3\frac{3}{7} \\ \hline \end{array}$$

36) $7\frac{1}{3} \div 1\frac{5}{6}$

37) $34.41 - 7$

38) $45.96 + .318$

39) $\frac{48}{49} \times \frac{7}{8}$

40)
$$\begin{array}{r} 8\frac{7}{12} \\ 3\frac{1}{8} \\ + \quad 2\frac{3}{4} \\ \hline \end{array}$$

41) 20% of 80 = ?

42) 25% of 120 = ?

43) 6% of 300 = ?

44) 60% of 300 = ?

45) 150% of 80 = ?

46) 40% of $75.00?

47) 4% of $75.00?

48) 30% of $900.00?

49) 3% of $900.00?

50) 37% of $641.27?

- 185 -

REVIEW—SOLVE THE FOLLOWING

1) $8\frac{3}{5}$
$+\ 2\frac{1}{2}$

2) $21.3 - 5$

3) $21.3 - .5$

4) 50% of 140 = ?

5) $\frac{14}{15} \times \frac{5}{7} =$

6) $7\frac{1}{4}$
$-\ 1\frac{2}{3}$

7) 75% of 140 = ?

8) $\frac{15}{16} \div \frac{5}{8} =$

9) $14.9 + .75$

10) $3\frac{3}{4} \times \frac{8}{9} =$

11) $7\frac{1}{2} \div 20 =$

12) $4\frac{5}{8}$
$+3\frac{5}{6}$

13) 25% of 140 =?

14) $3\frac{1}{3} \times 1\frac{4}{5} =$

15) $24.8 + .79$

16) $24.8 + 6$

17) 40% of 360 = ?

18) $6\frac{1}{4} \div 3\frac{3}{4}$

19) $\frac{19}{20} \times 1\frac{2}{3} \times \frac{8}{38}$

20) 80% of 400 = ?

21) 6
$-\ 3\frac{1}{5}$

22) $\$47.75$
$\times\ \ \ .5$

23) 23.47
$\times\ .003$

24) $5\frac{1}{3}$
$+\ 7\frac{4}{5}$

25) $417.76 - 9.5$

26) $15\overline{).12}$

27) $8\frac{2}{3}$
$-\ \ \ 5$

28) 9% of $10,785.00 = ?

29) $24 \div 5\frac{1}{4}$

30) $18.3 + 7$

31) $18.3 - .7$

32) $\$125.97$
$\times\ \ \ .007$

33) 10% of 971 = ?

34) $.004\overline{)15}$

35) $2\frac{1}{2}$
$+\ 3\frac{1}{3}$

36) $.09\overline{)21.6}$

37) $1\frac{1}{2} \div 1\frac{3}{4} \times \frac{1}{8}$

38) $18\frac{5}{6}$
$+\ 9\frac{7}{9}$

39) $9\frac{3}{4}$
$-\ 2\frac{9}{10}$

40) 1% of 750 = ?

41) $24.17 + 15$

42) $.015$
$\times\ \ .006$

43) $8\overline{)\$325.67}$

44) $4\frac{7}{15}$
$-\ \ 3\frac{5}{6}$

45) 8% of $150.00 =?

46) $\$750.37$
$\times\ .0009$

47) $312 - 9.87$

48) $.09\overline{)\$3641.38}$

49) $4\frac{1}{2} \times \frac{7}{8} \div 3\frac{6}{16}$

50) $8\frac{1}{2}$% of $150.00

REVIEW—SOLVE THE FOLLOWING

1) $2\frac{1}{2}$
   $+ \quad 1\frac{4}{5}$

2) $17.3 - .8$

3) $17.3 - 8$

4) $\frac{15}{16} \times \frac{8}{9}$

5) 20% of 75

6) $\frac{4}{5} \div \frac{8}{9}$

7) $\quad 25.3$
   $\times 1.4$

8) $8\overline{).012}$

9) $3\frac{1}{2} \times 18$

10) 10% of 900

11) $14.4 + 31$

12) $\quad 4\frac{1}{8}$
    $- 1\frac{3}{4}$

13) $\quad 2\frac{3}{5}$
    $+ 1\frac{3}{4}$

14) 15% of 60

15) $217.3 + .94$

16) $\frac{14}{21} \times \frac{8}{12}$

17) $2 - 1.483$

18) 25% of 92

19) $\quad 24\frac{3}{7}$
    $- \quad 16\frac{2}{3}$

20) $\quad 34.34$
    $\times .003$

21) $4\frac{1}{3} \div 1\frac{1}{6}$

22) 8% of 420

23) 80% of 420

24) $3\frac{1}{5} \times \frac{10}{32}$

25) $14.31 + 7 + 1.947$

26) $\quad 4\frac{5}{8}$
    $+ 21\frac{5}{12}$

27) $.007\overline{)448}$

28) $26 + 3.4 + 15.83$

29) $\quad 9\frac{2}{5}$
    $+ 3\frac{3}{8}$

30) 150% of 80

31) $\quad 10\frac{1}{6}$
    $- 4\frac{3}{4}$

32) $18 \div 1\frac{1}{5}$

33) $25 - 17.8$

34) $\quad 2415$
    $\times .0008$

35) $\quad 14\frac{5}{9}$
    $+ 24\frac{5}{6}$

36) 75% of 600

37) $8\frac{1}{3} \times 3\frac{3}{5}$

38) $\quad \$91.43$
    $\times .004$

39) $.09\overline{)42.3}$

40) $\quad 20$
    $- 7\frac{3}{5}$

41) $75\overline{).03}$

42) $\quad 20\frac{3}{5}$
    $- 7$

43) 30% of 90

44) $281.376 - 8.4$

45) $\$50 - \$13.71 - \$24.68$

46) $2\frac{4}{5} \div 7$

47) $\quad .008$
    $\times .014$

48) $15\overline{).0606}$

49) $12\frac{1}{2}\%$ of 720

50) $\frac{49}{50} \div 4\frac{1}{5} \times 4\frac{2}{7}$

REVIEW—SOLVE THE FOLLOWING

1) $14.3 - .9$

2) $14.3 - 9$

3) $15.147 + .7$

4) $15.147 + 7$

5) $8 - 3.56$

6) $\begin{array}{r} 4.3 \\ \times\ .5 \\ \hline \end{array}$

7) $\begin{array}{r} .67 \\ \times\ .034 \\ \hline \end{array}$

8) $9\overline{).02736}$

9) $.004\overline{)2}$

10) $24\overline{)1.2}$

11) $\begin{array}{r} \frac{3}{5} \\ +\ \frac{3}{4} \\ \hline \end{array}$

12) $\begin{array}{r} 2\frac{1}{3} \\ +\ 1\frac{3}{8} \\ \hline \end{array}$

13) $\begin{array}{r} 7 \\ -\ 2\frac{3}{7} \\ \hline \end{array}$

14) $\begin{array}{r} 4\frac{3}{5} \\ -\ 2 \\ \hline \end{array}$

15) $\begin{array}{r} 9\frac{1}{8} \\ -\ 2\frac{4}{5} \\ \hline \end{array}$

16) $\frac{4}{9} \times \frac{3}{8}$

17) $3\frac{1}{2} \times 1\frac{1}{7}$

18) $\frac{9}{10} \div \frac{3}{5}$

19) $3\frac{1}{3} \div 2\frac{1}{2}$

20) $\frac{24}{25} \times 1\frac{2}{3} \div 1\frac{3}{5}$

21) $\$20 - \$3.47$

22) $\$50 - \$39.73$

23) $\$1.42 + \$2.79 + \$4$

24) $\$5 + \$7.47 + \$.52$

25) $\$50 - \$17.49 - \$19.61$

26) $\begin{array}{r} \$95.55 \\ \times\ .5 \\ \hline \end{array}$

27) $\begin{array}{r} \$73.33 \\ \times\ .07 \\ \hline \end{array}$

28) $\begin{array}{r} \$45.35 \\ \times\ .0006 \\ \hline \end{array}$

29) $8\overline{)\$641.04}$

30) $9\overline{)\$75.38}$

31) $\dfrac{M}{15} = \dfrac{91}{105}$

32) $\dfrac{24}{N} = \dfrac{60}{35}$

33) $\dfrac{42}{28} = \dfrac{N}{34}$

34) $\dfrac{15}{75} = \dfrac{225}{R}$

35) $\dfrac{57}{38} = \dfrac{21}{T}$

36) $\dfrac{36}{45} = \dfrac{52}{Z}$

37) $\dfrac{25}{.003} = \dfrac{A}{15}$

38) $\dfrac{B}{.6} = \dfrac{.03}{12}$

39) $\dfrac{3/4}{7} = \dfrac{15}{L}$

40) $\dfrac{.24}{K} = \dfrac{2/5}{.9}$

41) 40% of 120 = ?

42) 4% of 120 = ?

43) 10% of 360 = ?

44) 50% of 360 = ?

45) 25% of 360 = ?

46) 20% of 360 = ?

47) 75% of 360 = ?

48) $37\frac{1}{2}$% of 360 = ?

49) 8% of $3875.00 = ?

50) $8\frac{1}{2}$% of $3875.00 = ?

REVIEW—SOLVE THE FOLLOWING

1) $17.6 + 2.49$

2) $14.9 - 7.84$

3) $18 - 3.5$

4) $15.1 + 7.6 + 9.84$

5) $21.97 - 8$

6)
$$\begin{array}{r} 1.7 \\ \times\, .8 \\ \hline \end{array}$$

7)
$$\begin{array}{r} .52 \\ \times\, .03 \\ \hline \end{array}$$

8) $9\,\overline{\smash{)}.1854}$

9) $.004\,\overline{\smash{)}3.3}$

10) $.002\,\overline{\smash{)}175}$

11)
$$\begin{array}{r} 9\frac{1}{3} \\ -\,1\frac{3}{5} \\ \hline \end{array}$$

12)
$$\begin{array}{r} 6\frac{1}{8} \\ +\,3\frac{5}{12} \\ \hline \end{array}$$

13)
$$\begin{array}{r} 15 \\ -\,7\frac{5}{9} \\ \hline \end{array}$$

14)
$$\begin{array}{r} 26\frac{7}{8} \\ +\,9\frac{3}{4} \\ \hline \end{array}$$

15)
$$\begin{array}{r} 24\frac{7}{8} \\ -\,15\frac{14}{16} \\ \hline \end{array}$$

16) $\frac{3}{15} \times \frac{5}{9}$

17) $4 \times \frac{3}{8}$

18) $2\frac{1}{3} \div 1\frac{1}{2}$

19) $6 \div \frac{4}{5}$

20) $5\frac{1}{3} \div 1\frac{7}{9}$

21) $\$20 - \$3.44$

22) $\$50 - \$21.79$

23) $\$6.21 + \$7.80 + \$5$

24) $\$3.43 + \$2.25 + \$15.32$

25) $\$20 - \$3.94 - \$6.78$

26)
$$\begin{array}{r} \$49.49 \\ \times\quad .05 \\ \hline \end{array}$$

27)
$$\begin{array}{r} \$145.44 \\ \times\, .0007 \\ \hline \end{array}$$

28)
$$\begin{array}{r} \$56.75 \\ \times\, .004 \\ \hline \end{array}$$

29) $8\,\overline{\smash{)}\$156.40}$

30) $7\,\overline{\smash{)}\$499.16}$

31) $\dfrac{M}{12} = \dfrac{5}{4}$

32) $\dfrac{15}{N} = \dfrac{25}{30}$

33) $\dfrac{18}{12} = \dfrac{T}{32}$

34) $\dfrac{9}{5} = \dfrac{108}{K}$

35) $\dfrac{24}{Z} = \dfrac{16}{34}$

36) $\dfrac{25}{45} = \dfrac{15}{R}$

37) $\dfrac{27}{36} = \dfrac{81}{B}$

38) $\dfrac{95}{38} = \dfrac{85}{A}$

39) $\dfrac{64}{49} = \dfrac{C}{14}$

40) $\dfrac{7}{3} = \dfrac{A}{5}$

41) 45% of 300 = ?

42) 80% of 360 = ?

43) 8% of 360 = ?

44) $12\frac{1}{2}$% of $7000.00 = ?

45) 24 = 60% of ?

46) 57 = 75% of ?

47) $24.50 = 25% of ?

48) 36 = ? % of 45?

49) 75 = ? % of 300?

50) $36.04 = ? % of $450.50?

REVIEW—SOLVE THE FOLLOWING

1) $.7 + .27 + .9$

2) $3.3 - .64$

3) $8.5 + 4.7 + 6$

4) $15 - 3.433$

5) $25.741 - 8$

6) $\begin{array}{r} .05 \\ \times\ .03 \\ \hline \end{array}$

7) $\begin{array}{r} 12.5 \\ \times\ .6 \\ \hline \end{array}$

8) $7\overline{).343}$

9) $.003\overline{)132}$

10) $4.8\overline{)1.2}$

11) $\begin{array}{r} 5\frac{3}{4} \\ +\ 1\frac{2}{3} \\ \hline \end{array}$

12) $\begin{array}{r} 6 \\ -\ 2\frac{3}{5} \\ \hline \end{array}$

13) $\begin{array}{r} 4\frac{5}{8} \\ +\ 1\frac{2}{3} \\ \hline \end{array}$

14) $\begin{array}{r} 7\frac{1}{4} \\ -\ 2\frac{3}{5} \\ \hline \end{array}$

15) $\begin{array}{r} 9\frac{3}{8} \\ -\ 7 \\ \hline \end{array}$

16) $\frac{5}{6} \times \frac{3}{5}$

17) $4\frac{3}{4} \times \frac{8}{38}$

18) $\frac{7}{9} \div \frac{14}{15}$

19) $4\frac{1}{5} \div \frac{7}{10}$

20) $5\frac{1}{3} \times \frac{6}{7} \div 4\frac{5}{7}$

21) $\$20 - \$.54$

22) $\$20 - \$7.75$

23) $\$20 - \$19.13$

24) $\$3.45 + \$2.65$

25) $\$4.89 + \$10 + \$3.17$

26) $\begin{array}{r} \$95.00 \\ \times\quad .09 \\ \hline \end{array}$

27) $\begin{array}{r} \$2540.00 \\ \times\ .11 \\ \hline \end{array}$

28) $\begin{array}{r} \$75,000.00 \\ \times\ .095 \\ \hline \end{array}$

29) $15\overline{)\$3601.20}$

30) $7\overline{)\$635.66}$

31) $\dfrac{A}{42} = \dfrac{20}{28}$

32) $\dfrac{9}{6} = \dfrac{39}{B}$

33) $\dfrac{91}{65} = \dfrac{49}{M}$

34) $\dfrac{51}{34} = \dfrac{N}{38}$

35) $\dfrac{3}{5} = \dfrac{57}{T}$

36) $\dfrac{24}{R} = \dfrac{120}{75}$

37) $\dfrac{.45}{18} = \dfrac{X}{.6}$

38) $\dfrac{.003}{15} = \dfrac{9}{T}$

39) $\dfrac{\frac{3}{4}}{\frac{2}{3}} = \dfrac{8}{M}$

40) $\dfrac{2\frac{1}{2}}{.45} = \dfrac{B}{72}$

41) 150% of 80 = ?

42) 15% of 80 = ?

43) 1.5% of 80 = ?

44) 24 = ? % of 120?

45) 35 = ? % of 56?

46) 75 = 60% of ?

47) 51 = 75% of ?

48) 9% of $24,500.00 = ?

49) $9\frac{1}{2}$% of $24,500.00 = ?

50) $12\frac{1}{2}$% of $120,000.00 = ?

REVIEW—SOLVE THE FOLLOWING

1) $14.7 - .8$

2) $14.7 - 8$

3) $14.7 + .8$

4) $14.7 + 8$

5) $8 - 1.47$

6) $\begin{array}{r} .14 \\ \times .7 \\ \hline \end{array}$

7) $\begin{array}{r} .08 \\ \times .007 \\ \hline \end{array}$

8) $\begin{array}{r} \$42.37 \\ \times .6 \\ \hline \end{array}$

9) $4\overline{).1236}$

10) $.003\overline{)15}$

11) $\begin{array}{r} 4\frac{1}{8} \\ + 1\frac{1}{2} \\ \hline \end{array}$

12) $\begin{array}{r} 9\frac{1}{4} \\ - 3 \\ \hline \end{array}$

13) $\begin{array}{r} 9 \\ - 3\frac{1}{4} \\ \hline \end{array}$

14) $\begin{array}{r} 6\frac{5}{7} \\ + 4\frac{1}{2} \\ \hline \end{array}$

15) $\begin{array}{r} 8\frac{1}{6} \\ - 5\frac{7}{8} \\ \hline \end{array}$

16) $\frac{7}{8} \times \frac{24}{28}$

17) $4\frac{1}{3} \div 5\frac{1}{5}$

18) $\frac{9}{10} \times 1\frac{1}{3}$

19) $6\frac{1}{4} \div 50$

20) $\$56.72 \times \frac{3}{4}$

21) $4^2 =$

22) $7^2 =$

23) $2^3 =$

24) $9^3 =$

25) $5^3 =$

26) $10^4 =$

27) $6^2 =$

28) $25^2 =$

29) $5^5 =$

30) $2^{10} =$

31) $.4^2 =$

32) $.03^4 =$

33) $1.2^3 =$

34) $(\frac{1}{8})^3 =$

35) $(\frac{2}{5})^4 =$

36) $\sqrt{64}$

37) $\sqrt{36}$

38) $\sqrt{81}$

39) $\sqrt{225}$

40) $\sqrt{100}$

41) $\sqrt{1089}$

42) $\sqrt{121}$

43) $\sqrt{729}$

44) $\sqrt{324}$

45) $\sqrt{196}$

46) $\sqrt{\frac{4}{9}}$

47) $\sqrt{\frac{64}{169}}$

48) $\sqrt{\frac{1}{361}}$

49) $\sqrt{.0025}$

50) $\sqrt{2.89}$

REVIEW—SOLVE THE FOLLOWING

1) $3^2 =$ 6) $8^3 =$ 11) $.3^2$

2) $5^2 =$ 7) $9^4 =$ 12) 1.3^2

3) $3^3 =$ 8) $5^4 =$ 13) $.02^4$

4) $4^5 =$ 9) $10^7 =$ 14) $(\frac{1}{4})^2$

5) $2^2 =$ 10) $6^3 =$ 15) $(\frac{3}{5})^3$

16) $\sqrt{9}$ 21) $\sqrt{576}$ 26) $\sqrt{1764}$

17) $\sqrt{25}$ 22) $\sqrt{676}$ 27) $\sqrt{.04}$

18) $\sqrt{169}$ 23) $\sqrt{400}$ 28) $\sqrt{.0196}$

19) $\sqrt{144}$ 24) $\sqrt{625}$ 29) $\sqrt{25/49}$

20) $\sqrt{289}$ 25) $\sqrt{961}$ 30) $\sqrt{9/225}$

FIND THE MISSING SIDE OF EACH RIGHT TRIANGLE
HYPOTENUSE   LEGS

31) 5 cm − 4 cm − ?

32) 13″ − 12″ − ?

33) 15 ft. − 12 ft. − ?

34) ? − 24 yd. − 18 yd.

35) 25 m − 7 m − ?

36) ? − 15 cm − 8 cm

37) ? − 48″ − 14″

38) ? − 24″ − 10″

39) 45 ft. − 27 ft. − ?

40) ? − 52 cm − 39 cm

FIND THE MISSING ANGLE IN EACH TRIANGLE

41) 40° − 75° − ?

42) 51° − 47° − ?

43) 60° − 60° − ?

44) 90° − 30° − ?

45) 57° − 63° − ?

46) 100° − 40° − ?

47) 35° − 45° − ?

48) 41° − 59° − ?

49) 29° − 29° − ?

50) 130° − 15° − ?

REVIEW—SOLVE THE FOLLOWING

1) $-12 + -5$

2) $-12 - -5$

3) $12 - -5$

4) $12 + -5$

5) $-12.1 - -5$

6) $12.1 - -.5$

7) $-12 - -5\frac{3}{4}$

8) $1.2 + -5$

9) $-1.2 - -.5$

10) $.12 - 5$

11) -12×-4

12) $-.12 \div 4$

13) $-12 \div -.04$

14) $.12 \times -.04$

15) $1.2 \div 40$

16) $-18 \times -\frac{3}{4}$

17) $-\frac{3}{5} \div 1\frac{1}{3}$

18) $-5\frac{3}{5} \div 1\frac{3}{4}$

19) $.144 \div \frac{8}{9}$

20) $.144 \times \frac{8}{9}$

21) $\dfrac{M}{8} = \dfrac{12}{16}$

22) $\dfrac{5}{3} = \dfrac{M}{51}$

23) $\dfrac{8}{M} = \dfrac{20}{15}$

24) $\dfrac{13}{91} = \dfrac{15}{M}$

25) $\dfrac{M}{42} = \dfrac{25}{15}$

26) $\dfrac{M}{\frac{1}{2}} = \dfrac{80}{10}$

27) $\dfrac{.8}{M} = \dfrac{15}{18.75}$

28) $\dfrac{.04}{M} = \dfrac{.03}{.9}$

29) $\dfrac{\frac{5}{8}}{2\frac{1}{2}} = \dfrac{M}{36}$

30) $\dfrac{.75}{\frac{3}{8}} = \dfrac{M}{14}$

31) $\dfrac{.3}{.18} = \dfrac{4.5}{M}$

32) $\dfrac{10,000}{M} = \dfrac{3,000,000}{8,000,000}$

33) $\dfrac{\frac{1}{2}}{\frac{3}{5}} = \dfrac{\frac{2}{3}}{M}$

34) $\dfrac{14}{.07} = \dfrac{M}{35}$

35) $\dfrac{18}{M} = \dfrac{.36}{1.44}$

36) 40% of 700 = _____?

37) 4% of 700 = _____?

38) 25% of 145 = _____?

39) 125% of 600 = _____?

40) $8\frac{1}{2}$% of 300 = _____?

41) 45 = _____ % of 50?

42) 28 = _____ % of 21?

43) 40 = _____ % of 64?

44) 76 = _____ % of 95?

45) 13 = _____ % of 20?

46) 56 = 80% of _____?

47) 73 = 25% of _____?

48) 51 = 60% of _____?

49) 51 = $37\frac{1}{2}$% of _____?

50) 51 = 150% of _____?

REVIEW—SOLVE THE FOLLOWING

1) $-8 + -7$

2) $-8 - -7$

3) $8 + -7$

4) $8 - -7$

5) 9×-7

6) $-21 \div 3$

7) $-35 \div -7$

8) -8×-7

9) $-6 + -7 - -3$

10) $-24 \div -6 \times 5$

11) $-9 + 7\frac{1}{2}$

12) $-9 - -7\frac{1}{2}$

13) $-9\frac{1}{2} + -7$

14) $9\frac{1}{2} - 7\frac{1}{4}$

15) $-.5 \times -4.2$

16) $-.34 \div 2$

17) $-85 \div -.17$

18) $240 \times -\frac{2}{3}$

19) $-25 \div 1\frac{2}{3}$

20) $-17 - -5.3 + 9.4$

21) $\dfrac{N}{5} = \dfrac{21}{35}$

22) $\dfrac{12}{N} = \dfrac{15}{10}$

23) $\dfrac{24}{20} = \dfrac{N}{15}$

24) $\dfrac{13}{91} = \dfrac{10}{N}$

25) $\dfrac{28}{42} = \dfrac{N}{51}$

26) $\dfrac{N}{144} = \dfrac{16}{36}$

27) $\dfrac{42}{56} = \dfrac{33}{N}$

28) $\dfrac{34}{51} = \dfrac{38}{N}$

29) $\dfrac{4}{3} = \dfrac{3}{N}$

30) $\dfrac{3}{N} = \dfrac{2}{13}$

31) $\dfrac{3}{7} = \dfrac{N}{2}$

32) $\dfrac{\frac{3}{4}}{8} = \dfrac{N}{32}$

33) $\dfrac{.25}{40} = \dfrac{N}{50}$

34) $\dfrac{.14}{.7} = \dfrac{2.8}{N}$

35) $\dfrac{\frac{2}{3}}{N} = \dfrac{\frac{3}{4}}{4}$

36) 30% of 120 = _____?

37) 25% of 84 = _____?

38) 10% of 360 = _____?

39) 70% of 600 = _____?

40) 7% of 600 = _____?

41) 15 = _____ % of 25?

42) 15 = _____ % of 250?

43) 39 = _____ % of 52?

44) 24 = _____ % of 64?

45) 52 = _____ % of 65?

46) 20 = 80% of _____?

47) 45 = 150% of _____?

48) 75 = 75% of _____?

49) 3 = 12½% of _____?

50) 60 = 2½% of _____?

REVIEW—SOLVE THE FOLLOWING

1) $16.4 + 7$

2) $16.4 - .7$

3) $\begin{array}{r} 9\frac{1}{2} \\ + 1\frac{2}{3} \end{array}$

4) 30% of 80 = ?

5) $\frac{12}{15} \times \frac{6}{9}$

6) $4\frac{1}{2} \div \frac{3}{4}$

7) 60% of 350 =

8) $\begin{array}{r} 6 \\ - 1\frac{5}{9} \end{array}$

9) $\begin{array}{r} .005 \\ \times .015 \end{array}$

10) $\begin{array}{r} 8\frac{1}{3} \\ + 1\frac{4}{5} \end{array}$

11) 20% of 657 =

12) $417.51 - 9.9$

13) $8\overline{).036}$

14) $.007\overline{)217}$

15) $\begin{array}{r} \$95.95 \\ \times .07 \end{array}$

16) 25% of $854.70 =

17) $27.65 + 24$

18) $\begin{array}{r} 9\frac{1}{4} \\ - 3\frac{5}{7} \end{array}$

19) $4\frac{1}{4} \times 8$

20) $\begin{array}{r} 8\frac{3}{4} \\ + 5\frac{5}{8} \end{array}$

21) $8 + -5$

22) $-8 + -5$

23) $-8 - -5$

24) -8×-5

25) 8×-5

26) $24 \div -8$

27) $-24 \div -8$

28) -9×-7

29) $-36 \div 4$

30) $-8 \times -7 \times -6$

31) $-1\frac{3}{4} + \frac{5}{8}$

32) $2 - -3\frac{1}{5}$

33) $-18 \div -\frac{2}{3}$

34) $-1\frac{1}{3} - -2\frac{1}{4}$

35) $-\frac{8}{9} \times -\frac{3}{4}$

36) $-2.5 + 4$

37) $-50 \div -.05$

38) $18.3 - -6.5$

39) $-1.8 \times -.3$

40) $15.4 \times -.4$

41) $8 \times -5 + -8$

42) $8 + -5 \times -7$

43) $-6 \times 3 + -5 \times -2$

44) $-9 + -4 \times -6$

45) $8 \times -\frac{1}{2} + -7$

46) $-8(5 \times -4 + 3)$

47) $-10(-8 + 3 \times 3)$

48) $-5(-6 + -8 \times -7)$

49) $-6 + -4(-9 + 3 \times 5)$

50) $-8(-3 \times -5 + -6) + -7$

REVIEW—SOLVE THE FOLLOWING

1) $84 + -7$

2) $-84 - -7$

3) $-84 + -7$

4) $84 - -7$

5) 84×-7

6) -84×-7

7) $-84 \div 7$

8) $-84 \div -7$

9) $16.1 - 9$

10) $16.1 - -.9$

11) $-16.1 - -.9$

12) $1.61 - 9$

13) $.52 \div -4$

14) $5.2 \times -.4$

15) $-52 \div -.004$

16) $-52 \times .004$

17) $-9 - -1\frac{1}{2}$

18) $9 - -1\frac{1}{2}$

19) $-9 + -1\frac{1}{2}$

20) $9\frac{1}{2} + -1$

21) $-36 \times \frac{3}{4}$

22) $-36 \div -\frac{3}{4}$

23) $36 \times -\frac{3}{4}$

24) $1\frac{1}{5} \div -\frac{3}{8}$

25) $-\frac{4}{5} \div -20$

26) $N + 9 = 34$

27) $N - 17 = 5$

28) $3N = -87$

29) $\frac{1}{3}N = -87$

30) $5M + 8 = 63$

31) $7M - 17 = 25$

32) $25M + 87 = 12$

33) $15L + 7L = 88$

34) $25L - 13L = -84$

35) $21L + 11L = -96$

36) $14K = K + 65$

37) $19K = -3K + 110$

38) $24K = 27K + 51$

39) $9J + 7 = 4J + 52$

40) $6J - 31 = J + 74$

41) $14J - 9 = 17J + 243$

42) $9A = .9A + 162$

43) $B + 3\frac{3}{4} = 1.8$

44) $.09C + 36 = 108$

45) $20E - 18 = 4E - 18.32$

46) $45F + F = 20F - 104$

47) $.9H + 30 = \frac{3}{4}H - 75.9$

48) $28R + 15R - 37R = .003$

49) $1\frac{1}{2}T = \frac{4}{5}T + 35$

50) $9Y + 45 = 9.03Y - 450$

REVIEW—SOLVE THE FOLLOWING

1) $-24 + -6$

2) $-24 - -6$

3) $24 - 6$

4) $24 - -6$

5) $-24 + 6\frac{1}{4}$

6) $24 + -6\frac{1}{4}$

7) $-24 - -6.3$

8) $-2.4 + 6.3$

9) $-.24 + 6.3$

10) $.24 - -6.3$

11) $24 \times -.06$

12) $-.24 \times -.06$

13) $-2.4 \times .6$

14) $-24 \div 6$

15) $-.24 \div -6$

16) $24 \div -.006$

17) $-24 \div -.06$

18) $18 \times -\frac{2}{3}$

19) $-18 \div -1\frac{1}{5}$

20) $-\frac{3}{4} \times -\frac{5}{8}$

21) $-\frac{3}{4} \div \frac{5}{8}$

22) $3\frac{1}{5} \div -8$

23) $3\frac{1}{5} - 8$

24) $-3\frac{1}{5} - -8$

25) $-3\frac{1}{5} + -4.75$

26) $M + 8 = 17$

27) $A - 9 = 37$

28) $T + 15 = 6$

29) $3H = 84$

30) $-4I = 112$

31) $9S = 432$

32) $7F + 13 = 104$

33) $5U + 16 = -79$

34) $-15N + 31 = 196$

35) $6A + 7A = 91$

36) $17N - 9N = 144$

37) $9D - D = 192$

38) $7E = E + 198$

39) $5X = 7X + 48$

40) $14C = -8C + -242$

41) $8I + 3 = 2I + 45$

42) $9T - 14 = T + 70$

43) $15I + 41 = -5I + 49$

44) $19N - 1 = 94$

45) $19G - G = 90$

46) $Y = -7Y + 120$

47) $\frac{3}{4}Y - 9 = 27.36$

48) $.5Y + 30 = 95$

49) $1\frac{1}{2}Y + 17 = Y + 71$

50) $25Y - 17Y + 6Y = 9Y + .35$

REVIEW—SOLVE THE FOLLOWING

1) $15 + -3$

2) $-15 + -3$

3) $-15 - -3$

4) $15 - -3$

5) 15×-3

6) -15×-3

7) $-15 \div 3$

8) $-15 \div -3$

9) $-8 + -4.7$

10) $-8 - -4.7$

11) $-\frac{3}{4} \times 1\frac{3}{5}$

12) $-12 \div -1\frac{1}{2}$

13) $-7\frac{1}{3} + 4\frac{3}{5}$

14) $5\frac{4}{7} - -1\frac{2}{3}$

15) $-.12 \times -.5$

16) $-.12 \div 8$

17) $12 \div -.008$

18) $-.8 + -4.7$

19) $-.8 - -4.7$

20) $5\frac{1}{2} \div -3\frac{2}{3}$

21) $-\frac{49}{75} \times -\frac{15}{28} \div -\frac{7}{20}$

22) $15 - 7 - 8.3$

23) $51 \div -.0003$

24) $-4.1 - -5 + -12.34$

25) $-5\frac{3}{4} + 2.7 + -3\frac{4}{5}$

26) $F + 9 = 25$

27) $I + 3\frac{3}{4} = 2\frac{1}{3}$

28) $T - 1.7 = -7$

29) $T - 28 = -5\frac{1}{2}$

30) $\frac{3}{4}S = 18$

31) $-8T = .72$

32) $-1.2R = -84$

33) $I + \frac{5}{8} = \frac{1}{5}$

34) $7N + 5 = 33$

35) $-6K + -9 = 33$

36) $4L + 75 = 74$

37) $5E + 7E = 108$

38) $5A - 7A = 108$

39) $9N = N + 144$

40) $9D = -D + 75$

41) $\frac{4}{7}S + 9 = -19$

42) $7E - 5 = 3E + 15$

43) $8L + 95 = 11L + 38$

44) $9B - B = -100$

45) $6Y - 3Y = Y + -34$

46) $\frac{3}{5}F + 18 = 6.12$

47) $1\frac{3}{4}I - 30 = 40$

48) $5R - 3R - 2R = 4R - 56$

49) $\frac{3}{8}S = \frac{1}{8}S + 75$

50) $15T - 48 = -3T + 96$

REVIEW—SOLVE THE FOLLOWING

1) $18.4 - .9$

2) $18.4 - 9$

3) $46.317 + 8.4$

4) $\begin{array}{r} 6.3 \\ \times .04 \\ \hline \end{array}$

5) $\begin{array}{r} \$74.37 \\ \times .05 \\ \hline \end{array}$

6) $15\overline{).3}$

7) $.15\overline{)3}$

8) $\begin{array}{r} 7\frac{1}{3} \\ + 16\frac{4}{5} \\ \hline \end{array}$

9) $\begin{array}{r} 7 \\ - 2\frac{3}{5} \\ \hline \end{array}$

10) $\begin{array}{r} 15\frac{1}{8} \\ - 5\frac{5}{6} \\ \hline \end{array}$

11) $\frac{14}{15} \times \frac{5}{7}$

12) $\frac{3}{4} \div \frac{8}{9}$

13) $3\frac{1}{4} \div 3$

14) 80% of 75 = _____ ?

15) 8% of 75 = _____ ?

16) 24 = what % of 40?

17) 42 = 60% of _____ ?

18) $8\frac{1}{2}$% of \$7500.00 = _____ ?

19) $-8 + 13$

20) $-8 - -13$

21) $-8 + -13$

22) $-5 - -9 + -7$

23) $-3\frac{3}{4} + 2\frac{7}{8}$

24) $-9\frac{1}{3} - 4\frac{5}{8}$

25) $-9\frac{1}{4} - -6\frac{3}{8}$

26) -9×-4

27) 9×-4

28) -9×4

29) $-42 \div 3$

30) $-42 \div -3$

31) $42 \div -3$

32) $-9\frac{1}{3} \div 4\frac{2}{3} \times -\frac{3}{4}$

SOLVE THE FOLLOWING PROPORTIONS, EQUATIONS, AND INEQUALITIES

33) $\dfrac{B}{9} = \dfrac{14}{21}$

34) $\dfrac{12}{7} = \dfrac{A}{91}$

35) $\dfrac{24}{35} = \dfrac{144}{T}$

36) $M + 35 = 4$

37) $9N = -36.18$

38) $4R + 3R = R + -42$

39) $10L - 7 = 18$

40) $6Z + 4 = 9Z + 4.12$

41) $A + 7 > 5$

42) $6B + 1 \leq 13$

FIND THE AREA AND PERIMETER (OR CIRCUMFERENCE) OF THE FOLLOWING

43) Rectangle 14 ft. by 8 ft.

44) Square 13 inches a side

45) Triangle - base 20 cm, altitude 16 cm, other sides 22 cm, 25 cm

46) Right Triangle - Legs 20 m and 15 m, hypotenuse 25 m

47) Parallelogram - base 40 in., altitude 25 in., other sides 30 in.

48) Trapezoid - bases 27 cm and 23 cm, altitude 15 cm, other sides 20 cm, 24 cm

49) Circle - R = 30 m. Use 3.14

50) Circle - D = 28 ft. Use $\frac{22}{7}$

REVIEW—SOLVE THE FOLLOWING

1) $-9 + 7$

2) $-9 - 7$

3) $-9 - -7$

4) $9 - 7$

5) $-5\frac{1}{3} + 4\frac{2}{5}$

6) $-7\frac{3}{8} + -6.5$

7) $-4.17 + 6 - -9 + -21$

8) -8×1.2

9) -8×-12

10) $-4\frac{1}{2} \times 2\frac{2}{3}$

11) $-12 \div \frac{3}{4}$

12) $-36 \div -\frac{2}{3}$

13) $-.2 \times 40$

14) $-75 \div -.005$

15) $4\frac{1}{2} \times -3.3$

SOLVE THE FOLLOWING EQUATIONS, PROPORTIONS, AND PERCENTS

16) $M + 9 = 54$

17) $9N = -54$

18) $4T - 3 = 89$

19) $9B + 7B = -144$

20) $8A = A - .42$

21) $15T + 3 = 7T + -105$

22) $\dfrac{18}{15} = \dfrac{6}{R}$

23) $\dfrac{91}{25} = \dfrac{A}{30}$

24) $\dfrac{B}{47} = \dfrac{24}{23\frac{1}{2}}$

25) $\dfrac{-36}{.9} = \dfrac{.8}{M}$

26) $\dfrac{18}{N} = \dfrac{25}{100}$

27) 25% of 80 is what?

28) $14 =$ _____ % of 35 ?

29) $39 = 75\%$ of what number?

30) 18% of $7500.00 = _____ ?

31) $300.00 = 30% of _____ ?

32) What is a 15% commission on a $7,500.00 sale?

FIND THE FOLLOWING SIMPLE INTEREST

33) $3500.00 at 9% for 2 years.

34) $5000.00 at 12% for 30 months.

FIND THE DISCOUNT AND SALE PRICE OF THE FOLLOWING:

35) Regular price $30.00. Discount 25%

36) Regular price $9500.00. Discount 20%

37) Regular price $675.00. Discount 15%

38) $3^2 =$ _____ ?

39) $4^3 =$ _____ ?

40) $2.5^2 =$ _____ ?

41) $5^4 =$ _____ ?

42) $\sqrt{64}$

43) $\sqrt{576}$

FIND THE PERIMETER (OR CIRCUMFERENCE) AND AREA OF THE FOLLOWING:

44) Rectangle 25 ft. by 20 ft.

45) Square $4\frac{1}{2}$ cm A side

46) Right triangle - legs 21 in. and 28 in. hypotenuse 35 in.

47) Rhombus - sides 40 m, altitude 30 m

48) Trapezoid - bases 40 ft. and 60 ft., altitude 30 ft., other sides 45 ft. and 50 ft.

49) Circle - R = 100 cm. Use 3.14

50) Circle - D = 42 in. Use $\frac{22}{7}$

SOLVE THE FOLLOWING PROBLEMS WITH PROPORTIONS. ROUND TO
NEAREST HUNDREDTH.

1. Greg can ride the 24 miles to Cathlamet in two hours on his bike. If he rides
   at the same rate, how long will it take him to ride his bike the 36 miles to
   Battleground?

2. Kathy uses 3 cups of sugar to make 48 of her famous Minnesotian cakes.
   She has five cups of sugar in her sugar canister. How many Minnesotian
   cakes can she make?

3. Jose usually strikes out three times for every eight times he bats. If he batted
   192 times in his senior season, how many times did he strike out?

4. Tom loses four golf balls in eighteen holes of golf. During his vacation in
   Ephrata he played 108 holes of golf. About how many golf balls do you
   think Tom lost on his Ephrata vacation?

5. Fumiko can get 36 miles to the gallon in her new car. How many gallons
   of gas will it take her to drive the 432 miles from Gardena to Sacramento?

6. It takes Sherri 45 minutes to run the four miles around the lake. If she has
   only 30 minutes to run before soccer practice, how far can she expect to run?

7. Chuck, Ken and Mitch average one win in every five team golf matches. If
   they play 15 team golf matches this winter, how many do you expect they
   will win? How many do you expect them to lose?

8. Lone Eagle sold 1440 steaks in three months. If sales stay at the same
   rate, how many steaks can he expect to sell from May 1st to September
   30th.

9. Steve can drive the 183 miles from Castle Rock to Corvallis in three hours.
   If he drives at the same speed, how long will it take him to drive the 1098
   miles from Castle Rock to Glendale?

10. Shannon bought fertilizer for her garden. Six pounds of fertilizer covers 150
    square feet. Shannon's garden is 200 sq. ft.. How much fertilizer does
    Shannon need?

11. Alexandra uses one and one half pounds of powdered sugar to make 64
    pieces of microwave fudge. How many pounds of sugar does she need to
    make 192 pieces of microwave fudge?

12. Willie can mow four lawns in six hours. If he has contracted to mow ten
    lawns a week, how many hours will it take him?

13. UCLA scored 28 touchdowns in its first eight football games. After their
    bowl win, UCLA will have played a 12 game schedule. If UCLA scores at
    the same rate, how many touchdowns will they score in their season?

SOLVE THE FOLLOWING WITH PROPORTIONS. ROUND TO THE
NEAREST TENTH.

1. Kevin hits three home runs every eight baseball games. How many home runs
   will he hit in a thirty-two game season?

2. Al sells 24 shirts for every 16 that Dale sells. During the month of December
   Al sold 72 shirts. How many did Dale sell?

3. Pierre Laberge averaged 24 points a game during his senior basketball season
   at R.A. Long High School. If Pierre scored 528 points during the season,
   how many games did he play?

4. Charlie Craig can drive the 455 miles from Longview to Wallace in six and
   one half hours. How long will it take Charlie to drive the 2100 miles from
   Longview to St. Cloud?

5. Eldon from Kalama can pick forty-five pounds of strawberries in six hours.
   If he works two ten hour days, how many pounds of strawberries can he pick?

6. Tim averages four birdies every twenty-seven holes of golf. How many
   birdies should he get in the "Big Six Man" 108 hole golf tournament?

7. Alfredo figures he needs three gallons of weed killer to cover a 1.8 acre truck
   farm. How many gallons will he need to cover David Yanai's 240 acre lettuce
   farm?

8. Chin Lee averages 30.6 miles to a gallon in his new sports car. Chin's gas
   tank holds 15 gallons. How far can he expect to go on a tank of gas? How
   many tanks of gas will Chin need to drive the 2295 miles from Portland to
   Detroit?

9. Running Brook types 108 words in five minutes. How many words can she
   type in an hour? In an hour and a half? In eight hours?

10. It takes one and half pounds of ground beef to make tacos for the Farkle
    family of six. David and Carol Farkle are planning a taco party. There will
    be sixteen at the party. If their friends eat like their family, how many
    pounds of ground beef will they need?

11. Francisco can make 288 enchiladas from 30 pounds of Argentine
    cured roast beef. He sells 8640 enchiladas a month in his Buenos Aires
    cafe. How many pounds of cured roast beef does he need? If Argentine
    cured roast beef comes in 1.5 pound cans, how many cans does he need?

12. Beaudreau's wins three out of four home baseball games, but only two out
    of five away games. If Beaudreau's plays twenty home games and fifteen
    away games during it's season, find Beaudreau's: 1. Home wins 2. Away wins
    3. Total wins 4. Total losses. 5. Home winning percentage. 6. Away
    winning percentage. 7. Season winning percentage.

SOLVE THE FOLLOWING

1. Becky shot 8 free throws. She made 7 of them. What percent of shots did she make?

2. Dawn was a softball pitcher. She struck out 68% of the batters she faced. How many would she strike out if she faced 25 batters?

3. Megan saw 6 calico cats. This was 40% of all the cats she saw. How many cats did she see?

4. Carla earned a 94% on a 50 problem test. How many did she miss?

5. Pat can lift 160 pounds. He weighs 120 pounds. What percent of his body weight can he lift?

6. A new soap claims to kill 97% of the bacteria on one's body if used regularly. Joe used the soap for a year. If he started with 1,500,000,000 bacteria, how many would he have left on his body?

7. Charlie lost 28 pounds. If this was 13 1/3% of his body weight, how much did he weigh before he lost the weight?

8. About 40% of a golf score are putts. If Mick shot an 84, about how many putts did he have? If Mick had 50 putts, about what would his score be?

9. Alex and Kevin fight about 12½% of the time. If they are awake for 16 hours, how long will they be fighting?

10. On a video game, Elizabeth was shooting ducks. If she shot 48 ducks and missed twelve, what was her percentage of success? Of missed ducks?

11. Seventy-five percent of Mr. Trinkle's first period math class had all their assignments turned in. If there are thirty-two students in his first period class, how many students were not missing assignments? How many students were missing assignments?

12. Dash scored 95% and Carrie 92% on a math test. If Carrie missed 18 problems on the test, find: 1. How many Carrie got right? 2. How many Dash got right? 3. How many Dash missed? 4. How many problems were on the test?

13. Bill and Betty had 200 computer problems last month. Tim, the outside computer ace, was called in by Bill 12 times and by Betty 28 times to solve these problems. Find the percent that: 1. Bill called Tim in. 2. Betty called Tim in. 3. The total that Tim was called in.

SOLVE THE FOLLOWING PERCENTS WITH PROPORTIONS. ROUND TO
THE NEAREST TENTH.

1.   There were 66,500 fans for the UCLA-Washington football game in Husky
     Stadium. Husky Stadium holds 70,000. What percent of Husky Stadium was
     full? How many empty seats were there?

2.   Mai had an "A" on 80% of her assignments. The rest were "B's". If Mai
     turned in 45 assignments, how many were "A's"? How many were "B's"?

3.   Luis spent $294 on ski equipment. He paid 70% of the listed price. What
     was the listed price of the ski equipment? How much money did Luis save?

4.   It is 970 miles from Portland to Los Angeles on Interstate 5. Seventy
     percent of those miles are considered non-mountainous. How many of the
     miles are considered mountainous? How many are considered non-
     mountainous?

5.   In his last twenty golf rounds Ric's average score was 75, of which 30 were
     putts and 15 were drives. What percent of Ric's score were putts? What
     percent were drives?

6.   Arturo's Taco House saved 40% on $800 worth of ground beef purchases at
     Nishimoto's Quality Meats. Find: 1. How much Arturo saved? 2. How
     much Arturo paid for the ground beef?

7.   It is 20% closer to take I-5 through Portland than to take I-205. If I-205
     is 25 miles, how many miles will I-5 save you? How far is it through
     Portland on I-5?

8.   Mr. Estes from Texas misses on 75% of his football predictions. Last year
     he had 135 losing football predictions. Find: 1. How many total football
     predictions he made? 2. How many winning predictions he had? 3. His
     winning percentage?

9.   Olivia got 32 problems correct on Mr. Fitts' math test. If Olivia's
     score was 80% correct, how many problems were on the test? How many
     problems did Olivia miss?

10. Seventy percent of Stanley's ties are ugly. If 35 of his ties were
     declared ugly by the Monticello "Fashion" Committee, how many total ties
     does Stanley have? How many "decent" ties does he have?

11. Mick is nineteen, single, drives a sports car, and lives in Seattle. For a
     certain time period he pays $900.00 for his auto insurance. Jan is 31,
     married, drives an old clunker and lives in Kalama. Her insurance is 65%
     less than Mick's. What does Jan pay? How much less is her insurance than
     Mick's.

12. Helen makes 45% of her free throws. She made twenty-seven free throws
     during basketball season. How many free throws did she shoot? How
     many did she miss?

SOLVE THE FOLLOWING WITH PROPORTIONS. ROUND TO THE NEAREST TENTH.

1. Armand Gonzales completes 60% of his passes. In his senior season at Gardena High School he attempted 420 passes. How many did he complete? How many incomplete passes did he throw?

2. Dannybob Craig saved $60.00 on a purchase of hillbilly music recordings at D.J. O'Connor's Country Music Shop in Pikesville. The listed price of Dannybob's purchases was $300.00. Find: 1. What percent Dannybob saved? 2. What Dannybob actually paid for her purchases?

3. At the West Covina Lanes, Brute usually picks up 60% of his splits. In the Bruin Alumni League last year Brute picked up 27 splits. How many splits did Brute have last year? How many did he not pick up?

4. Mitch and Beverly drove the 650 miles on Route 23 from Asheville to Detroit. Beverly drove 35% of the time. Find: 1. What percent Mitch drove? 2. How many miles Mitch drove? 3. How many miles Beverly drove?

5. At Monticello Middle School, 30% of the faculty are Washington State Cougar football fans. These 18 Cougar fans usually dress up in Crimson and Grey after Washington State wins. How many are on the faculty at Monticello? How many are not Washington State Cougar fans?

6. Terri drove 259 of the 370 miles from Castle Rock to Spokane. Steve drove the rest. What percent of the miles did: 1. Terri drive? 2. Steve drive?

7. Pat sold 150% as many golf shirts as Carmen. If Carmen sold 40 shirts, how many did Pat sell? How many more shirts than Carmen did Pat sell?

8. Rosemary Tanaka got a 40% discount on curios for her import-export shop in Redondo Beach. The curios were posted at $1200.00. How much did Rosemary pay? How much did she save off the listed price?

9. Lath and Squeak posted golf scores at the Longview Country Club 90 times last year. Lath "claims" that Squeak was absent from the posting sessions 27 times. What percent was Squeak absent? How many times was Squeak present?

10. Escondido Tony usually tells nine bad jokes for every three good ones. What percent of Tony's jokes are good? Bad? If Tony told 120 jokes in September, how many of them were good? Bad?

11. Ronnie T. from Malvern can hit his golf ball 30% farther than Glenn from Touchet. Teevee from Rainier can hit his golf ball 90% of Ronnie T.'s distance. Goosee from Eugene hits his ball 20% farther than Glenn. Glenda from Goble can hit her golf ball only 80% as far as Glenn. Kathy from St. Cloud hits her ball 15% farther than Glenda. If Glenn hits his golf ball 200 yards, find the other five golfers distances.

SOLVE THE FOLLOWING. ROUND TO THE NEAREST TENTH.

1. Jill and Emily are Husky fans. Most Husky fans lose an average of three friends a year. If Jill roots for the Huskies 66 years and Emily roots for them for 71 years, how many total friends will they lose in their lifetimes?

2. A grain car on a freight train will hold 1½ tons of wheat. A freight train leaving Seattle has 42 grain cars, but only 2/3 of them are full. How many pounds of wheat is the train hauling?

3. Greg took a math test with 40 questions on it. If he missed 6 questions, what was his percent correct on the test?

4. The Bruins' punter kicked the ball four times for a total of 158 yards in his first game. If he punted the ball ten times in the next game with the same proficiency, how many total yards did he kick for that game?

5. Terri bought 6 lbs. of pumpkin seeds for $1.44. Terri needs 8 more lbs. of pumpkin seeds for her pumpkin patch. How much will the 8 lbs. of seeds cost? How much will she spend for the pumpkin seeds altogether?

6. Jason wants to paint two rooms in his house. The dimensions of the rooms were 12 ft. by 10 ft. and 14 ft. by 13 ft. The ceilings were 8 ft. ceilings. If a quart of paint covers 150 sq. ft., how many quarts of paint would it take to paint both rooms? The smaller room? The larger room?

7. Chris was a football fullback. If he carried the ball for gains of 4.2, 6.8, 3.8, 2.1, .9, and 16.8 yards, what was his total yardage? What was his average per carry?

8. A plumber worked from 8:20 AM to 1:05 PM on a plugged drain. If he charged $32.00 an hour, how much did he charge for the job?

9. LaBerge's were going to buy a van. The van they wanted was $21,500. The bank they wanted to finance through needed a 20% down payment, plus 7% sales tax on the total purchase, plus license fee of $450.00. How much money did they have to pay the bank to finance the loan for the van?

10. There was a power blackout during the rainstorm. The Bloom's power went off at 7:00 AM. They went to work and returned home at 5:30 PM. If their clock said 12:00, how long was their power off? What if the clock said 11:00? 1:00? 12:30? 8:45?

11. Patty's recipe for "Calexio Lemonade" calls for ten limes for every three quarts of lemonade. She figures that it will take six gallons of lemonade for her softball team during the Yuma tournament. How many limes does she need?

206

SOLVE THE FOLLOWING. ROUND TO THE NEAREST TENTH.

1. A motorhome averages about eight miles to the gallon. One summer, the Andersons drove their motorhome 280 miles to Sun Lakes, 110 miles to Spokane, and 430 miles back home. To the nearest gallon, tell how many gallons of gas did their motorhome require?

2. The Arveson's checking account charges $.25 for each check written. There is a monthly service fee of $5.00. If they wrote 15 checks one month, how much was their total service charge for the month? If this was an average month, what was their service charge for a year?

3. A heavy equipment operator gets $24.50 an hour. Drew worked 13 hours on a mud slide. If he gets time and a half for everything over eight hours, how much did he make for the job?

4. It cost $24.00 for admission to an amusement park for a day pass. If Lena went on 15 rides, what was the average cost per ride?

5. Nicole has to read four books a month for a pizza certificate. She also needs to read two books a week for her reading class requirement. Assuming four weeks to a month, how many books should she read in nine months?

6. In 1989 the Parkins' bought eight and one half cords of wood for $60.00 a cord. In 1990 they bought five and one fourth cords for $76 a cord. How much did they pay for wood in 1989? For both years together?

7. A family barbeque has been planned. The menu and costs were as follows:
   12 lb. of steak at $3.58 a lb.
   1 1/2 gallons of potato salad at $4.56 a gallon.
   28 ears of corn at 12 for $1.00.
   4 gallons of lemonade at $1.25 a gallon.

   1. How much would this cost?
   2. They planned to serve 24 people for the barbeque. If at the last minute six more decided to come, how much would this increase the cost? What would be the new cost of the barbeque?

8. Find all 8 golfers scores. Tim shot 16 strokes better than Chet. Ed shot two more than Tim. Mike shot halfway between Tim and Ed. Damian shot halfway between Tim and Chet. Don shot four more than Ed. Ken shot halfway between Tim and Don. The Gapp shot twelve higher than Damian. Chet's eighteen hole golf score was 90.

207

SOLVE THE FOLLOWING. ROUND TO THE NEAREST TENTH.

1. The average annual rainfall for the following ten major U.S. cities is: Seattle 40", Miami 68", Houston 52", New Orleans 64", Los Angeles 18", San Francisco 24", Chicago 28", New York 53", Philidelphia 49", Denver 20". Find the average rainfall of the following cities: 1. The three wettest. 2. The four wettest. 3. The three dryest. 4. The four dryest. 5. The four middle wettest. 6. The two Gulf Coast. 7. The three farthest west. 8. The three farthest east. 9. All ten.

2. The average rainfall for the following European cities is: Moscow 23", Oslo 39", Stockholm 35", Helsinki 29", Copenhagen 40", Berlin 31", Paris 37", London 36", Madrid 18", Warsaw 26". Find the average rainfall of the following cities: 1. The three wettest. 2. The four wettest. 3. The three dryest. 4. The four dryest. 5. The middle four wettest. 6. The four Scandinavian. 7. The three farthest east. 8. London, Paris, and Berlin. 9. All ten.

3. Amy went shopping on the day after New Years. She went to a store that was having a store-wide clearance sale. She bought the following items at the corresponding discounts.
    A blouse for $15.00 at 10% off.
    A skirt for $25.00 at 50% off.
    A pair of shoes for $45.00 at 20% off.
    A sweater for $44.60 at 15% off.
    A coat for $93.00 at 33 1/3% off.
    6 pairs of stockings for $6.00 each at 30% off.
    A pair of jeans for $29.95 at 35% off.

    A. Find how much she paid for each item. Then find her total bill. If she bought this in a state with a sales tax of 7%, how much tax did she pay? What is her total bill now? She paid $10.00 on the bill and charged the rest. If she paid the rest at the end of one month with a one and one half percent interest charge, how much interest did she pay? What was the total amount Amy paid for her shopping trip?

    B. If Amy bought the same things but they were all at 40% discount instead of the discounts listed above and the sales tax was 8%, find her total bill.

4. Double calorie cookies sell for $1.44 a dozen. How much will the following amounts of cookies cost? 1. 4 cookies. 2. 24 cookies. 3. 60 cookies. 4. 6 cookies. 5. 8 cookies. 6. 18 cookies. 7. 36 cookies. 8. 144 cookies. 9. 1000 cookies.

SOLVE THE FOLLOWING. ROUND TO THE NEAREST TENTH.

1. Judy needed one gallon of paint for each 300 square feet of her deck floor. If her back deck is 25 ft. by 30 ft., Find: 1. How many square feet of deck Judy has? 2. How many gallons of paint she needs?

2. One can of flea spray will kill fleas in a 150 sq. ft. area. Ginger really needs to kill fleas in her living room (12 ft. by 14 ft.), her kitchen (8 ft. by 10 ft.) and her family room (15 ft. by 20 ft.). Find: 1. Area of the living room. 2. Area of the kitchen. 3. Area of the family room. 4. The number of flea spray cans Ginger needs.

3. Gopher State Mosquito Spray kills Mosquitos in a 400 sq. ft. area. Jackie plans to spray her lawns before a family reunion. Her lawns are all rectangles with the following dimensions: front (15 ft. by 50 ft.), side (10 ft. by 25 ft.), back (20 ft. by 50 ft.). Find the area of each of her lawns and how many cans of Gopher State Mosquito Spray Jackie needs.

4. Edyth makes 75% of the bridge hands in which she gets the bid. In the Chula Vista Tournament she got the bid fifty-two times. How many bids did she make?

5. Eighty-five percent of the students at Dana Jr. High choose hot dogs when they are available at the cafeteria. If 420 students were in the cafeteria on Monday, how many hot dogs did the cafeteria serve?

6. The Ken Koch company sells 75% of their prizes east of the Mississippi River. Of this 75%, only 30% is east of the Appalachians. If the Ken Koch company sold 60,000 prizes last year, find how many prizes were sold: 1. West of the Mississippi. 2. East of the Mississippi. 3. East of the Appalachians. 4. West of the Appalachians and east of the Mississippi.

7. Jim and Jackie drove the 104 miles from Lakeville to the Pirate Cove Restaurant. Twenty-five percent of the miles were surface streets where Jim could only average 52 MPH. The other 75% of the miles were on freeways where Jim could average 65 MPH. Find: 1. How many miles were on surface streets? On freeways? 2. The number of minutes Jim drove on surface streets? On freeways? Total?

8. Jose's last ten math scores were: 95, 80, 94, 76, 90, 98, 85, 97, 94, 88. Find the average of: 1. All his test scores. 2. His highest three test scores. 3. His lowest three test scores. 4. His middle four test scores. (round to the nearest tenth.)

9. Yesterday's low temperatures were: Chicago 25, Detroit 20, Cleveland 22, Minneapolis 5, Milwaukee 20, St. Louis 30, Indianapolis 28, Cincinnati 25, Pittsburgh 24, Buffalo 18. Find the average of: 1. All ten cities. 2. The three coldest cities. 3. The four coldest cities. 4. The three warmest cities. 5. The four warmest cities. 6. The middle four cities. 7. The five cities on the Great Lakes. (round to the nearest tenth of a degree.)

SOLVE THE FOLLOWING. ROUND TO THE NEAREST TENTH.

1. Find the number of wins each team had at the end of the basketball season. Stanford had six less wins than UCLA. Arizona State had two less than Stanford. Oregon State was halfway between UCLA and Stanford. Washington was halfway between Stanford and Arizona State. Oregon had two more wins than Washington. Washington State was halfway between Oregon and Oregon State. California had two thirds as many wins as UCLA. USC had one half as many wins as Washington State. Arizona had nineteen wins, which was one more than Stanford.

2. Find the number of wins each baseball team had at the end of the season. Seattle had six more wins than Minnesota, 21 more than Chicago, and 31 more than Texas. Oakland had one half as many wins as Seattle. Kansas City had eleven more wins than Chicago and four less than California. Milwaukee had two thirds as many wins as California. Boston was half way between Milwaukee and Minnesota. Baltimore had four fifths as many wins as Boston. Detroit had five sixths as many wins as Minnesota. Milwaukee had three fourths as many wins as Cleveland and two thirds as many as Toronto. New York had 74 wins, which was 22 less than Seattle.

3. Milo split up the $600.00 profit amount the employees at his bakery. Gregori got 20%, Lena 10%, Anna 15%, and Nickolas 25%. Milo kept the rest. Find everyone's share of the profits.

4. Jose split up the $1440.00 profit from his produce stand. Each employee got the following share. Ronaldo 1/5, Luigi 1/10, Carmela 1/8, Juan 1/4. Jose kept the rest. Find everyone's share of the profits.

5. Mr. Cantello has a certain number of coins in his pocket. All the coins are nickles, dimes, or quarters. He has some of each type. There is more than one answer to each question. Find the number of nickels, dimes and quarters he has in his pocket if: 1. He has 15 total coins and they add up to $2.00 (3 different answers) 2. He has 20 total coins and they add up to $2.60. (3 different answers) 3. He has 25 total coins and they add up to $3.15. (5 different answers) 4. He has 26 total coins and they add up to $2.70. (6 different answers)

6. Find the following:
   1. Three consecutive numbers whose sum is 66.
   2. Three consecutive odd numbers whose sum is 69.
   3. Three consecutive even numbers whose sum is 102.
   4. Three consecutive multiples of five whose sum is 60.
   5. Three consecutive multiples of fourteen whose sum is 126.
   6. Five consecutive multiples of thirteen whose sum is 390.
   7. Three consecutive multiples of one half whose sum is 13½.
   8. Five consecutive multiples of 1.5 whose sum is 37.5.
   9. Five consecutive multiples of $.25 whose sum is $8.75.
   10. Five consecutive multiples of $1.25 whose sum is $31.25.

SOLVE THE FOLLOWING.

1. Find 3 consecutive integers whose sum is 63.

2. Find 3 consecutive odd integers whose sum is 63.

3. Find 3 consecutive even integers whose sum is 60.

4. Find 3 consecutive multiples of 5 whose sum is 60.

5. Find 2 consecutive integers whose sum is 145.

6. Find 3 consecutive integers whose sum is 105.

7. Find 2 consecutive even integers whose sum is 114.

8. Find 3 consecutive odd integers whose sum is 99.

9. Find 3 consecutive odd integers such that the sum of the first and third integers is 60.

10. Find 3 consecutive integers such that the sum of the first two is 8 more than 3 times the third.

11. Find 3 consecutive odd integers such that 8 times the first integer is 3 more than 3 times the third.

12. Find 4 consecutive even integers such that the sum of the first three is 24 more than the fourth.

13. Find 4 consecutive integers such that the sum of the first and fourth is 9 less than 4 times the second.

14. Find 3 consecutive even integers such that the sum of 5 times the second and three times the third is 70.

15. If 5 times a number is increased by 8, the result is the same as when 8 times the number is decreased by 10. Find the number.

16. If 25 is decreased by 4 times a number, the result is ten more than the number. Find the number.

17. The difference between two numbers is 11. Find the numbers if their sum is 55.

18. The greater of 2 numbers is 4 more than 3 times the smaller. If their sum is 32, find the numbers.

19. One number is three times another number. If the first is increased by 5, the result is 3 more than the second. Find the numbers.

211

SOLVE THE FOLLOWING.

1. The length of a rectangle is 4 inches more than its width. If the perimeter is 72 inches, find the length and width.

2. The length of a rectangle is two centimeters more than twice its width. If the perimeter is 40 cm find the length and width.

3. The length of a rectangle is 3½ times its width. If the perimeter is 108 inches, find the length and width.

4. The width of a rectangle is 4 less than its length. If the perimeter is 84 cm, find the length and width.

5. The perimeter of a soccer field is 320 meters. If the length is 10 meters more than twice the width, what are the dimensions.

6. The sum of the length and width of a rectangle is 72 feet. Three times the width is 4 feet less than twice the length. What are the dimensions?

7. Helen is now 3 times as old as Millie. Five years from now she will be only twice as old. What are their current ages?

8. Chan is 4 times older than his cousin. In 8 years he will only be two times older. How old are they both now?

9. Mr. Gomez is 25 years older than Mr. Kowalski. Four years from now Mr. Kowalski will be ½ as old as Mr. Gomez. What are their ages now?

10. Scott is now 24 and Shannon is 12 years old. How many years ago was Scott 4 times as old as Shannon was at that time?

11. The sum of Greg's age and Sherri's age is 42. Greg's age 14 years from now will be twice what Sherri's age was 11 years ago. What are their ages now?

12. In a math class of 29 students, there are 9 more boys than girls. How many of each are in the class?

13. Jill, Maria, and Ashley sold tickets to a rock concert. Jill sold 5 times as many as Ashley. Maria sold 4 more than Ashley. The total amount sold was 67 tickets. How many did each sell?

14. Paco weighs 4 pounds more than 3 times as much as his brother. The sum of their weights is 168 pounds. How much does Paco weigh?

15. Boris and Josh collect baseball cards. Together they have 360 cards. Boris has 30 more than ½ as many as Josh. How many does each have?

SOLVE THE FOLLOWING.

1. Kevin has $2.15 in dimes and quarters. He has 3 less dimes than quarters. How many of each does he have?

2. A piggybank has $3.60 in nickels and dimes. There are 48 coins in all. How many of each does it hold?

3. Louisa has 3 times as many dimes as nickels and twice as many quarters as nickels. She has $1.70 in all. How many of each coin does she have?

4. Mr. Nguyen has $129 in his wallet. He has $1, $5, and $10 bills. He has twice as many $5 bills as $1 bills, and 1/3 as many $10 bills as $1 bills. How many of each does he have?

5. Mrs. Rodriguez has $4.50 in change. She has 6 less quarters than nickels and 12 less dimes than nickels. How many of each does she have?

6. The units' digit of a two digit number is 6 more than the tens' digit. The number it names is 3 more than 3 times the sum of the digits. What is the number?

7. The units' digit of a two digit number is 4 less than the tens' digit. The number it names is 3 less than 9 times the sum of the digits. What is the number?

8. The tens' digit of a two digit number is 5 more than the units' digit. The sum of the digits is 9. Find the number.

9. How many pounds of dog food worth $.80 per pound must be mixed with dog food worth $.65 per pound to make a mixture of 60 pounds worth $.70 per pound?

10. How many pounds of cookies worth $1.40 a kilogram must be mixed with cookies worth $1.25 per killogram to make a mixture of 45 kilograms worth $1.30 per kilogram?

11. A total of 420 tickets were sold to the school play. Adult tickets were $4 and student tickets were $2.50 each. The total money taken in was $1,231.50. How many of each kind of ticket were sold?

12. San Antonio and Dallas are 270 miles apart. A car traveled from San Antonio to Dallas at the rate of 50 miles per hour. Another car traveled from Dallas to San Antonio at the rate of 40 miles per hour. How many miles did they travel before they met?

13. Two jets leave from the Honolulu airport at the same time in opposite directions. One flies 600 miles per hour and the other 750 miles per hour. How many hours later will they be 4,725 miles apart?

PRACTICE PRACTICE PRACTICE BOOK I

Whole Numbers	Money
Basic Facts	Fractions
Decimals	Prime Numbers
Rounding	Greatest Common Factors
Comparing	Least Common Multiples

Plus over 25 review and combination pages!

Just think of the topics listed above. Book I can provide you with an abundance of quality, organized, practice problems on these topics.

Classroom set:

Think of the time you will save if you have or share a classroom set of books.

Save ditto costs.

"The publication costs in our math department decreased enough in one year to pay for the books" Henderson, Kentucky

For more information contact: ST^2 Publishing
203 Si Town Road
Castle Rock, WA 98611
(360) 274-7242